WOW:
Words of Wisdom

WOW:
Words of Wisdom

Virginia Glover

Library of Congress Control Number: 2011913856
ISBN: Hardcover 978-1-4653-4736-7
Softcover 978-1-4653-4735-0
Ebook 978-1-4653-4737-4

This book was printed in the United States of America.

To order additional copies of this book, contact:
Xlibris Corporation
1-888-795-4274
www.Xlibris.com
Orders@Xlibris.com
81662

Contents

Dedication

This book is dedicated to my family, beginning with my Grandmother Christerson who instilled in me a love for the Bible, my Mom who was the essence of the perfect Sunday School teacher, my Dad who was an example of a loving father on this earth, my sister who gave me the first glimpse of heaven at her death, my husband who in my times of doubt never wavered, our daughter Lonnie whose love for the literature of the Bible has revealed so many truths to me, our son Mike who has always stood firm in his faith and passed it on to his children, our daughter Ginifer who with stubborn determination has overcome with joy and our son Chris who heard the call and answered "yes".

Acknowledgments

This work came about because of Pastor Bill Allen of Hilltop Bible Church, Clarksville, Arkansas, who gave me the chance to minister to the children and encouraged me to write down the devotionals I presented at Awana and the children's lesson at church. With the challenge to always find some wonderful lesson in my daily Bible reading as I read through the Bible, I discovered that not a day passed without some great truth presenting itself.

Invaluable editing was provided by my daughter, Lonnie McElroy whose years of teaching English, editing a paper and home schooling her four children gave her the insight to spark up the manuscript. I will always be indebted to her for her willingness and desire to "help out Mom".

Thanks goes to my grandson, Nate Puckett, who using his talent for design, created the cover.

Finally, I want to acknowledge my twelve outstanding grandchildren and their children who have made my life complete. As they serve their Master in the military, business world, education and home, they are gifted in music, art, sports and ministering to others. What more could a Grandmother ask for?

My prayer is that as you and your children share this book together you will know and love God more.

January 1

. . . . and Adam and his wife hid themselves from the presence of the Lord God among the trees of the garden. Genesis 3:8

Adam and Eve were disobedient. God told them that they could eat of every tree of the garden except the Tree of Knowledge of Good and Evil. But, guess what they did? The same thing we do sometimes—they DISOBEYED. When God called to them they were ashamed and felt guilty. They tried to cover or hide their sin from God. But we all know that God is with us every minute and we can't hide from Him.

The next time you are tempted to do something that you know you shouldn't, remember what happened to Adam and Eve. They lost the beautiful garden God had given them and their punishment was hard. They couldn't have their daily walks with God anymore. Don't you think they must have said a hundred times, "Oh, I wish I hadn't done what I was told not to do?"

You see, once we've disobeyed, we're just like Adam and Eve. We want to hide or make excuses or lie about what we did. However, we can't lie to God and it's so much better if we just obey our parents, teachers, and all others who have authority over us. Then we have the JOY that only God can give us. NOW THAT'S A GREAT FEELING!!!

Questions To Think About

1. What does it mean to obey?
2. What happens when we don't obey?
3. What happens when we do obey?

January 2

And Enoch walked with God; and he was not,
for God took him. Genesis 5:24

When I was a kid like you, I thought this was a great Scripture. I pictured this man, so perfect in every way, never getting angry, never wanting something that others had, never questioning what was happening to him, never being jealous of others, never doing anything bad. Then one day, as he was walking along talking to someone who was invisible, all of a sudden he just vanished into thin air. God just beamed him up to Heaven. He didn't have to die! This was really a big deal to me because I didn't want to die.

As I learned more about the Scriptures and listened to my pastor and other teachers, I began to realize that God didn't take Enoch straight to Heaven because he was PERFECT. Of course, not! The only perfect person who ever lived was Jesus. So why did Enoch get to walk with God and talk with God and never have to die? Could I be like Enoch and never have to die? This was important to me and I wanted to know! I was surprised to learn that Enoch got to walk with God because of his FAITH. You know what else I learned? Enoch is a picture of us when we become Christians. You know, we really never die either because Jesus is waiting for us as we cross over from this life to Heaven. He is there waiting for us to walk with Him and talk with Him just like Enoch.

We also know that when Jesus returns, if we are still living, we won't have to die. Like Enoch, we will get to walk with Jesus. Either way it makes us realize that we can grow in our FAITH. We don't have to wait until we die or until Jesus returns. The more FAITH we have, the closer we walk with Jesus right now. NOW THAT'S SOMETHING TO THINK ABOUT!!

Questions To Think About

1. What is faith?
2. What does walking and talking with Jesus mean to us now?

January 3

Thus Noah did according to all that God commanded him, so he did. Genesis 6:22

Noah was a great man. One little word in the Scripture verse today sets Noah apart from all the others of his day and most people of our own day. That word is ALL. "All" may only have three little letters but it is a VERY BIG word. When we think of "all", many times we have a different idea of what that includes. We say, "Is that all?" Or "I have to do that all the time." Or "Do I have to do all the work?" You get the picture. Sometimes the word all has a negative meaning attached to it. But with God and Noah it was a wonderful word that meant Noah was completely dedicated to whatever God told him to do. Remember, it had never rained when Noah started building the ark. You can imagine what people were saying about Noah, the funny looks he got, and the way they treated him. It must have been terrible. In spite of the hateful things people said, the jokes they made about him, and the way they refused to have anything to do with him, Noah did not stop OBEYING God.

Sometimes we think the people in the Bible are a special kind of people and that we can't be like them no matter how hard we try. Noah was just a person like us. We remember him today as a man of great faith because he made the choice to DO what God told him. We have a choice just like Noah. We can choose to OBEY God or to DISOBEY God. HOW WILL PEOPLE REMEMBER US? The right and best choice is always, OBEY JESUS!!

Questions To Think About

1. When asked to obey, what choices do you have?
2. How will people remember you?

January 4

And they said, "Come, let us build ourselves a city, and a tower whose top is in the heavens, let us make a name for ourselves ... Genesis 11:4

Have you ever heard anyone say, "When I get rich and famous . . . ?" It seems that deep down inside, most of us want a name that people will recognize when they hear it. There's nothing wrong with being well known, it's what you are known for that counts. For example, we all know the name Hitler, but we sure wouldn't want to be known for the same reason he is. We want a name we can be proud of. You may wonder how you can earn a name that will be remembered. Maybe it will be through excelling in sports, writing a best selling book, or inventing something amazing. However, even if you did become famous in one of these areas, after a few years only some would remember you.

You know, God is the only one who can give you an EVERLASTING NAME written in His Book of Life. Now that's a name worth having. Don't be like the people in our Scripture verse who wanted to glorify their own name by doing something great. We CAN do great things because God promises that with Jesus all things are possible. Just remember to give God the glory rather than keeping it all for yourself and He will give you the desires of your heart. Most importantly, you can always rest assured that God never forgets your name.

Questions To Think About

1. Why is a good name important? What is an "Everlasting Name"?

January 5

. . . there he built an altar to the Lord and called on the name of the Lord. Genesis 12: 8

In the Old Testament we read lots about altars. The altar was a place of sacrifice. An animal was sacrificed before God and placed on the altar and a believer's sins were covered. Altars were also used to burn incense. This represented the prayers of God's people.

You'll notice when you read the New Testament that God didn't tell the people to build altars. Have you ever wondered why? When Jesus died on the cross, He was the last sacrifice that would ever have to be made for our sins. Why? Because Jesus lived a perfect life—something none of us can do. He took all our sins on himself and paid for them. On the cross Jesus said, "It is finished." When He said this, He meant that no one would ever have to build an altar to make a sacrifice or burn incense again. Now, Jesus is our altar. His blood shed on the cross takes away our sins once and for all and we don't have to build an altar. We don't have to go to a special place or to a special person to have our sins forgiven or to talk to Jesus. We can call on His name any time, any place and He hears us.

The people of the Old Testament, like Abram in our Scripture verse, had to build altars and think about a Savior who would come in the future. We are BLESSED to have our Savior right here with us today. PRAISE HIM for being our sacrifice.

Questions To Think About

1. Why don't we have to build altars today?
2. What did it mean when Jesus said, "It is finished?"

January 6

And he [Abram] believed in the Lord and He [the Lord] accounted it to him for righteousness. Genesis 15:6

We hear a great deal about the word BELIEVE now days don't we? What do you think it means? Maybe you think to believe means: "having an idea that people say is true but can't prove" or "having an idea that has been proven to be true". The dictionary says the word believe means, "to accept as true or real, to have confidence in, or to trust".

Let's apply some of these definitions to real life situations. Your Dad might hand you a present and say, "This is for you." You believe him. You ACCEPT what he says and enjoy the present. Or you might say, "I believe this chair will hold me." This means you have CONFIDENCE in the chair and you sit down. Or you deposit money in the bank so you won't lose it. You TRUST the bank to keep it safe.

All of these things are part of BELIEVING. Like Abram in our Scripture, when we believe in Jesus we have to ACCEPT as truth all that He has said. We have CONFIDENCE that He will keep His promises. We put all of our TRUST in Him. Then Jesus will say because we "believed in the Lord . . . He accounted it to him [us] for righteousness." RIGHTEOUS! AND ALL WE HAD TO DO WAS BELIEVE!!

Questions To Think About

1. What does it mean to BELIEVE in Jesus?

January 7

Is anything too hard for the Lord? Genesis 18:14

There you are struggling over your homework and finally deciding, "It's just too hard, I can't do it." What about the time you were much younger and you wanted to do what the "big kids" did? You tried really hard to ride a bike, swim, catch a ball, or whatever it might have been and it was just TOO HARD. This happens to all of us. No matter how old, how big, or how smart we are there is always something that is just too hard for us.

Isn't it wonderful to know that nothing is too hard for the Lord! This is an awesome concept and one we might have trouble understanding, but stop and think of all He has done. First, He CREATED THE WORLD and everything in it. And, what about His MIRACLES: parting the Red Sea, healing the sick, raising the dead just to name a few. But He didn't stop there. He CAME into the world as a baby, DIED on the cross, and ROSE from the dead so that we could be forgiven and live with Him forever. How could you top that? Jesus will. He is COMING BACK for His children; that will be the LIVING END. Nothing is too hard for the Lord!

Questions To Think About

1. Today, think about how great God is.

January 8

And He said, "Do not lay your hand on the lad, or do anything to him; for now I know that you fear God since you have not withheld your son, your only son, from Me." Genesis 22:12

This is a wonderful story. Abraham planned to sacrifice his only son Isaac because God commanded him to. It was a test of Abraham's love and respect for God. As the Bible says, God stopped Abraham before he hurt his son. And God had already prepared a ram nearby as a substitute for Isaac. This act of obedience showed Abraham's love and respect for God.

Have you ever wondered if God knows that you love Him? I know I have. How can we show God that we love Him? Do you show Him by obeying—what about the little fit you threw to get your own way? Do you show Him in the way you treat others—what about ignoring the new kid instead of asking if he wants to be your friend? Do you show Him by what you say—what about repeating bad things about another person or making fun of someone? Do you show Him by spending time with Him—what about when you ignore God, never reading your Bible, never talking to Him, never going to church unless there's a party? We really need to check up on ourselves to make sure Jesus KNOWS that we REALLY DO love Him.

QUESTIONS TO THINK ABOUT

1. Read your Bible daily.
2. What does it mean to be more like Jesus?

January 9

Then he said, "O Lord God of my master Abraham, please give me success this day, and show kindness to my master Abraham." Genesis 24:12

Today's Scripture verse refers to Abraham sending his oldest and most trusted servant to find a wife for his son, Isaac. In this verse the servant is asking God to make his mission successful. Isn't it wonderful that we can ask God for help and that He can make us successful? He HEARS, LISTENS, and ANSWERS.

Suppose you are working on a project for school and you get to a certain point and nothing comes out right. You ask your Mom and she can't help. You ask your Dad and he's not sure. You discuss the problem with some friends, but they don't have the answer either. Suddenly, in tears, you cry out, "O Jesus, help me with this thing. I've got to make it work. I've done everything I know to do but I am completely stumped. Please lead me to the right information so I can finish my work. I give You all the glory. Amen." The next morning you get up and glance at "the project" sitting in the corner. Then it hits you, "This is what I need to do." Do you think this is an ACCIDENT?

Abraham's servant was successful in his duty for his master after asking God to help him. As surely as God helped Abraham's servant, He will answer your prayers. So, in your prayers, remember to praise and thank God, to ask Him for forgiveness, and to pray for others. This is the best way to be successful in everything you do.

Questions To Think About

1. *Why was Abraham's servant successful?*
2. *Why does God want us to pray?*

January 10

And Esau said, "Look, I am about to die; so what is this birthright to me?" Genesis 25:32

A birthright in Abraham's day was a big deal. It meant that the firstborn son inherited most of the family's fortune including a blessing from the father. In this verse Esau had been hunting. He was hungry and his Godly birthright meant nothing to him. All he could think about was his stomach. All he could think about was RIGHT NOW. When he gave up his birthright he gave up everything that is truly important.

Sometimes we fall into this trap. We don't want to wait for anything. We want to grow up faster, do what older kids are doing, go where older kids are going, have what other kids have, and we want it RIGHT NOW. I recently learned of three young men who burglarized a store because they wanted money RIGHT NOW to spend on things they wanted RIGHT NOW. They didn't want to wait to earn the money and pay for what they wanted. Their parents were ashamed and upset and now the young men have a police record. These boys had the same attitude as Esau.

So remember Esau. If your parents say that you have to wait for something or that you can't do something, go somewhere, or have what the other kids have, respect their rules. They know that WAITING is good for you. LATER, you will be glad you did.

Questions To Think About

1. Did Esau count the cost of giving up his birthright?
2. What are the consequences of giving away something you can't get back?

January 11

. . . and of all that You give me I will surely give a tenth to You. Genesis 28:22

Jacob awoke from a wonderful dream and realized that God was with him. Then, as our verse says, he vowed or promised to give God a tenth of all that he received. We can learn two important things from this Scripture. First of all, Jacob is saying that everything he has or will have comes from God. Jacob was so grateful, that he promised to give a portion back to God.

I know you have watched your parents put their tithes and offerings in the offering plate when it comes around each Sunday morning. Maybe you have asked for money from your parents so that you could put in something as well. Giving back to God is very much a part of worshipping Him, just like singing hymns, reading the Bible, and listening to the sermon. All these things glorify God and that is what worship is all about. So as soon as you are able to earn some money, you need to give part of it back to the Lord.

Questions To Think About

1. What does the word tithe mean?
2. Why should we give God a tithe?

January 12

Then God remembered Rachel, and God listened to her . . . Genesis 30:22

Have you ever wondered if God really knows who you are? Sometimes you might feel like He never listens to you and that you are just a "nobody". Nothing is farther from the truth. Could your parents forget that you are their child? That would never happen. We KNOW that God is ALWAYS with us, that He LOVES us, and that he will NEVER leave us because he tells us this time and time again in His Word. He is not like some people who make promises and don't keep them. God cannot lie. He always remembers us and listens when we talk to Him. In fact, God remembers us so well that He knows everything from the number of hairs on our heads to what we are thinking. He even knows our deepest secrets.

God remembered Rachel and listened to her when she wanted to give Jacob a son, and she did have a son—Joseph. You never need to wonder again if God knows you or listens to you. As with Rachel, He will never forget who you are or what you need.

QUESTIONS TO THINK ABOUT

1. How well do you know yourself?
2. How well does God know you?
3. Who knows you better?

January 13

May the Lord watch between you and me when we are absent one from another? Genesis 31:49

I'll never forget the day I said good-bye to my native friend, Lymtock. I met her while living on a tiny little island in the middle of the Pacific Ocean. We lived in the Marshall Islands for nearly four years and I made some very close friends, but Lymtock was a special friend. We shared so many good times together, laughing when we couldn't understand each other, and waiting for someone to interpret for us. We shared some sad times too when native traditions caused her to loose a child. I knew when we were preparing to leave the island to come back to the United States that I would have to say good-bye. I knew I would never see Lymtock again until we met in Heaven. The hour came when it was time to board the airplane. One last hug was all I could manage, but I'll never forget the words Lymtock said to me. "You pray for me and I'll pray for you."

It's been a long time since that day. I pray for Lymtock every time I think of her and I am sure she has prayed for me. Chances are that sometime in your life you will have to say good-bye to someone you will never see again on this earth. Isn't it a blessing to know that the Lord is so big, so awesome, that He can watch over all of us while we are away from each other?

Questions To Think About

1. Should we worry about those who are away from us? Why?

January 14

But Esau ran to meet him and embraced him and kissed him and they wept. Genesis 33:4

Remember how Jacob tricked his brother Esau out of their father's blessing? Jacob had to run away to another land because Esau was so angry he said he was going to kill him. Years later, Jacob decided to return home but he was afraid that Esau would still be angry with him. Our Scripture tells us that Esau ran to meet Jacob and all was forgiven.

Is there someone in your family who has done something wrong to you? Have you forgiven him for it? Maybe someone lied about you, stole something from you or got you into trouble with your parents. Or, maybe you need to go to someone and ask for forgiveness? Maybe you lied about him, stole something that belonged to him, or got him into trouble with his parents. Whatever the case, think about how awful you feel when anger lies between you and someone else. Think about how great it feels when all is forgiven and everyone is happy. If you need to forgive or be forgiven—DO IT! The Bible tells us not to let the sun go down on anger. It might be hard, but you will feel so much better. Remember, people know we are Christians when we have LOVE for each other.

QUESTIONS TO THINK ABOUT

1. Why is it important to forgive others?
2. Can you think of anyone you need to forgive or ask to forgive you?

January 15

And his brothers envied him . . . Genesis 37:11

Envy is the sin of wanting something that someone else has. That something could be a physical thing, it could be attention, or it could be a position another person has. Whatever it is when you wish it could be yours, that's envy. This is what happened to Joseph. Joseph's brothers envied him. Instead of loving him, as brothers should, they hated him so much they wanted to kill him. In fact, if a caravan of merchants hadn't come along and bought Joseph as a slave, he might have died in the pit where they threw him. You must be thinking, "That's HORRIBLE!" Or you might think, "How can anyone be so mean?"

You know, Joseph's brothers didn't just wake up one morning and say, "We hate Joseph, let's kill him." Little by little Joseph's brothers let their envy grow until it consumed them. Instead of talking to their father or asking the Lord to help them, they let their hatred grow until they murdered Joseph in their hearts and sold their own brother to foreigners as a slave. So many times horrible things start off small and grow because we feed them with more hatred.

We can do something to STOP the hatred that seems to be all around us today. HOW? I'm sure you know the answer already, but what is the opposite of hate? What is the opposite of hurt? What is the opposite of selfish? LOVE, KINDNESS, GIVING. So start praying and asking God to help you love your enemies, be kind to everyone, and give to those in need. In other words, BE A FRIEND.

Questions To Think About

1. How do envy and hatred get started?
2. What does the Bible say about loving those who hate you?

January 16

But the Lord was with Joseph and showed him mercy, and He gave him favor in the sight of the keeper of the prison. Genesis 39:21

How would you feel if you were thrown into prison for something you didn't do? Our Scripture today tells about Joseph being thrown into prison even though he was falsely accused. But Joseph knew that God was in control. He knew that God had a purpose behind his being in prison. God was watching over him. God caused the warden to like Joseph.

Sometimes it's hard to see what God has in mind when we are having tough times. Perhaps you or someone you know has lost a parent in an accident, through illness, or through divorce. Do you know someone who had to move and leave all of his friends because his dad got a new job? Or maybe you have tried to please your teacher and you just can't seem to no matter how hard you try. These things are difficult and they make us sad. Sometimes we don't understand and we wonder WHY? But, did you know that every single thing that happens to you goes through His hands first?

We shouldn't WORRY or BLAME someone for these kinds of things. Instead, we should be like Joseph and KNOW that God is always with us and will take care of us no matter what. WOW! That makes me feel much better. How about you? The Bible tells us that we can even have JOY in the bad times. When we talk to Jesus about our problems and listen for HIS ANSWER, we will have strength and peace during the hard times. SO BE A JOSEPH WHEN THINGS GO WRONG!

Questions To Think About

1. How should you react when things you can't control go wrong?
2. Think about the fact that God promises that nothing can separate us from His love.

January 17

So Joseph answered Pharaoh saying, "It is not in me, God will give Pharaoh an answer of peace." Genesis 41:6

Joseph was a great person, but he wasn't any different from you or me. He was born just like we are; he had a mom and dad and brothers and a sister. I'm sure he did "kid stuff" just like us. Yet he became one of the greatest men to ever live and no one who reads the Bible will ever forget Joseph.

Do you know why this "average person" became so great? To begin with, it was in God's plan for his life, and don't forget that God has a plan for your life too. In addition, Joseph did three things that aided him in becoming a great man. First of all, he was OBEDIENT. If you recall the story, Joseph had plenty of chances to sin against God, but he didn't and God always honors obedience. Secondly, Joseph always GAVE GOD CREDIT. He knew that God was the source of his ability and he was never afraid to tell people. Lastly, Joseph always put OTHERS first. He constantly did things to help those around him whether it was the prison warden or Pharaoh himself.

Joseph is an excellent example for us. We need to always remember to BE OBEDIENT, GIVE GOD THE GLORY, and PUT OTHERS FIRST. We may not become great in this life like Joseph did, but if we follow his example, we will have joy and peace in our spirits.

Questions To Think About

1. What fruit will be produced in our lives if we follow Joseph's example?
2. Joseph was a picture of Christ. What characteristics did Joseph have that reflected Jesus?
3. How can your life reflect Jesus?

January 18

. . . Peace be with you, do not be afraid. Your God and the God of your father has given you treasure in your sacks . . . Genesis 42:23

Have you ever been afraid or worried and not really known why? Sometimes deep down inside you have this worried feeling. You aren't sure why you have it but it keeps you from being happy. This is what happened to Joseph's brothers. Remember, they were the ones who sold him into slavery and lied to their father about what happened to Joseph. They were afraid that they were going to get into trouble because the money they had used to pay for the grain they bought in Egypt kept appearing in the grain sacks they were taking home. This would look like they had stolen the money and the grain; a crime punishable by death.

This same feeling can crop up in us when we have done something wrong and we haven't admitted our sin and asked God to forgive us. That feeling inside us is the Holy Spirit telling us we need to confess our sin. After we do, we realize we aren't afraid any more. Joseph's brothers had been living with a lie all those years and were full of fear. Our verse today says that Joseph's steward told the brothers not to be afraid. Jesus promises us today that if we will confess our sins he will faithfully forgive us and give us peace. Then we won't feel afraid any more.

Questions To Think About

1. How do you feel when you have confessed your sin and God has forgiven you?
2. How do we know God will forgive us when we ask Him to?

January 19

Moreover he kissed all his brothers and wept over them, and after that his brothers talked with him. Genesis 45:15

Have you ever gone to a family reunion and seen relatives that you haven't seen for a long time? You were so happy to see them you hugged and kissed everyone. But what if you had a disagreement with one of those relatives and the two of you refused to talk with each other. Perhaps both of you were so stubborn that neither of you would be the first to apologize and make up. Maybe this has never happened with a family member but has happened with a good friend. Are you both so angry and headstrong that neither of you will make up?

Joseph's brothers were in this exact situation. They found themselves face to face with the brother they had sold into slavery, but instead of a slave, he was now second in command of all Egypt. Joseph had the power of life and death over them. The brothers were afraid until they realized that Joseph wasn't angry with them. Once they understood this, they had a wonderful reunion.

It's so silly to hold grudges against others. You aren't hurting anyone but yourself. You end up denying yourself good times and wonderful memories. So if you have been avoiding someone or shutting him out of your life because of a grudge, what should you do about it? Get in touch with the relative or friend and talk out your differences and tell them how much you have missed them. YOU'LL BE GLAD YOU DID.

Questions To Think About

1. Why do we hold grudges?
2. What does God think about grudges?
3. Have you resolved any grudges or disagreements you have with others?

January 20

Joseph said to them, "Do not be afraid, for am I in the place of God?" Genesis 50:19

Have you ever had a day when it seemed that TROUBLE picked you out personally and followed you around trying to ruin your life? Do you wonder why in the world you live in this place, go to this school, have these brothers and sisters, these parents, and maybe even this church? We all know that everyone has bad days, but sometimes we just don't understand why God puts us where He does. Nothing seems to make sense; we have no ANSWERS and we need ANSWERS, right? Well, the easy answer is that we live in a fallen world and because of sin, bad things happen. But the second part of the answer is that we LIVE in this place, go to this SCHOOL, have the BROTHERS, SISTERS, PARENTS and CHURCH we have because GOD PLACES US WHERE HE WANTS US.

Yesterday we learned that Joseph forgave his brothers for all the evil they had done to him. He forgave them because even though the brothers sinned and did everything because they hated Joseph and wanted to hurt him, God was in control of the situation. God wanted Joseph in Egypt so that he could save the lives of his brothers and their families during the famine.

In today's scripture, Joseph reassures his brothers again that he has forgiven them and that they don't have to fear him. He tells them it was all God's plan for him to end up in Egypt. So when we can't see any reason for our circumstances, we need to remember that we are where God has placed us. Instead of being angry or rebellious we need to ask, "What can I learn from this? What is God trying to teach me?"

Questions To Think About

1. How did Joseph react to evil treatment?
2. What can we learn from Joseph?

January 21

The Lord gave, and the Lord has taken away;
Blessed be the name of the Lord. Job 1:21b

Job was a very righteous man and had a wonderful life. Everything he could possibly want or need was his. Suddenly, all in one day, he lost everything he had, his wealth, his children, and later even his health. He knew he had not sinned against God and at first he couldn't understand why all these bad things were happening to him. His friends kept telling him that he must have sinned and that God was punishing him. It wasn't until later, when the Lord himself came to Job, that Job understood.

Sometimes bad things happen to us and we wonder if we are being punished for something we have done wrong. Or, we wonder why we are being punished. We may even think that it isn't fair. Maybe we aren't allowed to go to a party or concert. Perhaps it's something more serious like loosing someone we love through death or divorce. Understand that we do reap what we sow. God does get us back on the right path by disciplining us, but not every bad thing that happens to us is because we have sinned. You remember all of our discussions about Joseph? Well, now we have another example—Job. Today's scripture gives us the assurance that God is always in control no matter what is happening around us or to us. And what's more, GOD KNOWS BEST! Because of this, we can ALWAYS TRUST GOD to work all things that happen to us for our good. So we don't have to worry about things that have happened in the past or things that might happen in the future. We can be happy knowing that the Lord is taking care of us.

Questions To Think About

1. Is it our fault when bad things happen to us?
2. Who is in control of all things?
3. Why should we not worry about the future?

January 22

But as for me, I would seek God . . . Job 5:8

Job was really suffering. He had lost everything and was covered in huge painful sores. Some of his friends came to comfort him, but they weren't doing a very good job of it. They kept telling him how bad he was and what he should do to be forgiven. Job was feeling worse by the minute.

When my daughter was young, she had a terrible case of the mumps. Her neck and jaws were so swollen it made her head look pointed. In fact, her head looked like a triangle. When her friends came to see her they all laughed at the way she looked and called her pinhead. Have you ever had friends like this who really let you down when you needed someone to make you feel better?

We can learn at least two things from Job's situation. First, we should never be like Job's friends that condemned him and we should never be like my daughter's friends who made fun of her. We must always keep in mind that we should treat others like we would want them to treat us. Secondly and most importantly, no matter how badly we hurt or how badly our friends make us feel we need to always, "Seek God." He is our COMFORTER. He will always help us through the hard times.

Questions To Think About

1. Why should we go to God with our problems?
2. How should we treat others who are going through difficult times?

January 23

. . . *But how can a man be righteous before God?* Job 9:2b

When you are sick and can't do all the things that you usually do, you have lots of time to think. This was happening to Job. He was beginning to think that maybe his friends were right. Maybe he was being punished for his sins, but he had always helped everyone in need and he thought he had a close walk with the Lord. Everything was all mixed up in Job's mind and he didn't understand.

As Job asked in our Scripture today, how do we become righteous before God? If we try to go out and do good things, will that make us righteous before God? Or, what if we just make sure that we don't do anything that's too bad, will that do it? The Bible says that the only way we can become righteous is to BELIEVE in JESUS. That sounds easy doesn't it? But what does BELIEVING in JESUS mean? It means KNOWING that Jesus lived—but that's not all. It means SAYING we believe He is God's Son—but that's not all. It means TRYING to be like Jesus—but that's not all. BELIEVING IN JESUS means accepting that we are sinners and can never, ever be good enough on our own to be righteous before God. It means that we understand that JESUS is the ONLY one who can give us His righteousness because he lived a perfect life, died on the cross to pay for our sins, and rose from the dead so we might have eternal life. When we ask Jesus into our heart to be our Lord and Savior—when we BELIEVE in JESUS—we are made righteous before God with the righteousness of JESUS.

Questions To Think About

1. Is it hard to become righteous before God?
2. Is Jesus in your heart?
3. If Jesus is not in your heart and you still have questions ask your parents or teacher to help you with your questions.

January 24

You shall call and I will answer You. Job 14:15

Do you ever wonder how Jesus "calls" us or "talks" to us? The most important way that Jesus "talks" to us today is through His Word, the BIBLE. Did you know that every possible question that has been or will be asked has already been answered in the Bible? Everything that you need to know to live your life God's way is in His Word. Of course, this means you have to read it and think about it and maybe even get your Mom and Dad to help you find the answer in the Bible if you can't find it on your own. We should also memorize Scripture so the Holy Spirit can "recall" it to our minds when we need an answer to a question or strength when we are tempted.

PRAYER is another way we "talk" to God. It is a great blessing from God that we can pray anywhere and anytime we want, and we should pray often. When we pray, we also need to be still and listen for the Holy Spirit who may bring to mind people or things we need to pray for. There are even examples of people waking in the night to pray for a missionary. At that exact time, halfway around the world, the missionary was rescued from some sort of evil. We know that God ALWAYS ANSWERS when we call on Him.

QUESTIONS TO THINK ABOUT

1. Take time this week to find a plan for reading God's Word daily.
2. Why should we read the Bible daily?

January 25

For I know that my Redeemer lives, and
He shall stand at last on the earth; . . . Job 19:25

According to this Scripture, there are three things that Job knew for sure and we can know these things as well. First, we know that we have a Redeemer. A redeemer is one who pays our debt. God is a just God; therefore, sin must be punished and paid for by someone. When Jesus died on the cross, he took all of the punishment we had earned on himself—He paid all the debt of sin that we owed—He REDEEMED us. Maybe you have read a story about someone who, in the "olden days", was thrown into debtor's prison. They could not be released until they had paid back all the money they owed to people. I always thought, "How can they pay the money back if they can't work?" Of course, they were incapable of paying back the debt themselves, so they had to rely on someone else. This is how we are. We are incapable of paying the debt of sin we owe, so we have to rely on Jesus to pay it for us or to REDEEM us.

The next thing that Job knew and we can know as well is that JESUS LIVES. This is why we celebrate Easter. We know that Jesus rose from the dead and is alive in Heaven with God right now. This is why we can talk to Him and depend on Him. He is alive and is ruling over all things.

The last thing Job tells us in this verse is that Jesus is coming again. We don't know when this will happen, but we do know that He is our King of Kings and He promised to come back some day. We know that we can trust Him to keep His promise because he always does. So, just as Job knew that we have a REDEEMER, that JESUS LIVES, and that JESUS IS COMING AGAIN, we can believe these things too.

Questions To Think About

1. Why do we need a Redeemer?
2. How do we know Jesus lives?
3. How do we know Jesus is coming again?

January 26

. . . *and the joy of the hypocrite is but for a moment* . . . Job 20:5b

Why is it that the local bully always wins? Why does the kid that lies, steels, and cheats get away with it? This Scripture has the answer. It may seem like the bully and the cheater always win. In fact, they may have a great time and win for a while, but they won't win forever. The Scripture says, *the joy of the hypocrite is but for a moment* . . . You see, these guys may think they are happy and they may be having a good time right now, but they will have to pay some day and when they do, the pleasure they have had will seem very short—only a moment. And, by the way, they may not really be having all that much fun. They may actually be quite miserable because they have no peace. They are living a life that will be full of regret.

Only Jesus can give us PEACE. And His peace is EVERLASTING. Only Jesus gives us a FREEDOM that lets us soar like eagles and a JOY that fills our lives with great memories. We can truly live a rich full life without regrets when we are obedient to the Lord.

QUESTIONS TO THINK ABOUT

1. Would you rather be the bully, the cheat, the unsaved, or the Lord's?
2. Can a bully or cheat change? What will it take?
3. What can you do to help someone who needs to change?

January 27

Behold the fear of the Lord, that is wisdom and to depart from evil is understanding. Job 28:28b

What is your favorite subject in school—RECESS doesn't count. Did you know that God has given each of us talents? If you haven't found yours yet, hang in there, you will. Usually we know our talent because it is something that is easy for us or something we never get tired of doing. But like Job, we need to learn that true wisdom and real understanding come from the Lord. This doesn't mean you can drop out of school. God gives you teachers and parents to help you develop your special gift. What this does mean is that you might be the smartest person around, full of worldly knowledge, but if you don't know Jesus you don't have true wisdom.

The dictionary tells us that wisdom is "understanding of what is true, right, or lasting, common sense; good judgment." Even if a person is highly educated and extremely smart, if they are not Christians, they can never have wisdom. They are unable to see what is really true because only those who *fear the Lord* have wisdom. Some day you might even encounter someone who says that truth is whatever you want it to be. They think if they want to do something and "it feels good" it must be right. In other words, they think right and wrong are open for discussion and it depends on the circumstances.

The Bible teaches that there is an absolute right and an absolute wrong. It has nothing to do with circumstances. Right and wrong have been decreed by God in His Word and nothing that any of us think can change it. Study God's Word—our road map for life—to know the difference between God's wisdom and worldly knowledge.

QUESTIONS TO THINK ABOUT

1. What is godly wisdom?
2. What is the difference between what the Bible says about truth and what the World says about truth?
3. Prepare yourself to recognize the difference between God's wisdom and the "wisdom of the World".

NOTES

January 28

Have I not wept for him who was in trouble?
Has not my soul grieved for the poor? Job 20:25

Our Scripture today tells us that Job had true compassion for those in trouble and for the poor. Let's look at compassion for a minute. The dictionary says compassion is, "the deep feeling of sharing the suffering of another in the inclination to give aid or support, or to show mercy." What does that mean? Think about the new kid who comes to your school and is really poor or maybe doesn't do well in class and no one wants to have anything to do with him. What should you do? Have compassion. In other words, befriend him, help him with his homework and maybe get your parents or church involved in helping his family with food, clothes, or whatever they need.

Be a Job this week and find someone you can help. You may have an opportunity to share the Gospel with him and gain, not only a friend, but a new brother in Christ as well.

Questions To Think About

1. Is compassion an idea or an action?
2. How can you show compassion to someone you know?

January 29

Let me not, I pray, show partiality to anyone; . . . Job 32:21a

It's easy when you are popular to forget about the kids who are never chosen for anything, who don't have any close friends, or who are ignored—maybe even by the teachers. You won't have to go far to find someone who fits this description. We all have a tendency to be partial to the people who are like us; the ones who dress like we do, make good grades like we do, go to the same church as we do, you know, the "in" crowd. On the flip side of the coin, maybe you show partiality to someone because they are popular, or are good looking, or have lots of money.

This isn't the way God intended it to be. As Christians, we are to treat all people the same. This doesn't mean we can't have a best friend. What it does mean is that we are NEVER to be rude or impolite to anyone. We should always be KIND to everyone. It is so easy to overlook others when we are wrapped up on our own little groups. Most people know the "Golden Rule" but few people live it. God wants us to learn to make kindness our LIFESTYLE and treat others as Jesus did.

Questions To Think About

1. What is the Golden Rule?
2. Why shouldn't we show partiality to some people?
3. Go out of your way this week to "make someone's day".

January 30

Where is God my Maker, who gives songs in the night? Job 35:10

Who is your favorite singer or singing group right now? Whose songs really give you a lift? Whose songs make you happy? Whose songs do you share with your friends? Whose songs truly touch your heart? Whose songs do you know all the words to? Whose songs do you really relate to? Whose songs do you sing all day long? No matter who that might be today, it probably won't be the same next year. You will either find another group or singer that you like better, the old group will go out of style, or you will grow tired of the "old songs".

In our Scripture, Job's friend reminds him that God, who created him, has also given him songs during his times of trouble. In other words, God is not ignoring Job's misfortune; He is giving Job comfort or peace in his heart. God's peace will make Job's heart "sing" if he will only listen. Unlike the songs that our favorite artists sing, which may make us happy momentarily, only God's "songs" can bring us true joy. When we are troubled we need to turn to God and ask Him to make our hearts sing.

Questions To Think About

1. What does it mean when Job's friend tells him that God *gives songs in the night*?

January 31

Everything under heaven is Mine. Job 41:11b

One of the first words we learn as a baby is MINE. We value possessions very highly. When we were living in the Marshall Islands we learned an excellent lesson in sharing. The natives believed in sharing everything. Whatever they had you could have. And even though they didn't have much, if someone needed something and someone else had it, they shared it. They never had any dispute over who owned what because they felt that they all owned everything together. The missionaries had a hard time building a school because if concrete blocks were stacked up waiting for the workmen to build walls and someone needed a concrete block they took it and used it. It was a switch for the missionaries to have to teach them "not to share".

We need to see that everything we have is really just loaned to us by God because He owns everything. You might say, "No, my parents gave me everything I have." There is a lot more to it than that. God has given your parents the ability to make money and blessed them with a job or business. He has also blessed their business so that they have an income, which provides the money to buy you things you need and want. So be very thankful for all of the blessings that God has shared with you. Remember, "Every good and perfect gift is from God."

QUESTIONS TO THINK ABOUT

1. Who gives us our daily bread? Are you thankful?

February 1

But Moses said to God, "Who am I that I should go to Pharaoh and that I should bring the children of Israel out of Egypt?" So God said "I will certainly be with you . . ." Exodus 3:11-12

"But I can't tell anyone about Jesus and what He means to me. I'm just a kid and no one would pay any attention to me. Besides I would be embarrassed." Have you ever thought this or even said it? Well, you're in good company because Moses told God something very similar, but God didn't let him off the hook. God promised Moses, "I will certainly be with you." In other words, God told Moses that with His help, Moses could do whatever task God put before him.

I know a ten-year-old boy who was bold enough to stand up in church and ask the entire congregation to pray for his father who was not a believer. He loved his father and wanted him to be saved so badly that he didn't care what people thought of him. But the people in the church admired him and prayed for his father. What if he had been too embarrassed to say anything? We might think, "Well that was in church and the people in church understand and expect that." Where else could the boy have asked for prayer? Besides, the boy said he was "scared to death" but he did it anyway because it was the right thing to do.

What are you afraid of? The Bible says that God will always be with us, so we have nothing to fear. Pray that God will give you an opportunity to share Jesus with someone this week. Remember, God wants you to be AVAILABLE. He will take care of the ABLE part; you just have to take advantage of the opportunity when it happens.

QUESTIONS TO THINK ABOUT

1. Should you be embarrassed to tell others that you are a Christian?
2. Should you be a certain age before you share the Gospel with someone?
3. If you did tell someone that you were a Christian, would your life match your testimony?

NOTES

February 2

And Pharaoh said, "Who is the Lord that I should obey His voice to let Israel go? I do not know the Lord . . ." Exodus 5:2

These are such sad words. I DO NOT KNOW THE LORD. At least Pharaoh was honest; he truly didn't know Him. Today, so many kids who are in and out of church say, "Yah, I know Jesus. See, I've got on a WWJD bracelet. Besides, I go on all the mission trips and to camp every summer." These kids know ABOUT Jesus, but they don't really KNOW Him. He doesn't live in their hearts. They want to DO all the fun things at church, but they don't want to do what it takes to get to KNOW Jesus. They don't understand that DOING a bunch of "good things" is not what BEING a Christian is all about.

First of all, to BECOME a Christian, we have to realize that we are sinners and can never be good enough or do enough good things to be saved. Secondly, we have to understand that the DEBT required to pay for our sin is DEATH. Jesus lived a perfect life so he had no debt of sin to pay. Instead, He paid the DEBT we owed for our sins with His DEATH. Thirdly, when we realize that we are sinners and that we can't pay our debt, we must repent and ask God to forgive us, and ask Jesus to come into our hearts and take control of our lives.

After we BECOME a Christian, we want to know our Lord better. It is like any relationship. When you meet someone and you don't know him very well, you want to find out all about him. It is the same thing with Jesus. We can spend the rest of our lives getting to know Him. We do this by READING THE BIBLE. The Bible is His story. We also get to know Him better by talking to Him. This of course is PRAYER. A closer relationship with Jesus will produce the "Fruit of the Spirit" in us. This fruit won't appear all at the same time, but will grow in our lives as we grow in Christ. You can find a list of this fruit in Galatians 5:22-23.

QUESTIONS TO THINK ABOUT

1. What does it mean to BE a Christian?
2. How can we have a relationship with Christ?
3. What is the fruit of the Spirit?

NOTES

February 3

Moreover the man Moses was very great in the land of Egypt: in the sight of Pharaoh's servants and in the sight of the people.
Exodus 11:3b

Do you know what you want to be when you grow up? When I was your age, I wanted to be an actress, partly because I loved to pretend, but also because I had a wonderful drama teacher who inspired me. As we think about our life's purpose, we often want important, famous people to know us and like us. We want to "rub elbows" with major league baseball players, famous singers, or even the President of the United States and the list goes on and on. Sometimes this happens, but most of the time the Lord has a plan for us that we would never think of choosing. Isn't it great that GOD KNOW BEST? The most exciting life plan for us is God's life plan.

Let's consider Moses. He didn't want to have any part of public life. He had run away from Egypt and the Egyptian court and was happily living the quiet life of a shepherd. While he was a simple shepherd, God told Moses that He had a different plan for his life. God wanted Moses to lead the Israelites out of Egypt. After answering Moses' many excuses, God said GO and Moses went. Understand that if Moses had been GREAT in the eyes of the Pharaoh he might have talked with him and worked out some sort of deal right away. However, Pharaoh didn't respect Moses and wasn't going to let several million slaves leave Egypt on the word of a mere shepherd. But as God unfolded His plan, Moses found himself in a position of authority that was GREAT in the eyes of the Egyptian people and eventually the Egyptians sent the Israelites away with a great horde of gold and silver and other precious things. What's more, the Egyptians knew that God was behind it all and that everything went according to His plan.

It's amazing how God always works out even the smallest details if we just follow Him. It really doesn't matter if the rich and famous and powerful people know us because GOD KNOWS US and has the perfect plan for our lives.

QUESTIONS TO THINK ABOUT

1. Begin praying that God will show you His plan for your life. (This is a lifelong prayer.)

NOTES

February 4

And Moses said to the people: "Remember this day in which you went out of Egypt, out of the house of bondage; for by strength of hand the Lord brought you out of this place." Exodus 13:3

Here you are at your friend's house. Let's call your friend Jessie. Your parents gave their permission for you to go to Jessie's house after school—but you didn't know that Jessie's parents wouldn't be there. Your parents have a rule that you can never go to anyone's house unless a parent or other grownup is present. You promised that you would always obey this rule. What are you going to do?

First, pray and ask God to give you strength to DO THE RIGHT THING. Now, the RIGHT THING is to tell Jessie that you can't stay at anyone's house if a parent isn't at home. Then, CALL YOUR PARENTS and tell them to pick you up or tell them you are on your way home. If Jessie is a true friend he will respect you and your parents' rules.

Isn't it great that just as the Lord brought His people out of bondage in Egypt, He is still bringing His children out of bad circumstances today? Jesus is always with us no matter what circumstance surround us and when we call on Him, He will ALWAYS give us the STRENGTH to DO THE RIGHT THING.

Questions To Think About

1. Would it matter if you stayed at your friend's and didn't tell your parents?
2. If you stayed, what would your actions say to your parents, to God, to your friend, to yourself?

February 5

The Lord is my strength and song, and He has become my salvation; He is my God and I will praise Him; My father's God and I will exalt Him. Exodus 15:2

This is part of the *Song of Moses*. What a great song this is. Let's look at this song and see if we can sing it from our hearts as Moses did. First, we need to ask ourselves some questions: Is the Lord my strength and song? Is He my Savior? Is He my God? Do I praise Him? Will I exalt Him? How we answer these questions will determine whether or not we can sing this song from our heart.

Let's expand these questions and apply them directly to our lives. As we ask ourselves these things, let's really think about them and answer them truthfully. Do I really depend on the Lord for strength to get me through all kinds of situations? Do I call on Him to help me in every circumstance? Does all that God does for me make me happy and thankful? When I sing praises to Him do I mean it from the bottom of my heart? Will I exalt Him by being obedient to those in authority over me?

Isn't it wonderful to know that the God of the universe is always with each one of us, that He knows each and every one of our problems, and that He cares about each one of us? Moses understood this and it made him want to sing. In fact, he did. Let's sing this song too!

Questions To Think About

1. Think again about all the questions in this devotional. Then sing!

February 6

"Behold, I will stand before you there on the rock in Horeb: and you shall strike the rock and water will come out of it, that the people may drink." Exodus 17:6

Do you know someone who complains constantly? No matter what happens he never seems to be happy or satisfied. The people Moses led out of Egypt were exactly like this. They complained about everything. God was so good to them. He had guided them, protected them, and fed them, and still they grumbled and demanded more. Poor Moses frequently had to go to the Lord and ask Him what he should do with these ungrateful people even though God GAVE them EVERYTHINNG they needed and more.

Do you know anyone like the Israelites who complains about everything? Complaining is a very bad habit that is easy to fall into. We are never satisfied when we take our eyes off of God and selfishly look only at ourselves. If we get some new clothes, we gripe because we really wanted a new bike; if we have cake for supper, we say we wanted chocolate chip cookies; if we get to have a friend over for a few hours after school, we whine because we can't have them spend the night. Why are we not satisfied? Is it our parents' fault? Maybe it's our sisters' or brothers' or teachers' or preachers' or . . . ? No, it is no one's fault but our own; we have a CHOICE. We can CHOOSE to complain or we can CHOOSE to be satisfied.

Questions To Think About

1. *Who gives us all that we have? Then, when we grumble, we are complaining about whom?*
2. *If we only think about what we want, we can't see the needs of others. This week, STOP, LOOK, and LISTEN. Then help someone else.*

February 7

"You shall not steal." Exodus 20:15

This is one of the TEN COMMANDMENTS and I know you've heard it many times and most of us feel we don't have any trouble with this one. Let's look at it a little closer and see if we REALLY do keep it. Stealing means taking something that isn't ours without asking the owner's permission. We may think we're perfectly safe on this one, but let's think about it. Have you ever kept the loose change you found lying around the house when you knew it wasn't yours, eaten cookies your Mom was saving for company, taken your brother's or sister's cool necklace, or kept a book you borrowed from a friend? We do these things without even thinking twice about it. The truth of the matter is, we are stealing.

So think about it before you *BORROW* that necklace or book. If you didn't ask first, then ASK PERMISSION. If you did ask, DON'T FORGET TO RETURN IT. This helps your friends and parents and sisters and brothers trust you and respect your WORD. This is why *You shall not steal.* Is one of the TEN COMMANDMENTS and is so important for us to follow.

Questions To Think About

1. What does this commandment mean (You shall not steal.)?
2. Is wasting time stealing?

February 8

Also you shall not oppress a stranger, for you know the heart of a stranger, because you were strangers in the land of Egypt. Exodus 23:9

Have you ever been a stranger? I mean have you ever moved to a new town, gone on a trip where you didn't know anyone, or stayed by yourself with someone you didn't really know? I'll never forget when I was your age and we moved to Arizona. We hadn't been there long when my sister got really sick and was in the hospital. My Mom and Dad took turns staying with her, but they worried about what they would do with me if they ever needed to be at the hospital together. An elderly couple that lived by us volunteered to take care of me if this happened. It was very nice of the couple to help out, but I was scared. I didn't really know them at all and I might have to live with them for a while.

The day did come when my parents were both needed at the hospital. I wanted to stay with my parents and sister, but I couldn't. So I went to live with that elderly couple. You know what? They were so nice to me. They played games with me, fed me things I really liked, and because he had been in the army he showed me how to polish my shoes, "the way we did in the army." My shoes outshined everyone's at school. Eventually, my sister got better and we were all able to come back home again.

I don't even remember the elderly couple's names, but I have never forgotten how nice they were to a family that needed help. This is what our Scripture today is all about. It means taking time to see those who are lonely, befriending those who are new at school or church, and making life a little nicer for someone else because of the way we treat them. This is WHAT JESUS WOULD DO.

Questions To Think About

1. What would Jesus do if He met someone who was lonely?
2. What are you going to do the next time you meet a kid who is all alone?

February 9

Then the Lord Spoke to Moses, saying; "Speak to the children of Israel, that they bring Me an offering. From everyone who GIVES IT WILLINGLY with his heart you shall take My offering." Exodus 25:1-2

I know you have heard people say; "Be a cheerful giver." This is what our Scripture today is talking about. Do you ever have any problem giving your Mom, Dad, favorite teacher, or special friend a gift? We usually want to give them a lot more than we can afford. Why is that? It's because we think so much of them. We treasure the relationship we have with them. I'll always remember the time a friend of mine gave me his top. It meant so much to me because, first of all, it was the only top I could make spin. Secondly, I knew how much he liked that top.

This is the same attitude God wants us to have when we bring our offering to Him. He wants us to give our offerings because we love Him and treasure the wonderful relationship we have with Him. He wants us to give our offering WITH OUR HEARTS.

QUESTIONS TO THINK ABOUT

1. What does it mean to give with our hearts?
2. Is an offering always money?

February 10

And they shall know that I am the Lord their God. Exodus 29: 46

In this Scripture God is telling Moses how things will be with the children of Israel and He ends with this wonderful statement, *"And they shall know that I am the Lord their God."* We might think, "So what's the big deal?" Well, just the fact that the children of Israel could say for sure that the Lord was their God was awesome. Why? Because everyone has a God in his life, but too often it isn't THE God of the Universe, THE God of the Bible. Sometimes it's this way because they have never heard of the Lord. Sometimes it's this way because they don't want the Lord in their lives. They don't want to turn from sin and run into the arms of our Lord.

Isn't it wonderful that the Scripture teaches that we CAN KNOW that the Lord is our God? When we repent, turn from our sin, and ask Jesus into our hearts to be our Lord and Savior, He will come into our lives and be our God. Then we KNOW that He is "the Lord our God."

Questions To Think About

1. What does it mean to "ask Jesus into your heart?"
2. Have you asked Jesus to be your Lord and Savior?

February 11

I have put wisdom in the hearts of all the gifted artisans . . .
Exodus 31:6b

When God gave the Israelites instructions for building His Tabernacle, He covered every detail. He wanted everything done a certain way and He made provisions for all the materials that the people needed to accomplish the task. Remember that in Egypt the people were sent away with gold, silver, precious stones, and lots of jewelry, just what they needed. But in addition to the materials to build the Tabernacle, God gave the people wisdom to create everything needed to complete the Tabernacle and its furnishings.

The GOOD NEWS is that He is still the One who puts wisdom in our hearts so that we can sing, play musical instruments, build things, paint great pictures, act, and write. The Lord is the giver of all good gifts and we should use them for His glory. God built His Tabernacle so that he could be close to and communicate with His people. He wants the same thing today. So develop your gift and use it to glorify the Lord.

QUESTIONS TO THINK ABOUT

1. What is your "gift"?
2. How can you use your gift to glorify God?

February 12

And I said to them, "Whoever has any gold, let them break it off." So they gave it to me and I cast it into the fire, and this calf came out. Exodus 32:24

In our Scripture today Aaron is telling Moses, who just came down from receiving the Ten Commandments, why Moses found the children of Israel worshiping a GOLDEN CALF. This is one of the most incredible lies ever told. Aaron, a religious leader and Moses' brother, saw God perform all of His miracles, yet there he is telling this terrible lie. It seems ridiculous that this is the best story that Aaron can come up with. Nobody would believe that story.

This is often what happens when we get caught doing something we shouldn't. We end up coming up with some pretty unbelievable stories. Have you ever told your teacher, "My dog ate my homework." Or what about, "I didn't want to write on the wall, they made me do it." Or, "I only did it because EVERYONE else was doing it." As the Scripture teaches, it doesn't matter who we are, how old we are or if we are a follower of God, all of us are capable of lying. This is exactly why we need to stop and think before we speak or act. And most of all we need to stay close to Jesus.

Questions To Think About

1. How do we keep from lying?
2. How can we stay close to Jesus?

February 13

So Moses gave a commandment, and they caused it to be proclaimed throughout the camp, saying, "let neither man nor woman do any more work for the offering of the sanctuary." And the people were restrained from bringing, for the material they had was sufficient for all the work to be done—indeed too much. Exodus 36:6-7

Moses had asked the people to bring the things they needed for building and furnishing the Tabernacle. Remember, they were told only to bring a gift if it were from the heart. They brought so much that Moses had to tell them to stop. Isn't that wonderful? Just think of all the things our churches could do if the people brought so much that the leaders had to tell them to stop. I have never heard of this happening and it tells us something about our giving and our hearts.

I know you don't have a lot of money right this minute, but you can do what the Bible says and give a tenth of what you do have. Then you can give your time, which is a truly great gift. Give your time to help the widows of your church with chores around their houses that they can't do. Or baby-sit for some new mother and father who can't afford to pay you. Or clean the church once a quarter.

Perhaps some day we will hear the announcement, "Let neither man nor woman do any more work for the offering of the sanctuary . . . for the material they had was sufficient for all the work to be done—indeed too much."

Questions To Think About

1. Do you give a tenth of what you have?
2. How can you give of your time?

February 14

Then they made the plate of the holy crown of pure gold, and wrote on it an inscription like the engraving of a signet: HOLINESS TO THE LORD. Exodus 39:30

The turban that the High Priest wore had a gold plate fastened to the front of it for all to see. This plate said HOLINESS TO THE LORD. Today, our High Priest is Jesus who is in Heaven reigning with God. We are the temple of the Holy Spirit and are all priests before the Lord. Even though we don't wear a sign that says HOLINESS TO THE LORD, we know that we should live holy lives so that others will know we belong to God. We know this because God doesn't change and He still tells us to be holy which means, "set apart".

What does it mean to be "set apart"? It means that we are to be different from the unbelievers in the world. We are to treat others differently, we are to help and care for others, and we are to love others. Today we are wearing the same sign as Aaron, but we see it in our actions, not on our foreheads. So BE A BLESSING AND BE BLESSED.

Questions To Think About

1. What do other people "read" in your life?

February 15

Then the cloud covered the tabernacle of meeting, and the glory of the Lord filled the tabernacle. For the cloud of the Lord was above the tabernacle by day and fire was over it by night, in the sight of all the house of Israel, throughout all their journeys.
Exodus 40:34, 38

Moses had built the tabernacle and its furnishings and prepared it exactly as the Lord had asked him to. When it was finished the Lord God in the form of a cloud by day and a pillar of fire by night came and dwelt with the children of Israel. He directed their lives with his presence.

The Lord is still here with us today. He doesn't take the form of a cloud by day and a pillar of fire by night; He indwells us. The Holy Spirit lives in us. That's pretty heavy stuff isn't it? But that is how God chose to have fellowship with His people after Jesus died on the cross and ascended into Heaven. It sounds like magic or nonsense to those who don't believe in Jesus, but for those of us who are Christians, we know it's true.

Last year I went to a performance by a Christian illusionist. After he had performed all of these wonderful tricks, like making lions, people, and even a helicopter appear or disappear on stage, he told us that all of these tricks were just illusions. He said none of it was REAL. He went on to say that he wanted us to meet SOMEONE who is REAL if we never had. That person is JESUS OUR LORD AND SAVIOR. He told us that Jesus lives in his heart and he invited us to ask Jesus to come into our hearts too. What a testimony! What an exciting show!

QUESTIONS TO THINK ABOUT

1. Does Jesus live in your heart?
2. Does Jesus direct your life as He did the Israelites so many years ago?

February 16

If a person swears speaking thoughtlessly with his lips . . .
Leviticus 5:4

The aim of Leviticus is to remind people that God said, "be holy because I am holy." The book tells of many different kinds of sin and in our verse today, a couple of things should be pointed out. The two things have to do with swearing and lying.

Have you ever been to a trial at the Court House and watched the witnesses take the stand and swear to tell the truth? If you tell a lie while you are testifying in court you can go to jail. I knew a man who wanted to help his friend who was on trial. He lied during his testimony and ended up having to spend thirty days in jail. This is what it is talking about when the verse says not to speak thoughtlessly and swear that what you say is true. However, it is not only important to tell the truth when you are "under oath", we should always tell the truth.

The Bible tells us that if we say we have never lied, the truth is not in us. So, we know that we all have the capacity and tendency to lie. Sometimes we lie to keep out of trouble or to keep from hurting someone's feelings or to make a bigger, better sounding story. Sometimes we even lie when there is no reason to. Thankfully, when we fail and end up lying we can repent and God will forgive us. But we need to remember that the goal is to not lie in the first place. So THINK ABOUT WHAT YOU ARE GOING TO SAY AND MAKE IT THE TRUTH!!

Questions To Think About

1. Is lying always verbal?

February 17

A fire shall always be burning on the altar; it shall never go out.
Leviticus 6:13

God has often used fire as a symbol for his presence. Remember God in the burning bush talking with Moses and the column of fire that led the Israelites by day out of Egypt? With the sacrifices, the fire showed that God accepted the sacrifice that looked forward to Jesus. Isn't it WONDERFUL that God SO loved us that He sent JESUS to make that sacrifice required to pay for ALL of OUR SINS?

The fire still burns for us today. God accepts us today because of Jesus' sacrifice. He loves us, takes care of us, encourages us, and teaches us. He provides us with all that we have and will take us home to live with Him someday. Today is the day to thank God for sending His Son to be our substitute sacrifice. Today is the day to begin spending time in His Word so we can know Him better. Today is the day to begin a life of prayer. Again, we should be SO THANKFUL FOR OUR SAVIOR.

QUESTIONS TO THINK ABOUT

1. How can we show our thankfulness for our Savior?
2. Is Jesus your Savior?

February 18

This is what the Lord spoke saying: "By those who come near Me I must be regarded as holy and before all the people I must be glorified." Leviticus 10:3

God told the people in our Scripture that He must be glorified or honored before ALL the people. Have you ever thought about what it means to honor the Lord? Honoring God doesn't have to be a GREAT BIG deal like getting up in front of church and saying a hundred memory verses, although this isn't a bad idea. We can honor the Lord in many ways that most people don't even think about. For example, it honors God when we have a good attitude around the house with our parents, brothers and sisters. It honors God when we don't complain if we are asked to help our little brother with homework or do the dishes or clean our rooms. It honors God when we cheerfully and immediately obey our parents in whatever they ask us to do. In other words, it honors God when we put others first. WOW, wouldn't this make a nice peaceful household. We honor the Lord when we don't have to be noticed for everything we do well. We bring honor to God when we are patient with others. We honor God when we let others have a say in how things should be done rather than always insisting we do things our way. If we just do these few things we will GLORIFY THE LORD BEFORE ALL THE PEOPLE.

Questions To Think About

1. Think of other ways to bring glory to God.
2. What must our heart be like to accomplish these things?

February 19

You shall therefore consecrate yourselves . . . Leviticus 11:43

To consecrate means to set apart as sacred. Sacred means to be devoted to a single holy purpose. So in this Scripture the Lord is commanding us to devote our lives to a holy purpose. You may think that you are too young to have a "holy purpose", but God never says that. Remember Jesus as a boy was "about His Father's business". He was obedient to his mother and father and grew in knowledge and wisdom. You can do this as well. Reading you Bible and putting to use what you learn as well as praying will help you.

RESPECT and OBEY all those in authority over you. This is another part of consecrating yourself. Listen when those in authority teach you and whatever you do, do it with God's holy purpose in mind. Remember, ONLY WHAT YOU DO FOR THE LORD LASTS. Everything else doesn't really matter.

Questions To Think About

1. What does it mean to "consecrate yourself"?
2. How can you devote yourself to a holy purpose? Now? In the future?

February 20

Now the leper shall cry, "Unclean! Unclean!" . . .
Leviticus 13:45-46

Leprosy is a terrible and highly contagious disease. People who had it in Bible times were supposed to warn others that they had the disease by yelling, "unclean" as they passed by them. It is not as common today, but we can learn a lesson from the leper of the Bible.

Although fewer people have leprosy today, many people we come in contact with have SPIRITUAL LEPROSY or are unclean on the inside. We can't tell by looking at them, but we can usually tell by the way they act. They have not been cured of their leprosy and made whole on the inside. They are sin sick and don't even know there is anything wrong. The only cure is Jesus. He is the only one who can heal their sin sick heart.

We need to pray for those who have spiritual leprosy. We need to bring them to church. We need to tell them that Jesus is the only One who can make them well. So PRAY and TELL.

Questions To Think About

1. What is spiritual leprosy?
2. Is there a cure for a sin sick heart?
3. Have you had the cure?

February 21

But the goat on which the lot fell to be the scapegoat shall be presented alive before the Lord, to make atonement upon it and to let it go as the scapegoat into the wilderness. Leviticus 16:10

In this Scripture God made a plan to show the Israelites through a picture how their sins would be covered. They were to take two goats and by casting lots, something like throwing dice, they would set aside one goat to be sacrificed and one goat to be the scapegoat. The priests placed their hands on the goat's head and turned him loose in the wilderness. The scapegoat symbolized the peoples' sins being carried away.

This pictured what Jesus would do for us when he came, lived a perfect life, and took all of our sin on himself when he died on the cross. Jesus was the sacrifice the goats pointed to. No other sacrifice would ever be necessary because Jesus fulfilled all the requirements for redeeming His people. We need to thank God for sending His Son, Jesus. We need to thank Jesus for being obedient and willing to die in our place. We need to thank the Holy Spirit for coming to comfort, teach, and indwell us after Jesus ascended into Heaven.

Questions To Think About?

1. What is a scapegoat?
2. Why did the people of the Old Testament need a scapegoat?

February 22

And if a stranger dwells with you in your land, you shall not mistreat him. Leviticus 19:33

Isn't it strange that when someone is different, we tend to stay away from him, ignore him, or may even be rude to him? The Bible tells us in today's Scripture that we are not to mistreat strangers. This command is so important to us. No matter where we meet someone new, we are to make him feel welcome. If you have ever been the "stranger" you know how it feels to not know anyone and how important it is to have someone make you "feel at home".

How can you do this? You need to include the new kids in your activities. Invite them to eat lunch with you. Offer to show them around the school and introduce them to other students. Don't forget to invite them to church. When someone comes to Sunday school or any church activity be sure to make him feel at home there too. Showing interest in OTEHRS and not always focusing on yourself is a wonderful way you can show your love for others. Don't let anyone feel UNWANTED. IT'S THE CHRISTIAN THING TO DO.

Questions To Think About

1. Can you think of other ways to make the "stranger" feel at home?

February 23

When you reap the harvest on your land, you shall not wholly reap the corners of your field when you reap, nor shall you gather any gleaning from your harvest. You shall leave them for the poor and for the stranger: I am the Lord your God.
Leviticus 23:22

When God commanded the people not to reap the corners of the fields He wasn't telling them to be sloppy in their work. He was telling them to save some of what He had given to them for the poor and others who were in need. Even though most of you are not farmers and are not in charge of a field of wheat, this Bible verse still applies. How? God is telling us to help the poor and needy.

As we have talked about before, this need is not necessarily physical. The need may not even be in someone who is poor. Perhaps someone needs your time or a certain talent that you have. Maybe the needy person just requires someone to listen to a problem or heartbreak and offer encouragement. That is a gift well worth giving. But how do we go about this? Look for people who seem to need help and do what Jesus did. When the woman at the well needed help, Jesus started a conversation with her. He listened to what she had to say then he told her how to find the TRUTH.

Besides giving time and attention, we can also give things. Make sure that shirt you hardly ever wear gets to someone who would love to have it. Or maybe you could find someone who needs those shoes you outgrew almost before you wore them. Look for opportunities such as this. When you share what you have, not only is someone else blessed, you are too.

Questions To Think About

1. Are there ways you can help your parents save money so that they can give more to the Lord?

February 24

You shall not oppress one another . . . Leviticus 25: 17

To oppress means to persecute someone. Lots of people are persecuted today. Christians are not to persecute others. We are not to be mean to anyone, not a stranger, someone who is different, our younger brother or sister, our friends we are angry with, or anyone we come into contact with. Sometimes we just "feel mean". We know it isn't right, but we don't care that we are being hateful to someone. God tells us, "DO NOT DO THIS." Ask God to help you get rid of this feeling quickly.

Have you ever seen a school bully picking on someone much smaller? Did you stand up for the little guy? This is an example of how we can be salt and light and help out the one who is being hurt. It doesn't have to be a physical fight. People can be really mean with words. We as Christians are to take up for those who are being persecuted and oppressed. And of course, we are never to give into our feelings when we want to hurt someone else.

We also need to pray for the Christians all over the world who are being persecuted right now as you read this. They are being mistreated and even killed simply because they love Jesus. Remember them in your prayers.

Questions To Think About

1. Have you ever thought of organizing a prayer vigil for the Christians around the world who are being persecuted daily?

February 25

If you walk in My statutes and keep My commandments, and perform them, I will give you peace and you shall lie down, and none will make you afraid. Leviticus 26:3, 6

Have you ever been really, really scared? I remember a time when I was. A friend of mine and I were home alone and I didn't expect my parents back for some time. Suddenly I heard what sounded like someone trying to break in. My friend and I locked ourselves in the bathroom. Footsteps crept down the hall, closer and closer to the bathroom door. My heart was in my throat and I thought I was going to faint when my Mom's voice said, "Honey, where are you?" Boy, was I relieved.

In our Scripture, God was telling the Israelites that if they kept His commandments, He would protect them from all the enemies that lived around them. They could lie down at night without fear of being hurt in any way. They could plant crops and raise cattle without the fear of being robbed. They would have peace, not fear.

It's terrible to live in fear. Sometimes we are afraid because we are being silly, like I was in the story I told you earlier. But sometimes we are afraid because we have broken God's commandments. When this happens we need to repent and ask God to forgive us. He will. Then we have peace that only comes from God and we are no longer afraid. When we keep the commandment, "Obey your Mother and Father", we can be sure that they will tell us things to do that will keep us safe. This is what it means when God tells us to keep His commandments and He will give us peace and we will not be afraid.

QUESTIONS TO THINK ABOUT

1. What does obeying have to do with fear?
2. What can we do to have peace?

February 26

Thus the children of Israel did: according to all that the Lord commanded Moses, so they did. Numbers 1:54

We learn in this verse that things were going great for the children of Israel. God had completed many miracles to make their lives as easy as they could be while they journeyed toward the Promised Land. This Scripture lets us know that God was blessing them because they were OBEDIENT. You might be thinking, "Oh no, not that obedient lecture again." Being obedient is such an important part of our lives that the Bible speaks of it often and the Israelites are a great example of how OBEDIENCE works.

As long as they followed the Lord's commands and did what He told them to do, things went well. Of course, this is because God always tells us to do the things that are best for us. However, it wasn't long before the Israelites started complaining—just a little. But this little complaint snowballed into an all out uprising against their leader Moses who took his orders straight from GOD. Then, all kinds of things began to happen to them.

The Bible tells us to be holy as God is holy. Obedience is the key. We can't be more like Jesus without knowing what He wants us to do and then doing it. Lets take a lesson from the Israelites and keep the Commandments—and the one you should be most concerned with right now is number five, *HONOR YOUR FATHER AND MOTHER.* You'll be so HAPPY when you do.

Questions To Think About

1. How can we be more like Jesus?
2. In what area of my life do I need to be more obedient to my parents?
3. What attitude qualifies as an obedient attitude?

February 27

Each according to his service and according to his task; thus were they number by him, as the Lord commanded Moses.
Numbers 4:49

This Scripture tells us that each of the Israelites who came out of Egypt was given a purpose and a task to do by the Lord and it is no different today. Always remember that God is the same today, tomorrow, and forever. So we can be sure that He has given us a purpose and a task to do while we are here on earth.

Jesus spelled out one thing we are to do. We are to go into all the world and make disciples. You might ask, "How can I go into all the world when I am just a kid?" You are IN part of the world so look around you and see if there is anyone who doesn't know Jesus. Remember the Disciples started in Jerusalem, you start wherever you are, sharing Jesus with people. I know fifteen young men who got together in college and prayed for a foreign country for several years. Now, all of them are in that country making disciples for Jesus. If you are faithful where you are, with what you have, God will do awesome things with your life.

QUESTIONS TO THINK ABOUT

1. Do you pray for opportunities to share Jesus with others?
2. Why is it important to remember that God never changes?

February 28

The Lord bless you and keep you; The Lord make His face shine upon you, And be gracious to you; The Lord lift up His countenance upon you, and give you peace. Numbers 6:24-26

In this Scripture, God told Moses to say this blessing over the children of Israel and ministers are still speaking it to their congregations today. What is Moses saying in this blessing? He is telling us that there are great benefits from God for Believers. He says that the Lord will bless us. Have you ever wondered why you weren't born to a poor family in Siberia? Maybe not, but the answer is that the Lord has blessed you greatly by putting you in your family. He did it for you. He blessed you even before you were born.

In addition, Believers are blessed because God, through Jesus can look on us and be gracious to us. Even though we continue to sin, God continues to look at us through His Son's blood. He sees us as being clean and promises to always forgive us when we repent. Also, Jesus is always with us—His shining face toward us. Jesus will NEVER LEAVE US. Besides these things, the Lord gives his children PEACE that is so good that no one in the world can understand it. We don't have to worry about a thing in the world. We don't have to fear the future because we KNOW that JESUS HAS A PLAN just for us.

Let's read this blessing again, and think of all that God has done for us.

Questions To Think About

1. How has God blessed us?

February 29

They brought their offering before the Lord . . . Numbers 7:3

Sometimes today we don't realize that giving an offering is part of worship. When God gave the Israelites all the rules and regulations in great detail that they were to go by in worship, He included an offering. In Bible times, the offering was usually an animal, grain, or whatever was of value to them. Besides giving money in church, we can also give things that are often more valuable than money to someone else. When someone is sick we can take him a meal. When an elderly person passes away, we can send a card to cheer the family. At Christmas we can share a meal or party with someone who has no relatives living close by. The list goes on and on. What it amounts to is being AVAILABLE to help others. So, PRESENT YOUR OFFERING BEFORE THE LORD.

QUESTIONS TO THINK ABOUT

1. What offering can you give to the Lord?

March 1

Now when Moses went into the tabernacle of meeting to speak with Him he heard the voice of One speaking to him from above the mercy seat . . . Numbers 7:8-9

Moses was very close to God. In fact, he actually spoke with God and God spoke to him. Today, God speaks to us in a different way. Moses didn't have God's written Word like we do; remember, he wrote the first five books of the Bible as the Holy Spirit inspired him. We have God's written Word and that is one of the ways He speaks to us. We can know God and how He wants us to live through reading and studying His Word. In the Bible we have the answers to all of life's questions.

In addition, as a Christian, we have the Holy Spirit living in us to teach us, guide us, and give us understanding. When we read the Bible the Holy Spirit helps us see and understand what we read. He brings to our mind the things God wants us to think about or learn at that time in our lives. The Holy Spirit never leaves us and if we "listen", the Holy Spirit will guide us in doing, saying, and thinking the things that please God most.

And of course, we talk to God and Jesus when we pray and tell Him what is in our heart. So we have ways to talk to God just like Moses. God wants to talk to us, teach us, and guide us through his Word, His Holy Spirit, and prayer. Isn't it wonderful that we can have this close personal relationship with God?

Questions To Think About

1. How do we "talk" to God today?

March 2

So it was, whenever the ark set out, that Moses said, "Rise up, O Lord! Let Your enemies be scattered, and let those who hate You flee before You." Numbers 10:35

The Ark of the Covenant was a special chest that God had instructed Moses to make. The chest held the Ten Commandments and was kept in the Holy of Holies in the Tabernacle. When the Israelites traveled they carried the Ark on two poles since God had forbidden anyone to touch it. The Ark was very holy because it was the place where God "dwelt with" or "met with" His people.

We don't have the Ark of the Covenant like the children of Israel because we have the Holy Spirit "indwelling us". God is always with us to lead us and protect us just like the Israelites in our Scripture. He is with us when we are at home. He is with us at school. He is with us when we are playing or hanging out with our friends. He is with us when we are far from home. Isn't it great to know that no matter where we are or what we are doing, God our Father is with us? It's awesome to understand that our God knows us by name and loves and cares for each one of us individually.

Questions To Think About

1. Where is God?
2. As Christians we can each have a personal relationship with God. How do the world's religions see a person's relationship with God?

March 3

Now when the people complained, it displeased the Lord . . .
Numbers 11:1

Some mornings when you get up are you really GRUMPY? Nothing is right. It's time to get up but you are still sleepy, you can't find the toothpaste, your favorite shirt is in the dirty clothes, you don't like what your Mom fixed for breakfast, and you have a test today that you really didn't study for that well. Of course, when these things happen, we COMPLAIN! And when they happen again, we COMPLAIN some more and pretty soon we are in the habit of complaining about almost everything. It's easy to fall into this sin. If we aren't wary we will end up with a very negative attitude and be in a "bad mood" all the time. As our Scripture says, this does not please God.

Why is complaining displeasing to God? Let's stop and think about it. If we complain, we are saying that we don't like the way things are going. In reality we are saying we don't like the way God is directing our life. God tells us in His Word, in EVERYTHING GIVE THANKS UNTO THE LORD. This means to thank God no matter what is going on in your life—it means to thank God in EVERYTHING.

The next time you start to complain, STOP and think, "Does this glorify the Lord?" It will change your attitude and your life.

Questions To Think About

1. What are we saying when we complain?
2. Why shouldn't we complain when things go wrong?

March 4

So they said to one another, "Let us select a leader and return to Egypt." Numbers 14:4

Talk about being ungrateful! Moses helped the Israelites escape from slavery in Egypt where they were underfed and mistreated in every way possible and they wanted to *select a leader and return to Egypt.* These very people had cried out to God about the Egyptians who demanded more and more from them but gave them less and less. God heard them and sent Moses to rescue them. He performed miracle after miracle before and after they were freed and yet they rejected God's leadership and WANTED TO GO BACK to Egypt. Back to slavery, back to a place where they couldn't worship God. Not only that, they wanted a NEW LEADER as well.

We can learn a great lesson from this passage. We have to remember that we were once a SLAVE TO SIN. So God sent His Son Jesus to free us and lead us to the Promised Land—Heaven. BUT, sometimes we lie to ourselves and think that our old life as a slave was better or more fun. We want to "go back to Egypt"—we want to dabble in sin. When we want to "play with sin", we are saying that we don't want Jesus for our Leader. We are saying we want to run things. We are being UNGRATEFUL too! Thankfully, God will convict us and forgive us when we repent.

Questions To Think About

1. Have you been ungrateful lately? What are you going to do about it?

March 5

. . . *And they fell on their faces.* Numbers 16:45

God was very angry at the Israelites for complaining about everything and wanting to go back to Egypt. He knew they deserved to be destroyed. So Moses and Aaron *fell on their faces* in prayer before God to plead with Him to show mercy to his people. Because of the prayers of these two Godly men, the people repented and God spared them.

Have you ever wondered if your prayers for someone REALLY do any good? Well, this is just one of many, many examples in the Bible of people interceding or praying for others. We see the result for ourselves. God tells us to PRAY FOR OTHERS and He will hear us. Make a list right now for all the people you should pray for. Include your parents, brothers and sisters, your pastor, the church, the leaders of America, all those in authority over you, Christian friends, friends who are not Christians, the kid who is mean to you, and the kid you don't like. The list could go on and on. Then spend time praying for these people. PRAYER IS A POWERFUL BLESSING GOD HAS GIVEN US—SO PRAY!

Questions To Think About

1. Why should you pray?
2. What should you pray about?

March 6

Then Edom said to him, "You shall not pass through my land . . .
Numbers 20:18

God's people were trying to get to the land that God had promised them when they came to the border of the Edomites. They asked for permission to pass through the land, but the Edomites said, "No." This meant trouble for God's people.

It's the same today. As Christians, we are trying to make our way to the "Promised Land"—Heaven—and along the way we are trying to make Earth a better place. But, we are constantly running into people who say, *you shall not* . . . This is the way of the world. As Christians we will have trials and troubles because we love Jesus. Just think back about how Jesus was treated. He told people the TRUTH. He showed people THE RIGHT AND GOOD WAY TO LIVE. He modeled for us how to WORSHIP and PRAY. He proclaimed the GOOD NEWS. He LOVED us and GAVE Himself for us. Do these sound like logical reasons for the world to hate Jesus? They did.

Jesus tells us in the Bible that the world, will hate us. He even tells us that we will be persecuted by the world because we love Him. Like the Edomites in the Old Testament, there will always be enemies of God who say to His children, "You can't do that. You can't have prayer in schools. You can't have the Ten Commandments in the courtroom. You can't sing Christian songs at Christmas." The list goes on. However, our enemies can never stop us from praying for them. REMEMBER, we are to pray for those who despitefully use us. JESUS DID!

Questions To Think About

1. Is persecution always physical?
2. Why should we pray for our enemies?

March 7

Then the Lord opened Balaam's eyes . . . Numbers 22:31a

It's easy to remember the story of Balaam's donkey because donkeys normally don't talk. But God used Balaam's donkey to teach Balaam a lesson. Balak the king of the Moabites paid Balaam to curse the Israelites, but the Lord told him not to. However, Balaam wanted the king's money so he decided that he would go through with the curse. Three times the Angel of the Lord stood in front of Balaam's donkey and the donkey stopped. Three times Balaam beat the donkey to try and make him proceed. The last time the donkey spoke to Balaam and Balaam's eyes were opened so that he saw what the donkey had already seen—the Angel of the Lord standing in front of them blocking the way.

Sometimes we are like Balaam. We have been told not to do something and we go right ahead and do it anyway. Maybe it's because we don't want anyone bossing us around. Rebellion rises up in our hearts and we are determined to do exactly the opposite of what we have been told. For example, maybe we have been told not to eat any more cookies. We take a cookie when no one is around and hide all the evidence we have been there. We get away with it. But somehow Mom discovers that a cookie is missing and asks us if we took it. We don't want to get into trouble so we lie. Eventually Mom figures out that we did take the cookie and then lied. We are in double trouble now because of our greed, just like Balaam.

God gives us parents and friends and others to look out for us so that we don't end up in double trouble. Like Balaam's donkey, they can see things that we can't see, like consequences down the road. God also gives us the Holy Spirit to convict us of our sin so that we won't continue to sin and get into worse trouble. So be careful not to sin, but when you do, pay attention to "Balaam's donkey"—the parents and others God has given you and the Holy Spirit—and repent and turn from your sin.

QUESTIONS TO THINK ABOUT

1. What does Balaam's donkey represent for us?
2. What should we do when we "Balaam's donkey" tells us not to do something?

NOTES

March 8

Therefor say, "Behold, I give to him My covenant of peace; . . . because he was zealous for his God . . ."

If we look up the word zealous in the dictionary, we'll see that it means to be motivated, enthusiastic and eager in pursing a goal, cause, or ideal. We all get motivated and enthusiastic over something. What is it that makes us want to strive for something and then enjoy every minute of the striving? The answer to that question is what we love.

The Scripture today is referring to a man named Phinehas. He was zealous toward the Lord. In other words he loved the Lord with all his heart. The Lord was everything to him. He loved to be with Him, work for Him, do whatever the Lord wanted him to do. He was *zealous for his God.* Because of this, the Lord rewarded Phinehas with peace.

Today, let's list ten things that we have been excited and enthusiastic about during the past year. Now let's rank the items on the list in order with number one being the thing we were MOST excited about. Let's look at our lists. What is in the number one spot? Where did Jesus fit in? Was He at the top of the list? If not, pray that God would help us to be more like Phinehas. Ask Him to make us more zealous for Him and His Word.

Questions To Think About

1. What does it mean to be zealous?
2. Have you been zealous for the Lord this past year?
3. What can you do to continue or remedy this situation?

March 9

. . . *You rebelled against My command to hallow Me at the waters before their eyes.* Numbers 27:14

In our Scripture today, God is talking to Moses just before He let him look into the Promised Land. Moses had led the Israelites all around the desert for forty years and the time had come for them to go into the Promised Land and take possession of it. However, Moses was not going into the Promised Land with the Israelites because he had disobeyed God. While Moses was leading them through the desert, the people began to complain because they had no water. God told Moses to speak to this rock and it would give them water. Moses was angry and he didn't listen to God. Instead of speaking, he struck the rock. This cost him the privilege of going into the Promised Land

We might think SO WHAT. WHAT'S THE BIG DEAL ABOUT THAT? This is a big deal because the Lord told him what He wanted him to do and Moses disobeyed. God did have a reason for not wanting Moses to strike the rock. The rock symbolized Christ and Moses had already struck the rock once and living water had come out of it. This symbolized Christ's death and he only had to die once to save us. But it wouldn't have mattered if we had never known why God told Moses not to strike the rock. IF GOD TELLS US TO DO SOMETHING WE MUST DO IT.

But how do we know what God wants us to do? He tells us in His Word. Every single thing we need to know about living a life for God is in His Word. So we should study it diligently and consistently so we will always know the TRUTH about how to live.

QUESTIONS TO THINK ABOUT

1. What must we always do?
2. How do we find out how God wants us to live?

March 10

And they said to Moses, "Your servants have taken a count of the men of war who are under our command, and not a man of us is missing. Therefore we have brought an offering for the Lord." Numbers 31:49, 50

In this Scripture the Israelites have just fought a big battle and have won. When they arrive back at camp they count and not one Israelite has been lost in the battle. They are all so grateful that they bring an offering to the Lord because they know He has protected them.

The Bible says that every good gift comes from God so when good things happen to us we should give thanks and bring an offering to God too. We might thing we don't have much to offer, but we need to remember that God isn't as concerned with the amount as He is with the fact that we give. We also need to remember that there are lots of ways to make an offering to the Lord. Our OBEDIENCE can be an offering and so can our PRAISE.

Most of us haven't lived through a battle, but it doesn't have to be anything that big and dramatic in order for us to bring an offering to the Lord. Perhaps we take a trip and arrive home safe and sound. This is a gift from God. Maybe we have a test in school and God helps us focus and keep a clear mind. This is a gift from God. Every second of every day is a gift from God. So we always have something to be thankful for. We always have some reason to bring an offering to God. Let's keep this in mind and do it.

Questions To Think About

1. Why should we bring offerings to God?
2. What qualifies as an offering?

March 11

. . . then take note you sinned against the Lord; and be sure your sin will find you out. Numbers 32:23

I once knew a girl, let's call her Jane, who wanted to go to a slumber party. She knew her parents wouldn't object to that, but she also knew that her parents had forbidden her to see a certain movie. Jane also knew that the girls at the slumber party were planning to go see that movie. Jane wanted to go to the party more than anything so she PROMISED her parents that the girls were all going to the mall. Jane and her friends went to the movie and the next day when she arrived home her mother asked her if she had a good time at the mall. Jane lied and said, "Yes."

A few days went by and Jane was feeling pretty cocky about the fact that she had "put one over" on her parents. That day her mother was doing the laundry and as she always did, she went through Jane's jeans' pockets. Guess what she found? She found the ticket stub to the movie Jane PROMISED not to see.

Jane's mother confronted her and she broke down and told her mother she was sorry. Jane knew it was wrong but she didn't want the other girls to be mad at her. Jane's mother forgave her BUT because of her disobedience and the fact that she couldn't trust Jane, she said that Jane was grounded and would miss an outing that she had really been looking forward to. The moral of this story and the lesson from today's Scripture is: *Obey and stay out of trouble.* Besides, even if no one here on earth ever finds out about our sin, JESUS KNOWS. Remember WE CAN'T HIDE FROM GOD.

Questions To Think About

1. Who always see us? Does He always see our sin?
2. What does the verse mean when it says *be sure your sin will find you out?*

March 12

. . . After the Passover the children of Israel went out with boldness in the sight of all the Egyptians. Numbers 33:3

In this Scripture, God had just freed the Israelites from slavery in Egypt. Remember, the Pharaoh would not let them go even after all the plagues until the first born of all the Egyptian children died including his heir. The Israelites were protected from this last plague by sacrificing a lamb and placing the blood over the doorposts and lintel of their houses. Then, when the Angel of Death passed through the land of Egypt, he passed over the houses with the lamb's blood and the people were saved. This is why it is called Passover—because the Angel of Death "passed over" their homes. This was a picture of Jesus—the Lamb of God—whose blood was shed for us when He died on the cross. Because of His blood we have "passed over" from eternal death in hell to eternal life in heaven.

The second part of this verse tells us that because of what God did for His people, they went out of Egypt with BOLDNESS. They weren't afraid any more. They marched right out of Egypt and left their slavery and their old life behind.

This incident should teach us two things. First of all, it should teach us how thankful we should be for what Jesus has done for us by dying on the cross in our place. Secondly, it should teach us that we don't need to be afraid any more. We should go out BOLDLY and witness to others. We can witness by simply telling others about Jesus. Or, we can witness by giving God and Jesus the credit for everything when talking with others. And certainly, we can witness by living a life that glorifies God. Others will notice.

Questions To Think About

1. What does the Passover represent?
2. How can we witness to others?

March 13

. . . As the Lord God of your fathers has spoken to you; do not fear or be discouraged. Deuteronomy 1:21

Discouragement is a very deadly thing. Discouragement can be caused by fear or it can be caused by weariness, but whatever the cause, it is not what God wants for his children. Fear of failing can cause us to want to give up before we even try. For example, when I was trying to learn to swim, which is very important for safety reasons, I looked at the water and thought, "I can never do it. I'm too afraid to jump in and even try. I guess I'll never know how to swim." This kind of fear leads to discouragement, which causes us to not even try.

The second kind of discouragement is caused by weariness or simply being frustrated and tired of trying to do something. I remember when I was trying to learn the multiplication tables. It seemed like I would never learn the "9's". I tried and tried until I was just too frustrated and tired to try any more. I thought I was just "dumb" in math and gave up.

God never intended for us to give in to discouragement. We need to pray and ask Him to strengthen us and give us courage when we are afraid. We need to pray and ask Him to calm and refresh us when we are frustrated and weary and help us to persevere. HE WILL! When discouragement freezes us, God's courage and perseverance frees us. With God's encouragement we can go on to do ALL HE HAS PLANNED FOR US TO DO.

And guess what, when I prayed and asked for courage, I did learn to swim. I am so thankful because I have enjoyed many wonderful hours swimming. And I did learn how to multiply by nine. When I prayed and asked God for help, He sent someone to show me a trick that helped me learn the "9's" in a few minutes. I am so grateful because I went on to work in a bank for twenty years. God tells us in this verse that we don't have to be afraid or discouraged. Let's not forget this GREAT PROMISE!

Questions To Think About

1. What does God say about fear?
2. What does God say about discouragement?

Notes

March 14

But from there you will seek the Lord your God, and you will find Him if you seek Him with all your heart and with all your soul. Deuteronomy 4:29

In today's Scripture Moses has just told the people the commandments of the Lord, which would teach them how to be obedient. The people heard all the laws and probably thought, how can we ever possibly do all of these things. But Moses goes on to tell them, SEEK THE LORD WITH HEART AND SOUL AND YOU WILL FIND HIM.

When the verse says SEEK GOD, it's doesn't mean that God is hiding from us like when we play Hide and Seek. God is always waiting for us and wants us to find Him. However, we won't even want to find God until the Holy Spirit has worked in our hearts and put the DESIRE to seek God in them. And if we push the Holy Spirit aside and pay no attention to Him, we will feel miserable because we are trying to run our lives without Him. Then we start to look for answers and we realize that we can't please God on our own and there is no way we can be holy without Jesus. This is when we are really SEEKING God with heart and soul.

God's part is to JUSTIFY us. Justify means we have been made right with God. Jesus did this for us when he died in our place and shed his blood on the cross. Once we have been JUSTIFIED, the Holy Spirit lives in us and teaches us how to follow God's commands. He also gives us the strength and grace to obey God's commands. So not only does God give us the desire to SEEK HIM, He really FINDS US and gives us the ability to OBEY His commands. THANK HIM FOR HIS GRACE!

QUESTIONS TO THINK ABOUT

1. What does it mean to seek God?
2. How do we "find" God?

March 15

And you shall do what is right and good in the sight of the Lord that it may be well with you . . . Deuteronomy 6:18

Don't you just love it when everything is going your way—you have lots of friends, you're making good grades on all your schoolwork, and your Mom and Dad have been bragging on you a lot? It sure beats not having any friends, making bad grades, and being in trouble with your Mom and Dad.

Today's Scripture says that if you do what is right and good in the sight of the Lord, it will be well with you.

So the question is what is right and good in the sight of the Lord. Thinking back, you've heard this one before over and over again—OBEDIENCE! You may be saying, "Oh no not again. Isn't there anything else you can talk about? Surely there is something else that's important in God's Word." But you know, if you really think about it, THE ONLY SIN IS DISOBEDIENCE. If you do all that God commands, then you are not sinning. That's why the "O word" is so important. That's the answer to what is right and good in the sight of the Lord—OBEDIENCE. It seems simple enough doesn't it? But without Jesus you can never be obedient. That's why having Jesus as your Savior is so important.

QUESTIONS TO THINK ABOUT

1. *What is right and good in the sight of the Lord?*
2. *What happens when you do what is right and good in the sight of the Lord?*

March 16

. . . What does the Lord your God require of you, but to fear the Lord your God, to walk in all His ways and to Love Him, to serve the Lord your God with all your heart and with all your soul and to keep the commandments of the Lord . . .
Deuteronomy 10:12, 13

Yesterday, we found out what we must do to have things go well with us and today, we are finding out what God requires of us. Do any of the five things listed in the Scripture seem familiar? First, we are to fear the Lord. Second, we are to walk in His ways. Third, we are to love Him. Fourth, we are to serve Him. And fifth, we are to keep His commandments.

Let's look at these. When we see the word fear, it refers to the way we are to act toward God. It means we are to be in awe of God. Awe means reverence and respect. We are not to call Him "our Buddy in the Sky" or "The Big Guy Upstairs". We are to approach him reverently and respectfully because HE IS GOD. Next, if we walk in His ways we do what He has told us to do. And of course this means that we are OBEDIENT. We are also to love Him more than anything or anybody else. The love we have for our Lord is a very special love. It is one that causes us to want to do anything and everything that He wants us to do. It is through obeying Him that we show how much we love Him. We are to serve Him. We can do this by using our talents for His glory. Lastly, we are to keep His commandments. When we keep His commandments we bring glory and honor to our Lord and He in turn blesses us. Thank Him for giving us such CLEAR instructions.

QUESTIONS TO THINK ABOUT

1. List the things that God requires of us.
2. Are you living these requirements?

March 17

You shall not at all do as we are doing here today—every man doing whatever is right in his own eyes— . . .
Deuteronomy 12:8

Imagine what it would be like if we didn't have any laws at all and everyone did whatever made him happy or satisfied that moment. There is a word for this—anarchy. Anarchy means that there isn't any form of law or order and all is confusion or chaos.

Let's look at an example. Let's say John has a brand new tennis racket. The kid down the street, Alan, comes along and says, "Hey, that's a cool racket and I want it because I don't have one." Alan is bigger and older and stronger than John, so he just takes the racket away from him and goes on his merry way. Taking the racket from John made Alan feel good because now he has a new racket. John on the other hand is feeling pretty rotten and probably mad too, because his new racket is gone.

God knew that this kind of situation would not be good for people. That's why he gave us His commandments and gave us the idea of a just government, one that operates on a Christian worldview. People who operate outside of the law, like terrorists, do what is right in their own eyes or what makes them feel good. They don't live by God's laws and they create confusion and chaos. So, let's remember that we are to DO WHAT GOD COMMANDS, NOT WHAT WE THINK IS RIGHT. If we live by this rule, we will always bring glory to God and joy and blessing into our own lives.

Things To Think About

1. *What is anarchy? Who promotes anarchy?*
2. *How should we always live?*

March 18

For the poor will never cease from the land; therefore I command you, saying, you shall open your hand wide to your brother, to your poor and your needy in your land.
Deuteronomy 15:11

Have you ever known anyone who was really poor? Have you known someone who didn't have enough to eat, very few clothes, and no way to get around? While this is bad enough there is something that hurts them even more—not having any friends. Could you put yourself in the place of someone from your school that's poor? Could you include him in your circle of friends? Could you not care what your other friends say about you when you include him? Could you invite him to Sunday school and Church? Could you ask him over for a meal? Could you tell him about Jesus and how important it is to you to be a friend of His? Could you? You could. WOULD YOU? Then you would be doing like today's Scripture says, you would be *opening your hand wide . . . to your poor and your needy in your land.* You would be giving him something money can't buy—TRUE FRIENDSHIP.

QUESTIONS TO THINK ABOUT

1. What is important about TRUE FRIENDSHIP?

March 19

When you go out to battle against your enemies, and see horses and chariots and people more numerous than you, do not be afraid of them; for the Lord your God is with you . . .
Deuteronomy 20:1

I know that we don't have enemies riding on horses or in chariots now days, BUT we all have enemies even if we aren't aware of them. I'm not talking about people in our neighborhoods who bully us or try to take things from us or who get mad at us for various reasons. I'm talking about ideas that are our enemies.

Yes, ideas can be some of our worst enemies. Ideas like: "The Bible isn't true. God may have created the earth but He did it through evolution. We don't have to tell our parents everything. Everybody sins, so we can do whatever we want and God will forgive us later. It's okay to cheat on a test the teacher really doesn't care." Any of these sound familiar? These are the enemies that can be just as deadly as knives, swords, arrows, or guns. These are deadly because they can lead us down a path to eternal death.

These types of enemies cannot be fought with guns and bombs. These enemies must be fought with WHAT GOD SAYS—THE BIBLE. The Word of God is the only place we can get the ABSOLUTE TRUTH every single time. So even though we will probably never have to face enemies on horseback or in chariots, we still don't need to fear. We need to combat our enemies with God's Word and *the Lord our God will be with us.*

Questions To Think About

1. What enemies are we likely to face?
2. Do you have answers from God's Word to the statements made in today's lesson? If not, find them.

March 20

You shall not have in your bag differing weights, a heavy and a light. For all who do such things, all who behave unrighteously, are an abomination to the Lord your God.
Deuteronomy 25: 13, 16

Have you ever copied someone's homework? Maybe you didn't have time to do it the night before. Besides, you let him copy your homework last week. This is just payback. As today's Scripture says, in Bible times, when a person sold an item, he weighed it. The person talked about in the Scripture had two sets of weights. For some, he would use the right weight and for some, he would use the lighter weight. Using the lighter weight cheated the individual out of what was due him. God hates this practice.

There are many ways to cheat, but probably the most familiar to you is cheating on schoolwork. When you look at someone else's homework or ask them an answer on a test it's cheating. When you let someone copy your homework or give them an answer on a test it's cheating. The Scripture says GOD HATES CHEATING. So what should you do when someone asks you to help him cheat? You tell him, "No." Later, if he wants to know why you wouldn't help him, you tell him, "Because God hates cheaters." You can also tell him that cheating is the same thing as stealing which is breaking one of the Ten Commandments. So, THINK BEFORE YOU DO ANYTHING. Would it please God? Would it break God's Law? If the answer to these questions is "YES", then don't do it!

QUESTIONS TO THINK ABOUT

1. What is cheating?
2. Have you cheated? If so repent and cheat no more.

March 21

And all these blessing shall come upon you and overtake you because you obey the voice of the Lord your God.
Deuteronomy 28:2

Have you ever dreamed of being a big time professional ball player or a famous movie star or singer? The blessing talked about in today's Scripture is even better than having all those dreams come true. You might be thinking, "How could it ever get any better than being rich and famous?" Remember that the Bible teaches that every perfect gift comes from God. So the blessing in today's Scripture will be GREAT and since it comes from God it will be perfect. If the blessing is perfect it will be exactly what you need to make you joyful and successful.

God's plan for you might include being a pro ball player or an actor or singer, but no matter what it is, if it's God's plan it will be perfect. So OBEY THE LORD and FOLLOW HIS PLAN and you will be an excited and fulfilled Christian.

Questions To Think About

1. What do we do to receive God's blessings?

March 22

And the Lord, He is the One who goes before you. He will be with you. He will not leave you nor forsake you; do not fear nor be dismayed. Deuteronomy 31:8

"You go first."

"No, you go first."

How many times have you said this to a friend just before you sat down in the seat of a roller coaster? Or maybe you have said this when you and your friend were lost and you had to ask a store attendant for directions. Perhaps you have said this when you have gone somewhere new with a friend and you simply wanted to find the bathroom. Whatever the situation, going first can sometimes be frightening.

Today's Scripture covers any and all of these situations. Of course, it is also talking about situations when you may actually be in danger, but Jesus is always with you, even when you ride a roller coaster. Another thing this Scripture teaches is that God will never abandon you. He will never skip out on you when things get rough. He will never leave you when you are hurting or in danger. The Lord has promised that He will be with you no matter what so you don't need to be afraid.

QUESTIONS TO THINK ABOUT

1. When is God with you?
2. Do we need to be afraid?

March 23

Now see that I, even I, am He and there is no God beside Me . . .
Deuteronomy 32:

You have probably read about all the gods that the Greeks believed in. They had a god for everything under the sun and even including the sun. Just so they wouldn't miss any gods, they had a memorial to the UNKNOWN god. But what does today's Scripture say? . . . *there is no God beside Me* . . . That means that there is no God other than the God of the Bible, Creator of the universe and all it contains. Aren't you glad that you don't believe in thousands of false gods? You don't have to be afraid that one of them might get angry and do something terrible to you if you don't please him.

One of the greatest blessings of being a Christian is the fact that you KNOW there is only ONE GOD. What's more, you know the ONE TRUE GOD who is RULER OF EVERYTHING. Furthermore, you know that God created you in His image so that you are able to COMMUNICATE with Him and KNOW Him and LOVE Him. The very fact that God wants to communicate with His children and knows them by name and loves them is mind-boggling. So thank Him for creating you and knowing you and loving you. Praise Him *for there is no God beside Him.*

Questions To Think About

1. Are there more gods than one?
2. Who is God?

March 24

All that you command us we will do, and wherever you send us we will go. Joshua 1:16

The people of Israel had wandered in the desert for 40 years. Now they were ready to cross over the Jordan River into the Promised Land. Moses had died and Joshua was their leader. As our Scripture says, the people promised to do what God commanded and to go anywhere he led.

We can learn lots from this verse. First of all, this verse tells us that God has given us commands that we are to follow. These commands and the way we should live are given to us in the Bible. We have no excuse. We can't say, "I didn't know what I was supposed to do." All the answers are in God's Word. We must do all that God commands us to do.

The second part of this verse says that we should go wherever God leads us. This means we are not to grumble and complain about where we are and we are not to put off our obedience. In other words, we can't say, "I'm in bad circumstances right now, but when I get somewhere else, then I will be obedient." We are not to put off the GOOD and settle for the EASY decisions in our lives. We KNOW that God is in control and will only do what is best for us. So we can GO WITH GOD and DO ALL THAT HE COMMANDS.

QUESTIONS TO THINK ABOUT

1. What does it mean to *do all that He commands?*

March 25

Achan took of the accursed things; so the anger of the lord burned against the children of Israel. Joshua 7:1

The soldiers of Israel had just conquered the city of Jericho and everyone was celebrating. They could hardly wait for the next battle. The army marched forth, confident they would take the city; after all, they were doing what God had commanded them to do. That day the army of Israel fell and they couldn't understand why God had abandoned them. They went to God and He told them. ONE MAN in the camp loved some worldly trinkets more than he loved God or his fellow Israelites. Hadn't God made it clear that when they captured the city of Jericho they were not to take anything but the silver and gold and they were to put it in the treasury of the Lord? But Achan just couldn't resist. He saw beautiful things that he wanted so he took them and hid them under his tent. We all know, and Achan knew too, that no one can hide from God. God had to deal with the sin and all of Israel suffered, not just Achan. Achan paid for his lust with his own life, and his whole family was executed as well. And we can't forget that many men died in the battle that Israel lost. So Achan's "personal sin" did have a big impact on others. It cost them their lives.

What does this teach us today? It shows us that our sin does affect other people. So we can't use the excuse that what we are doing isn't hurting anyone but us. We can't say, "No one will know." When we sin those around us are affected. Their trust in us is affected and our relationship is strained. Even when we repent, confess our sin, and Jesus forgives us, we still have a scar or mark left by the sin.

You know, the very next battle God told the men of Israel that they would win and that they could have all the riches they found for themselves. If Achan had been obedient and waited on the Lord, he would have had all he wanted and more. You see, God had a plan for that battle and He has a plan for us. So the next time you are about to do something that you know isn't right, think of Achan and all the trouble he caused, not only for himself, but also for so many people around him. Then DO THE RIGHT THING—OBEY THE LORD.

Questions To Think About

1. Can we see what the future holds? How should this affect how we live?
2. Should we let "circumstances" determine how we live?
3. What does it mean to live by principles?

Notes

March 26

. . . *but they did not ask counsel of the Lord.* Joshua 9:14

When God gave the Promised Land to the children of Israel, he told them that they had to go in and possess it. This meant that they had to conquer the cities one by one and get rid of all the people who lived there. This was God's judgment on the evil people of Canaan. The Gibeonites, one of the groups of people who lived in Canaan, tricked the Israelites into thinking that they lived far away outside the boundaries of the Promised Land. They did this so that the Israelites would make a treaty with them and promise not to destroy their cities. The Israelites thought this sounded like a good idea. It wouldn't hurt anything because they were outside the boundaries of the land of Canaan. The problem was the Gibeonites didn't live far away. They lived in cities that were supposed to be destroyed and the Israelites would have known this if they had only consulted God before making the treaty. When they found out that the Gibeonites lived in Canaan the Israelites were very angry and knew they had made a big mistake. Even though they made the Gibeonites servants, the Israelites suffered because of this sin.

This is an example of what happens so many times when we don't "live by principles" or go to the Lord and ask His guidance. Living by principles means that we take what God teaches us in His Word and apply it to our lives in every situation even when it appears to be the opposite of what the world would tell us we should do. It also means that we go to God and ask him to lead us in the paths we should tread, to open the doors of opportunities He wants us to take. And we know that no opportunity that contradicts the principles of God's Word is right even if it seems like a good idea at the time.

Don't get caught in a trap like the Israelites. They thought this opportunity was an open and shut case. All the outward signs were there. These people had worn clothes and moldy bread; of course they came from a long way away. But in the end, because they didn't go to God and ask His direction, the Israelites sinned. So STUDY GOD'S WORD, KNOW HIS PRNCIPLES, AND GO TO THE LORD IN PRAYER ABOUT EVERYTHING!

QUESTIONS TO THINK ABOUT

1. How can we learn God's principles?
2. Do we rely on circumstances to determine whether God's Word or His principles seem right?
3. If something you are taught in school or something you are told by friends contradicts the Word of God, what should you do? Which is right?

March 27

But to the tribe of Levi Moses had given no inheritance; the Lord God of Israel was their inheritance, as He had said to them.
Joshua 13:33

"When Grandmother's gone, I want all her brass stuff."

"Well, I want the tiger statue that sits on the back porch; it's always been in the family."

"Not me. I want the chalkboard that used to hang in the kitchen. I used to write on it when I was a kid."

"I want the lava lamp. It's cool."

Have you ever thought about what you want to inherit? The conversation above tells about some of the things my grandkids have said they want whenever the time comes. But we have a much greater inheritance than these "things" to think about. The tribe of Levi was selected by God to take care of all the things that dealt with the Tabernacle and the worship of God. In this Scripture, the Israelites are getting ready to enter the Promised Land to claim their inheritance and God reminds them all that the tribe of Levi will receive a much different inheritance than the rest. Their inheritance was not something you could touch or see. Their inheritance was the blessing of serving God.

So the next time you think about what you would like to have as an inheritance, don't forget that the most important one is not any possession like the things my grandkids say they want, or land, or even great wealth. The greatest inheritance of all is SALVATION and ETERNAL LIFE given to us by Jesus when he died for our sins and rose from the dead.

Questions To Think About

1. What do you want to inherit?
2. What do you want to leave for your children?

March 28

Give me a blessing . . . give me springs of water. Joshua 15:19

Achsah, the daughter of Caleb, was about to get married and as this Scripture tells us, she asked her father for land and for a blessing. Caleb was happy to give his daughter what she asked because he loved her. As I read this I thought about our Heavenly Father and how He loves us even more than Caleb loved his daughter. He gives us not only what we NEED but many times what we WANT. Just as Caleb was there for his daughter and blessed her with good things, our Heavenly Father blesses us beyond our wildest dreams.

So, is God your Father? If not, He can be. First, you must believe that you are a sinner and be deeply sorry for your sin. Tell God that you want to repent and turn away from your sins. Isn't it wonderful that He will forgive us and He will never remember our sins again? Then, we must understand that Jesus made it possible for us to become a child of God when He died on the cross for our sins and paid our debt that we could never pay ourselves. Remember God is holy and can have nothing to do with sin. But God didn't leave us to die in sin. He made a plan for us and sent Jesus to die in our place and pay off our debt. Like Achsah we also get a spring of "living water". That is the Holy Spirit who lives in us and helps us live for God.

QUESTIONS TO THINK ABOUT

1. Have you thanked God for sending Jesus to die for your sins?

March 29

How long will you neglect to go and possess the land, which the lord God of your fathers has given you? Joshua 18:3

CAN YOU BELIEVE IT? There were seven tribes of Israel who just lolly-gagged around and didn't claim the inheritance that God said they could have. Usually, when someone tells you that you have a gift coming, you can hardly wait to get it. You know how hard it is to wait to open presents at Christmas time. You start counting down the days early in the month. Or what about your birthday? Do you start dreaming and planning what you are going to get months ahead of time.

We are good at anticipating getting "things" we can touch and see, but how good are we at planning and pursuing things we can't see. What does this have to do with presents and "possessing the land"? Often times we forget about the greatest inheritance of all—ETERNAL LIFE IN THE REAL PROMISED LAND—Heaven. Have you neglected to "possess this land"? Are you headed into eternity WITHOUT GOD? Have you neglected to tell others about this inheritance? Don't be a lolly-gagger like those seven tribes of Israel.

Questions To Think About

1. What do you need to do to prepare for Eternity?
2. Do you know others who aren't prepared?

March 30

. . . Not a word failed of any good thing, which the Lord had spoken to the house of Israel. All came to pass. Joshua 21:41

Have you ever made a promise and then broken it? We all have sometime during our lives. It's easy to make a promise, but sometimes it's hard to keep that promise later. That's why this is one of the most wonderful verses in the Bible. This verse tells us that God will never break any promise He makes. Take time to search out all of the promises God makes in His Word. If you don't know how to look them up find an adult who can help you.

God made lots of promises to the people of Israel and He told them that He didn't choose them because they were good; He chose them because He is merciful. He brought them out of slavery in Egypt, performed many miracles to keep them safe, and gave them everything they needed to get to the land He had promised them. He did all this because He loved them and they had nothing to do with it. In some cases, God promised Israel certain blessings if they were obedient—like "If you keep My commandments, I will be your God and you will be My people." God always kept His end of the promise and much of the time when Israel didn't God, who is longsuffering, gave them lots of chances to repent.

Like the children of Israel, God has many promises for us today. God never changes and will always do what He says he will do. We do not deserve any of His promises, but He gives them to us freely because He loves us. And not a word of any good thing, which the Lord has spoken, will fail. ALL WILL COME TO PASS.

Questions To Think About

1. How does this verse give us hope?
2. Does it give you peace?

March 31

. . . Choose for yourselves this day whom you will serve, but as for me and my house, we will serve the Lord. Joshua 24:15

We have a lot of choices to make every day don't we? We have to decide what we are going to wear, which cereal we are going to eat for breakfast, and whether or not we will listen to our teachers. Our lives are filled with choices and the choices we make will determine what will happen in our lives. The subjects we choose to study now will give us certain opportunities when we get out of school. The things we choose to eat will make us health or sickly later on. The things we choose to believe will formulate what we think and how we will relate to the world. When we think about it we begin to realize how important it is to make the right decisions.

Making the right decision is what Joshua is talking about in this verse. He understood how important choices are and his life reflected the good decisions he had made. When he went as a spy into the land of Canaan, he believed God would do what He had promised. He and Caleb stood against the other ten spies, believing they could conquer the land because God had said they could and both were blessed because of it. Joshua worked with Moses and continued to make wise choices and he became the leader when Moses died. It was Joshua's decision to ALWAYS follow the Lord that put him in the leadership position and it was his decision to ALWAYS follow the Lord that made him successful when he became the leader. It is also apparent that he was the leader of his household and he saw to it that they made the right decisions as well.

The only way we can BE SURE that we are making the right choices is to TAKE EVERYTHING TO THE LORD. This means that we check God's Word to see if our choice follows all of the principles taught in the Word. Then we PRAY. God will lead us to make the right choices when we ask because WE ARE HIS CHILDREN and He loves us. He wants us to do the right thing even more than we want to do it. So remember that every little choice we make today determines where and what we will be tomorrow.

QUESTIONS TO THINK ABOUT

1. Why should we be concerned with the choices we make?
2. How do we know we are making wise choices?

NOTES

April 1

Thus let all your enemies perish, O Lord! But let those who love Him be like the sun when it comes out in full strength.
Judges 5:31

DO YOU LOVE THE LORD? I'm sure you do or you probably wouldn't be reading this. So the real question is, since you love the Lord, do you SHINE LIKE THE SUN? You may think this is a silly question but let's look at what the sun does and then decide if it's silly.

First of all, without the light of the sun all plant life would die. Without the sun, plants couldn't make the food that nourishes them and then they couldn't fulfill their ultimate purpose of feeding us. Next, without the sun's light we would be unable to see anything. Lastly, the sun gives us warmth and keeps everything on earth from freezing. There are many other benefits of sunshine but these three are enough to talk about for now.

So how does this relate to us? The Bible says that we are to shine like the sun when it comes out in full strength. We are to shine the light of GOD'S TRUTH into the lives of others so that they can fulfill their ultimate purpose in life. How do we do this? First, we must be kind and loving. This shows others that we have something different about us. Then, we can tell them about the SON and how to receive His blessings, because without the SON in our lives there is no SUNshine. Remember that light helps us see in the darkness. God's Word is "a lamp unto our feet" and helps us see in the darkness of this world so that we can be a light to others. Have you ever wondered why some people can't see that some certain act is a sin? It's because they are still in darkness. We can help them find Jesus who is the Light of the World. Finally, we know that everyone needs warmth. No one wants to be treated coldly. We can spread the loving warmth of Jesus when we share Him with others. These are just a few of the ways that WE can SHINE LIKE THE SUN WHEN IT COMES OUT IN FULL STRENGTH!

QUESTIONS TO THINK ABOUT

1. Can you think of other reasons we need sunshine?
2. Why is Jesus called the LIGHT OF THE WORLD?

NOTES

April 2

. . . I am the Lord your God . . . But you have not obeyed My voice. Judges 6:10

These are very sad words. The Lord is talking to the children of Israel. They have been disobedient and they know it. Have you ever been disobedient when your parents told you to do something? Sometimes we just get lazy and put other things ahead of our parent's instructions. Other times we are just stubborn and simply don't want to obey. We want to do what we want.

Being stubborn and not wanting to obey cultivates a spirit of disobedience in our hearts. The problem is that we establish this as a pattern of behavior or in other words, we create a habit. When we establish something as a habit it gets easier to do the next time and the next time. And since we still live in the flesh in a fallen world, there are times when we do slip back into our old ways of sin. So how can we stop this spirit of disobedience and cultivate a spirit of obedience?

One way that will help us to establish a pattern of obedience is to ASK GOD each day to help you make the right decisions and do the right things—just for the day. We have to take one day at a time and sometimes less than a day, because we can't seem to handle more than that. The earlier in life we make PRAYING AND ASKING for GUIDANCE a habit, the easier it will be to remain faithful all of our life. So START TODAY!

Questions To Think About

1. Do you have habits you need to encourage? To change?

April 3

So Abimelech came as far as the tower and fought against it; and he drew near the door of the tower to burn it with fire. But a certain woman dropped an upper millstone on Abimelech's head . . .
Judges 9:52-53

Do you dream of doing something heroic. I guess we all picture ourselves saving the day and being declared a hero by our friends and family. But many of us will never be in a position to do something heroic like the woman in our verse today. However, we can all be heroes; we can be heroes for Jesus. How? One way is by doing something that we have talked about a great deal already. We can be a friend to the friendless and share Jesus with them. This is being a real hero—sharing the Gospel with someone so they might be saved from eternal punishment.

Remember, you may never go into battle or be in a life-threatening situation but you can certainly be a hero just by putting others first and sharing Jesus with them. You may not know it now but some day the Lord will say to you, "Well done, good and faithful servant."

Questions To Think About

1. How can you be a hero?
2. Is it more important to save a physical life or the soul that lives forever?

April 4

We have sinned! . . . deliver us this day, we pray. Judges 10:15

Our Scripture today tells us three things: First, we sin; second, we can pray; and third, the Lord can deliver us. The first part of the verse is obvious to us because we all know through experience that we sin. But, because God loves us and is merciful, He didn't leave us in our sin. He sent His Son to redeem us. Jesus paid for our sins with His Death, conquered death when he arose, and is now ruling at the right hand of God. Jesus is the very reason we can be saved. He is the reason we can pray and ask God to deliver us and forgive us for our sins. He is the reason that God will forgive us.

It is so awesome that God promises to forgive us if we ask Him. God's forgiveness is really important when we start thinking that we are pretty good and we haven't done anything bad this week. In the Old Testament God told the Israelites to offer sacrifices for their UNKOWN SINS. This means that we commit sins that we don't even realize are sins. So we need to remember when we pray to ask God to forgive us for ALL of our sins, even the ones we don't know about. If we PRAY, God will HEAR us and FORGIVE us when we ASK. So pray OFTEN.

Questions To Think About

1. Why is it so important to ask God to forgive us for our sins?
2. Why does God forgive us?

April 5

. . . O Lord God, remember me, I pray! Strengthen me, I pray, . . . Judges 16:28

When you get into trouble what should you do? You should go to your Dad and tell him all about it. Then, even though he scolds you, he will forgive you and tell you that he loves you. Even if all earthly fathers don't react in this way, our Heavenly Father will. This is exactly what happened in our Scripture today. Samson is praying this prayer. All his life, Samson was rebellious. He always wanted what he didn't or shouldn't have. Remember how he sinned and told Delilah his strength was in his hair and she cut it off? Then, the Philistines captured Samson, put out his eyes, and held him prisoner for many years. Even though Samson had sinned terribly, God did remember him and strengthen him.

We need to guard against being rebellious and discontent. We need to be content with what we have and focus on thanking God for it. For example, if we have the second newest bike on the block, we should thank God for it and be happy we have it. We also need to be careful what we ask for. Samson wanted the woman Delilah. It was against God's law for him to have her, but he wanted her and took her anyway. We need to be sure that we never ask for something that would cause us to sin, lead us into sin, or cause us to stumble in our Christian walk. Maybe getting to be a cheerleader or captain of the football team at school is all you want. Will this position help you to glorify God. Will it cause you to become proud and ignore people who need you to be their friend? Will it lead you into sinful behavior? Will it help you glorify God?

God dealt with Samson and his sin, but it wasn't until Samson was BLIND that he could really SEE. We need to ask God to help us to really SEE and to protect us from being BLIND to sin. We need to ask Him to REMEMBER us and STRENGTHEN us so that we can LIVE OUR LIVES FOR HIS GLORY.

Questions To Think About

1. Ask yourself all of the questions in today's lesson when you desire something new in your life.

Notes

April 6

In those days there was no king in Israel; everyone did what was right in his own eyes. Judges 17:6

This Scripture points out how important it is to have a godly leader. Living in a FREE nation sometimes leads us to think that we don't have to answer to anyone, but we need to remember that there is a chain of command in our lives. The Bible tells us that we are to have as our head—GOD, who is the highest authority in our lives. We learn this from the first commandment. God gave us all of our instructions in His Word, so we should study the Bible to know how we should live.

We have other authorities in our lives besides God. Our highest earthly authority is our parents until we establish our own homes. We are to obey them just as we would the Lord. We don't have the right to do what is right in our own eyes. God set our parents over us to teach us, guide us, and when needed, to discipline us. God wants us to grow in wisdom and stature and favor with God and man just like Jesus did and he placed our parents here to help us accomplish this goal.

In addition, we need to obey the laws or rules set up by the church, the government, school, even the clubs we belong to as long as they don't contradict God's laws. We need to respect the authority and laws in our lives and live to God's glory.

Questions To Think About

1. What should you do if someone tells you to do something that God says is wrong?
2. What does it mean to respect authority?

April 7

. . . and the congregation gathered together as one man before the Lord . . . Judges 20:1

It is so important to be unified and of one mind with the Lord as our leader. As a Christian we should be of one mind not only when we go to church, but in every aspect of our lives. For example, in our families we should gather together as ONE MAN BEFORE THE LORD. This helps us to communicate with God and each other. We will UNDERSTAND each other and be able to talk together about anything and everything. THIS IS THE WAY THE LORD WANTS A FAMILY TO BE.

It is also important to be of one mind with our friends. This puts a big responsibility on us to choose friends who are Christians and who live as God would have them live. We should never choose someone to be a close friend who can't or won't stand with us before God as ONE MAN. THIS IS THE WAY THE LORD WANTS FRIENDS TO BE. Remember the example that Jesus set for us in all of our relationships. He had a few men gathered together AS ONE MAN BEFORE HIM—the twelve apostles.

Questions To Think About

1. What does it mean to come together as one man before the Lord?
2. Are you united in mind before the Lord with your family?

April 8

All that you say to me I will do. Ruth 3:5

Although Ruth spoke these words to her mother-in-law Naomi, they are words that we should speak to our Lord. If we do as Ruth did, wonderful things will happen to us just as they did to Ruth. Because of her obedience, Ruth was blessed with a son, but not just any son. Ruth's son Obed was the father of Jesse who was the father of David who became king of all Israel. But more than that, she was in the tribe and ancestral line, which God chose as the line of Christ. This was a great blessing.

We need to say "all that you say to me I will do" to Jesus and then do it. So how are we going to know what Jesus tells us to do? We must study God's Word daily and pray and ask Him for wisdom. A good place to learn how God wants us to live is the book of Proverbs. It is a very simple and practical instruction manual from God to us. There are thirty-one chapters in the book and one way to learn it is to read one chapter of Proverbs every day of the month. We have to remember that when we read God's Word we need to pay attention to what we are reading and then we need to go out and live it. Through prayer and study of God's Word, like Ruth, we will be equipped to say, "All that you say to me, I will do."

Questions To Think About

1. How can we learn how God wants us to live?
2. Why is it important to obey God?

April 9

Speak, Lord, for Your servant hears. I Samuel 3:9

Samuel said these words when he was just a young boy. He heard the Lord calling to him and he thought it was Eli, the priest. Eli told him that he had not called; it was the Lord. The Lord speaks to us today in a different way, but He speaks to us nonetheless. How? The Lord speaks to us through His Word and he does this in several different ways. One way He speaks to us through His Word is when the pastors and teachers at church expound or teach from the Word. SO LISTEN! He speaks to us when our parents teach us His Word. SO LISTEN! He also speaks to us when we study His Word. SO LISTEN! From now on when God speaks to us through His Word, we need to LISTEN and then LIVE what we have learned.

Questions To Think About

1. Name some ways in which God speaks through His Word.
2. Do you listen to God's Word?

April 10

. . . prepare your hearts for the LORD, and serve Him only; and He will deliver you . . . I Samuel 7:3

This Scripture is just as true today as it was in the days of Samuel. How do we know? The Bible says that God NEVER changes, so we know that what was true in Samuel's day is still true today. Therefore, what we need to know is how do we prepare our hearts for the Lord? The key is REPENTANCE. This means getting rid of anything in our lives that would be displeasing to God. That means working on always being kind, loving, patient, joyful, and anything that would be pleasing to God. When we fail, we REPENT and ask God to forgive us. Then we start again working on being kind, loving, patient, joyful, and so on. We also need to call on God and ask Him to help us to be strong and to protect us from giving in to sin when we are tempted.

This verse also says that we are to serve God only. This means putting God first in everything that we do and say. If some other activity interferes with family devotions or church, we choose church over the other thing. It also means studying God's Word so that we will know what is pleasing to God and then walking in obedience to what we learn. Studying God's Word includes listening and paying attention to what our parents teach us from the Bible, what our Sunday School teachers teach us from the Bible, and what our Pastor teaches us from the Bible.

God always takes care of us, so we should respond by obeying Him.

Things To Think About

1. Have you thanked God for blessing you so much, just like he did Samuel?
2. Why is it important to believe that God never changes?

April 11

". . . that we also may be like all the nations, . . ."
I Samuel 8:20

How often have we all said, "But everyone else is doing it", or "but everyone has one", or "but I want to be like everyone else, I don't want to be different"? Well, Israel was like this too. They wanted to have a king like all the other nations around them. It seemed like a good idea to them to have a king to judge them and lead them into battle. But they already had a KING. His name was Jehovah and his earthly representatives were the Judges of Israel. Samuel was one of these judges. By asking for an earthly king, the Israelites were rebelling against God's plan. God told the people all the bad things that would happen if they had a king like all the other nations, but they wanted one anyway. So God told Samuel to let them have their king.

We have talked before about the fact that God has a plan for each of us. In His plan He has placed our parents in authority over us until we have our own households. We are to listen to our parents and be obedient to them. We are not to follow the advice, dress, or actions of the "stars of this world". They will fade away and soon we will wonder what we ever saw in them. We will wonder why we wanted to sing their songs, wear their fashions, talk like they talked, act like they acted, or even be identified as "one of them." When we insist on being like everybody else we are rebelling against God's authority in our lives. And even if our parents don't directly say we can't do this or that we should ask ourselves, "Is this of God? Would I act this way if Jesus were standing right beside me?" Remember, HE IS! We need to remember to HAVE JESUS AS THE PATTERN FOR OUR ACTIONS AND APPEARANCE.

Questions To Think About

1. What was the pattern of Jesus life?
2. Are there things in your life that don't match up to the pattern of Jesus? What are you going to do about them?

April 12

Only fear the Lord and serve Him in truth with all your heart; for consider what great things He has done for you.
I Samuel 12:24

Have you really ever stopped to think about all the things that the Lord does for you each and every day of your life? To begin with He is the one who actually keeps you alive. He gives you every breath you take. He is with you every second of every day through everything that happens to you and everything that you experience. Remember the time you were in an accident and you came out of it with just a scratch. Jesus was there! He protected you from greater harm. Have you considered this great thing He did for you? Remember when your best friend didn't like you any more and how much it hurt? Jesus was there! He comforted you. Have you considered this great thing He did for you? Remember when your dog died and you missed him so much? Jesus was there! He helped you remember the good times and be happy. Have you considered this great thing He did for you? Remember the time you had to move to a new school or church and you didn't know anyone? Jesus was there! Before long you had new friends. Have you considered this great thing He did for you? Or maybe you are lonely right now. Jesus is with you! He will be your friend. Consider this great thing He will do for you.

Jesus is always with you doing GREAT THINGS for you and you don't even realize it. He blesses you with good times and helps you grow through the bad times so you have faith to face even bigger things that will come your way. As the Scripture says your response to the GREAT THINGS He has done for you is to love and serve the Lord in truth with all your heart. Serve him out of a heart full of love and thankfulness.

Questions To Think About

1. Why should you serve the Lord?
2. What can you do to serve the Lord in TRUTH with all your heart?

April 13

For rebellion is as the sin of witchcraft, and stubbornness is as iniquity and idolatry. I Samuel 15:23a

Saul was the first king of the Israelites. Soon after he established his power, he started taking things into his own hands instead of consulting God. He became very proud and arrogant and thought he could do anything he wanted to do. Then one day, before he went into battle, God told him not to take any spoil or any of the enemy's possessions. Saul rebelled against God's command and took some sheep because they were quality stock. He completely ignored what God had told him.

When Samuel came to him and confronted him about taking the sheep Saul came up with an excuse. He told Samuel that he wasn't taking the sheep for himself; he was planning on sacrificing those sheep to the Lord. RIGHT! Saul must have forgotten that he was lying to God because of course God knew what was in his heart and he knew what he had planned to do—keep the best sheep for himself. So Saul was caught in his sin. Instead of repenting Saul continued to rebel and to stubbornly do what he wanted. Each time he rebelled it became easier to rebel the next time.

We can learn a big lesson from Saul. We need to obey God's Word. This of course means obeying our parents—it's one of the TEN COMMANDMENTS. When we disobey our parents we are rebelling against God. Think about that. It's not just our parents we are ignoring; we are thumbing our nose in rebellion at almighty God! Each time we rebel or sin without repenting, it becomes easier to sin or rebel the next time our parents tell us to do or not do something. We might think, "I'm just INDEPENDENT." The truth is we are rebellious.

The rebellious Saul had a sad ending to his life. He continued in his sin and rebellion, each time straying farther and farther from God's truth. His rebellion against God lost him his kingdom and it also led to the death of his son Jonathan. So let's think about what we are really doing before we decide to do what we want instead of what our parents and God's Word tell us to do.

QUESTIONS TO THINK ABOUT

1. What is rebellion?
2. Whom are we rebelling against when we choose to sin?

NOTES

April 14

So Absalom said to Hushai, "Is this your loyalty to your friend? Why did you not go with your friend?" II Samuel 16:17

It's great to have friends. Maybe you have lots of friends or maybe you just have a couple or only one really close friend. The important thing is that you have friends. Have you ever thought how it would be if you didn't have a friend? Sometimes there are people who say they are our friends, but when someone else comes along who is more exciting or has more "cool stuff" than we do, they forget about us and go off with their "new friend". Or, there are those who call themselves our friend and really like us—as long as they always get THEIR WAY.

Hushai had always been a trusted friend in King David's household. Then when Absalom, David's son, tried to take over his father's kingdom, Hushai came to Absalom and offered to serve him. Absalom asked Hushai why he was deserting David and was no longer his friend. Absalom didn't know that David sent Hushai to pretend to be Absalom's friend so he could spy on the camp. Hushai was a true friend to David.

We have a true friend who will never leave us. This friend is Jesus. Sometimes we forget this and start feeling sorry for ourselves because we don't have a friend, but all we have to do is turn to the Lord and talk to Him as we would any good friend. He will listen and help us with our loneliness. So when we start feeling this way we need to remember our BEST FRIEND FOREVER is Jesus.

Questions To Think About

1. Do you talk to Jesus every day?

April 15

And David behaved wisely in all his ways and the Lord was with him. I Samuel 18:14

David was a great man and in this verse we find out why. As the verse says, he behaved or acted wisely in ALL his ways. Wouldn't it be great if we could say the same thing about ourselves? I have to admit that I have not always acted wisely. How about you? Do you ever let your feelings govern how you act instead of God's Word? For example, when you're tired or don't feel well are you a grouch to everyone around or are you longsuffering as God's Word says we should be? Sometimes when you are irritated do you withdraw into your own little world and ignore everyone or are you kind as God's Word teaches. Are there times when you don't get your way and you pout or stomp out of the room like a spoiled brat or do you put others first and consider their wants and needs before your own as God's Word teaches?

Maybe none of you act this way, but I have to confess that I have. You know, it all goes back to selfishness. The next time you act UNWISELY, check your attitude and see if it can be traced back to SELF. In other words, are you being selfish and thinking only of yourself, or are you putting other's first. The Bible tells us a child is known by his ACTIONS. So in all you DO obey God like David did and your actions will speak louder than words as a testimony for God.

QUESTIONS TO THINK ABOUT

1. Where do you go and what do you do to find out how to live wisely?

April 16

Whenever I am afraid, I will trust in You. Psalm 56:3

Have you ever been in a situation when you were really afraid? Your heart was pounding and it felt like you were going to explode if something didn't happen right away? It's okay to be afraid. God gave you this "warning system" inside to let you know when you are in danger. The difference for Christians is where do you go for help when you are afraid? Of course if you're in danger and can escape or call on other people to help you, you should always do that, but most importantly you should turn to Jesus. God's Word says you can always trust in Him.

Trust is a wonderful thing. We trust things and people all the time. We TRUST our car will take us where we want to go. We TRUST the food we eat will be good for us and not make us sick. We TRUST our parents will take care of us. The list goes on and on. But, sometimes things or people don't do what they are supposed to do. JESUS ALWAYS WILL. HE NEVER FAILS US. We can TRUST in HIM. Jesus knows what the future holds and he knows what is best for us. So we don't need to be afraid or worry because GOD IS IN CONTROL and He promises in His Word that He makes *all things work together for good to those who love God, to those who are the called according to His purpose.* If we are children of God and love the Lord we can TRUST HIM IN ALL THINGS!

Questions To Think About

1. How do we know we can trust God in all things?

April 17

You love evil more than good, lying rather than speaking righteousness. Psalm 52:3

When I was a kid, a new girl my age moved into the neighborhood on the street behind us. When she first got there I was nice to her and wanted her to be my friend. She would come over to my house to play almost every day. Before long we started noticing that things around the house were missing. Also that summer my cousin came for a visit and one afternoon the three of us decided to go to town with my Mom. We had a great time shopping, eating ice cream, and just messing around. When we got home, my cousin couldn't find her purse. We looked everywhere for it. She was sure she had it when we got into the car to come home, but we called all the places we had shopped just to make sure. No one had seen her purse. She was really upset because it had all the money her Dad had given her to spend during her visit. That evening we went to pick up some bread for supper and guess what. There on the back seat was my cousin's purse, but all the money was gone. My "friend" had taken the money and put the purse back.

I wish I could say that the girl on the next block learned her lesson and she never stole anything again, but later on she was caught stealing something more valuable and ended up in juvenile court. She loved evil more than good as our Scripture says. She started off taking small things. Then when she wasn't caught she moved on to bigger more expensive things and ended up living a life of crime. Eventually she was sent to prison. The Bible tells us to FLEE EVIL and TEMPTATION and be sure that you always choose good over evil and truth over lying.

QUESTIONS TO THINK ABOUT

1. Do you FLEE evil and TEMPTATION?
2. Do you choose good over evil?
3. Do you choose truth over lying?

April 18

I will praise You, O Lord, among the peoples; I will sing to You among the nations. Psalm 57:9

Have you ever thought about being a missionary? When I was young I wanted to be a missionary in some far off land where I could have a great adventure. To tell the truth, I was probably thinking more about the adventure than praising and singing to the Lord. It wasn't until I was older that I realized we don't have to leave home to be a "MISSIONARY". The word missionary comes from the word mission, which means having an assignment to accomplish. This means that every Christian is a missionary because we all have an assignment to accomplish. Christ has given us His name, so we are His representatives on earth to everyone. This includes our fathers, mothers, sisters, brothers, other relatives, friends, and other Christians. These people are usually pretty easy for us to love. But what about people we don't like, people who have been mean to us, people who are different from us, people who are dirty, people who are stuck-up, people in authority who misuse their power. Our faith and witness are really tested in the way we treat EVERYONE.

So, you can see that YOU ARE A MISSIONARY right now, this very minute. You are representing Jesus to others all the time. Are you "singing and praising" God for his bountiful blessings, goodness, mercy, justice, judgment, truth, and almighty power over all things so that others can see Jesus in you? If you claim Jesus as your master, the world will see a picture of Jesus through you. What does He look like to others when they look at Him through you?

Questions To Think About

1. What does Jesus look like to the world when they see a picture of Him in your life?
2. How should we live as "missionaries" or representatives of Jesus on earth?
3. Are you living like a representative of Jesus?

April 19

May the Lord repay every man for his righteousness and his faithfulness; . . . I Samuel 26:23

When David prayed this prayer he held the life of King Saul in his hand and he chose not to kill him. He prayed that God, in his own time, would deal with Saul. Even though Saul had tried to kill him many times, David always treated Saul well. God told Saul that because he had rebelled against Him he would loose the kingdom to David and be killed in battle. The consequences of Saul's rebellion against God were catching up with him. God is still teaching us this lesson today. What lesson? WE REAP WHAT WE SOW. This means that there are consequences for our actions.

When Samuel anointed Saul as the first king of Israel, Saul had everything. He was good-looking, powerful, wealthy, victorious in battle, and he could have done great things for God. But Saul was not a righteous man and was not faithful to God and His Law. He came to a terrible end. David, on the other hand was humble, faithful, and loved God and His Law. He made some terrible mistakes in his life and paid dearly for them, but he always repented and God always forgave him. In fact, God said that David was a man after His own heart.

Our lesson is simple. All of our actions, thoughts, and attitudes have consequences. If we live an evil life, we will reap evil consequences. If we live for the Lord we will reap blessings. Sounds simple doesn't it? But temptation is always around us so we must CHOOSE who we are going to follow just as Saul and David did. FOLLOWING AND DEPENDING ON THE LORD = RIGHTEOUSNESS = FAITHFULNESS = BLESSINGS FROM GOD.

Questions To Think About

1. Whom will you choose to follow today?
2. Whom will you choose to follow the rest of your life?

April 20

Now David was greatly distressed, for the people spoke of stoning him, . . . But David strengthened himself in the Lord his God.
I Samuel 30:6

David and his men were far away when the Amalekites raided their homes and took all of their women, children, and possessions. When they returned home, David's men blamed him and talked of stoning him. The same thing happens today. When something bad happens we always want to BLAME someone. Usually the first thing we say is, "I didn't do it." Then we BLAME someone else.

Sometime in your life you will probably experience this. When a project you proposed or are in charge of doesn't work out the way others think it should, you will be BLAMED. You probably won't have to worry about anyone trying to stone you, but people may say terrible things about you. It seems to make them feel better. The terrible things they say will hurt your feelings and you will have to be careful not to get caught up in the BLAME GAME—they blame you, you blame them, on and on and on.

When you are blamed for something you should react as David did. He SRENGTHENED himself in the Lord his God. You need to stop and think why the problem occurred in the first place. You need to ask yourself what you should and could do about it. Is someone else at fault? If so, present the facts not feelings about the person. Most importantly, before you do anything, do what David did. Get on your knees and talk to the Lord about it. Ask for His guidance and wisdom in dealing with the situation. Love those who persecute you and BLAME you and God will strengthen you.

Questions To Think About

1. Why is it destructive to "play the blame game"?
2. Does blaming others for problems produce progress?

April 21

. . . *David inquired of the Lord,* . . . II Samuel 2:1

All through the Old Testament we are told that David was "a man after God's heart". Why? I'm sure it was because David always repented when he sinned and he asked the Lord what to do in just about every circumstance. Some of the things David asked about seemed very small; things that he could have dealt with himself rather than bothering God. But instead, he went to God before he made his decision. This should be our goal in life. We should be thankful for the privilege of being able to go directly to God with everything; then, we should GO TO GOD FOR ADVICE ON EVERYTHING. Isn't it amazing that God is interested in everything that we do and everything that happens to us?

How do we get answers or learn God's advice? We learn God's advice through prayer, teaching, and God's Word. God's Word has answers and advice for all of our questions. Questions such as: "Who should I hang around with at school?" or "Why should I read my Bible everyday?" or "What difference does it make if I watch an R-rated move?" or "Why do I have to help the lady down the street when I hardly even know her?" or "Why should I tell someone I'm a Christian when I know they'll make fun of me?" or "I have my own friends why do I have to be nice to everybody?" or "What's wrong with saying certain words? They aren't that bad. Besides, everybody says them and they don't mean anything by them."

So inquire of the Lord. Ask your parents and teachers how God would answer your questions. Listen to the pastor as he tells you what God's Word teaches. Study the Bible and find the answers to your questions on your own or with your parent's help. Ask God to open your "eyes to see and your ears to hear" the truth. Inquire of the Lord and He will teach you how to live for Him.

QUESTIONS TO THINK ABOUT

1. Do you know God's answer to the questions above? If not search for them.

April 22

. . . David inquired again of God . . . So David did as God commanded him, . . . So David went on and became great, and the Lord God of hosts was with him.
I Chronicles 14: 14, 16; II Samuel 5:10

When I was a kid we used to joke around and say, "When I become great . . ." and then we would fill in the blank with what we were going to do when we grew up and "became great". It seems that most of us want to be a great person some day. There isn't anything wrong with wanting to be a great person necessarily, except that many people equate greatness with "rich and famous". The idea of greatness has nothing to do with being rich or famous. Let's look at David as an example and see how he became a great man.

The first thing we see in David's life is the fact that he went to God for guidance in the decisions he made. Too often we don't go to God with our needs until we've tried everything else and as a last resort we pray. Secondly, we see that David didn't just ask God for guidance, he OBEYED God's direction. Obedience is the KEY to becoming GREAT. Sometimes we KNOW what we should do but we want to try it OUR way first. We know how that always ends up. We have to consistently rely on God for direction and help. We can't rely on God when we are in trouble and then go our own way when things are going smoothly. We have to PERSEVER through smooth and rough patches. That means that we OBEY NO MATTER WHAT. When things are going our way or when they aren't. This is what made David great this is what will make us great. Sometimes fame and riches accompany greatness, but sometimes they don't. True greatness is how God views us. When we always seek God's will and then obey it, we will be great in God's sight like David.

Questions To Think About

1. What does it mean to live a life of obedience?
2. Is it more important to be great in men's eyes or God's eyes?

April 23

For you are my lamp, O LORD; The LORD shall enlighten my darkness. II Samuel 22:29

Have you ever been in a REALLY dark place? A cave? A photography dark room? A closet? It's kind of scary. No one likes to stumble around in the dark unable to see. God knows this and provides us with a LIGHT, or LAMP as our verse says, so that we can see the right path. When David sang this song of praise to the Lord, he had been rescued from his enemies. He was praising God for rescuing him from a very dark place—the middle of his enemies. We should thank God for the same thing today because he is still shining a light all around us to enlighten our paths and rescue us from "dark places".

God's LAMP for us today is His Word. He gives us all the instructions we need to live our lives for Him. When we think we are "in the dark" and don't have a light or friend to guide us safely through the rough times, we need to look to Jesus and remember that He is the Light of the World. He lights our path and guides us every step of the way. So we need to turn to Him when we are floundering in darkness surrounded by enemies. His Word will LIGHT our way.

Questions To Think About

1. Who is the Light of the World? Why is He called this?
2. What is the "Lamp for our feet"? What does that mean?

April 24

Give to the Lord the glory due His name; Bring an offering, and come into His courts. Psalm 96:8

Let's look at the verbs in this verse. They stand out because they are things we, as worshipers of the Lord, must do. The verse is not a suggestion. It doesn't use IF we give . . . The verse commands us to GIVE. Then the verse tells us what to give. The verse tells us to give glory to Him. We can do this through our singing, our prayers, our praise, and the testimony of our lives. The Lord wants to hear our voices singing, even if we can't carry a tune. He wants to hear our prayers; they are like incense to Him. He wants to hear our thankfulness for all the blessings He has poured out on us. He wants to hear us tell others about Him. He wants us to live a life that glorifies Him.

The second thing the verse commands us to do is to BRING an offering. If we earn an allowance or money from odd jobs around the house or neighborhood, we should give part of it to the Lord. Most importantly, we should bring our offering to the Lord with a cheerful heart.

The final verb in the verse is COME. We need to come together with other Christians when we praise God and bring our offerings to Him. This is what we do when we go to church on Sunday. We fellowship with other Christians and enjoy the blessings of worshipping together. As we read this verse and think it through we can see that when we give God the glory due his name He turns it around to bless us. What a GREAT GOD we serve.

Questions To Think About

1. How do we give God the glory due His name?
2. Why should we give God the glory due His name?

April 25

Glory in His holy name; Let the hearts of those rejoice who seek the Lord! Seek the Lord and His strength; Seek His face evermore!
Psalm 105:3, 4

Remember playing hide and seek? Remember searching diligently in every nook and cranny for those who were hiding? This is what David is talking about in this Psalm. We are to search diligently for the Lord, the most important find we can ever make. What's more, He will always be found IF WE SEEK HIM. We seek Him and it makes us glad. We seek His strength to make us strong.

David says to *seek His face evermore.* That means that we are to continually seek God. We do this through PRAYER, BIBLE STUDY, SERMONS, and CHRISTIAN FELLOWSHIP. As a Christian we should rejoice, because Jesus is "by our side" always. Rejoice! For if we seek Him, WE WILL FIND HIM.

QUESTONS TO THINK ABOUT

1. How do we seek God?
2. What benefits do we gain from seeking the Lord?

April 26

You have given a banner to those who fear You, that it may be displayed because of the truth. Psalm 60:4

Banners are neat things. I love to see banners stretched across the road in parades naming the bands that march behind them. I love the banners flying high at the Olympic Games indicating each nation's athletes. I love to read about Medieval Times when the knights' banners identified them to their allies in the midst of the fiercest battles. Banners have always played an important part in letting others know who and what a person stands for. They even had banners in Bible days.

Isn't it exciting to learn from this verse that we have a banner? Yes, God has given His children a banner. Those who fear Him are the soldiers of the cross and we carry His banner. What does a banner do? It shows who or what a person stands for. Our banner is being named a Christian. We must display our banner through our lives. So as Christians, we show that we stand for God and His Word by the way we live and honor God and His Word.

Why are we glad to be called Christians and to be identified with Christ? Our verse says we want to be called Christians because of the TRUTH. God's truth is the ETERNAL TRUTH and this is what the Christian banner stands for.

Questions To Think About

1. What is the Christian's banner?
2. Why does God give us a banner?

April 27

. . . Blot out my transgressions. Wash me thoroughly from my iniquity, and cleanse me from my sin. Psalm 51:1, 2

Isn't it wonderful that when we repent of our sin God will forgive us? What would it be like if we couldn't be forgiven for our sins? The burden of guilt and the memory of the sin would be hanging over us forever. Even if we felt sorry for what we did, the burden would still be there. Being forgiven—being free from this burden is a freedom like no other. It makes us feel so good and clean inside.

When we think about God's forgiveness it should also make us stop and think about what it cost. Jesus' death paid for our sin. We should thank God that he was willing to send his only Son to give His sinless life for our sinful ones.

We should not take sin lightly. The fact that we choose to sin should grieve us. The fact that God loves us so much that He will forgive us should inspire us with peace, joy, and love for Him and others.

Questions To Think About

1. What did it cost God to forgive our sins?
2. How should we feel about God's forgiveness?

April 28

Then the King said to her, "What troubles you?"
II Samuel 14:5

The King in this verse is David. David's son had killed one of his brothers and had run away to another country to escape being killed in return. The woman was asking David to let his exiled son come home. During this time, the King was all-powerful. He had the power of granting life or death to anyone who lived in his country. David found himself in a terrible position. His own son had murdered one of his other sons. What could he do? What should he do?

When we think about it we begin to realize that this is what God had to deal with when He sent His ONLY son to die a criminal's death for the rest of His children—US! God, who is all-powerful in Heaven as well as earth, gave His holy and sinless son to die for His unholy and sinful children. What's more, Jesus came to earth and died willingly because He loved us too.

Because God is holy and just, He didn't just say, I'll let everyone off the hook. No one will have to pay for his sin. Someone had to pay and of course we know it was Jesus. So we should be very thankful for God's gift of salvation. But what if we don't have Jesus as our Savior? The Bible tells us that the wages of sin is death. This means that without Jesus to pay the price for our sin we will have to pay the price. The price is death and this death is eternal separation from God in never-ending torment. See what God has saved us from—thank Him every day for saving us—because we deserve death.

Questions To Think About

1. Is Jesus your Savior? If not, ask your parents or pastor to tell you how He can be.
2. Why should we be thankful for our salvation?

April 29

"*. . . The people are hungry and weary and thirsty in the wilderness.*" II Samuel 17:29

This verse tells us of a time when David had to flee from his palace because his son Absalom was threatening to kill him and take over as king. David's loyal followers went with him into the wilderness and they suffered in three ways. They suffered from hunger, weariness, and thirst. When we sin and we try to hide from God because we don't want to confess our sin, this is what happens to us. We suffer. We get HUNGRY for the FELLOWSHIP we had with the Lord before we sinned. We grow WEARY because we have lost our JOY. When we are separated from God by sin we don't have the "joy of the Lord". We are THIRSTY for LIVING WATER. We don't have the daily "renewing of our mind" by the Holy Spirit because of the barrier of sin separating us from Him.

Any sin causes this separation. The sin doesn't have to be BIG like murder; it can be talking back to our parents. Then sometimes we become stubborn and want to run into the wilderness instead of asking for forgiveness. This means that instead of going to our parents and confessing that we were wrong we go to our friends and tell them how mean our parents have been. When we do this we don't feel better. Instead we feel hungry and weary and thirsty! The only solution is to do things God's way. When we sin, we need to go to God first and ask for forgiveness. Then we need to go and ask forgiveness from the person we have sinned against. When we do this our fellowship with God and the other person is restored. We have been forgiven and as we talked about in an earlier lesson, being forgiven is the greatest feeling in the world.

Quesitons To Think About

1. What happens when we try to run and hide from our sin?
2. What is the remedy for this?

April 30

I cried to the LORD with my voice, and He heard me from His holy hill . . . I will not be afraid . . . Psalm 3:4, 6

In this verse David is thinking back about the time he spent running from his son and he remembers how he cried out to the Lord to deliver him from harm. God did protect David and restore him to the throne. King once more, David is telling the world that even though he wasn't always faithful, God is. David tells us that God's faithfulness doesn't depend on us. When God promises to protect and care for us we can know beyond any shadow of doubt that He will. So like David we have nothing to fear.

God is faithful but that does not mean that we won't have consequences for our sin. David sinned. This sin led to his son's hatred and desire to kill him. When David cried out to the Lord, God did deliver him from death. However, it cost David the life of his son and David loved Absalom in spite of Absalom's desire to kill him.

We need to learn from this that when we sin we should go IMMEDIATELY and ask for forgiveness. And God will forgive us, but we need to remember that choosing to sin brings with it consequences. And if we are stubborn and refuse to repent that is another sin added to the first which will also have consequence.

Thankfully, God is patient with us. But let's remember to keep a tender hear toward Him and run to him when we sin to ask his forgiveness and to restore us to His fellowship.

Questions To Think About

1. What happened as a result of David's sin?
2. Why should we be quick to admit, confess, and repent of our sin?

May 1

. . . After that God heeded the prayer for the land.
II Samuel 21:14

Sometimes we have a tendency to just pray for ourselves and for our immediate family and we don't think about anything else. As this verse teaches us, God will also hear our prayers for our LAND. Why is this important? It means that we can pray for our leaders and whether they are Christians or not God will use them to do what is good for His children. Or, if there is a drought or flood or tornado or hurricane, we can pray for our LAND and God will hear and do what is good for His children. God wants us to come boldly to is throne and pray for our LAND. He will hear us and will HEAL OUR LAND. So when we pray, let's remember to pray for the leaders of our nation, town, church, school. Let's remember to pray for the physical Land as well.

QUESTIONS TO THINK ABOUT

1. Why should we pray for our land?

May 2

. . . *His mercies are great!* II Samuel 24:14

David had sinned. So the Lord gave him three choices as to the punishment for his disobedience. The first two choices God gave David would be delivered through men. God would deliver the third choice. David chose the third because he believed that God was more merciful than man. He was right—God is infinitely more merciful than man.

We should be so glad that God is merciful because if we always got what we deserved we would be in big trouble. God knows that *our spirit is willing but our flesh is weak.* This means that we all know the difference between right and wrong and we usually really want to do what is right, but sometimes we give in to our selfish desires and choose to sin. This is when God's mercy becomes very important. When we ask for forgiveness, because we are His children and Jesus has paid our debt of sin, God will forgive us.

However, we should never let this weakness become an excuse to sin. We need to become stronger Christians. We do this by regularly studying His Word, praying, listening to our parents, pastor, Sunday School teachers, and others who are giving us Godly advice. We also grow in the Lord when we OBEY what we learn. If we just soak it in and never put into practice what we learn we haven't accomplished anything. But when we OBEY what we have learned we grow stronger in our faith and in our desire to be obedient. What a great blessing that we serve a merciful God.

Questions To Think About

1. Why should we thank God for His mercy?
2. How can we grow in the Lord?

May 3

Arise and begin working and the Lord be with you.
I Chronicles 22:16

These were the words King David spoke to his son Solomon when God chose Solomon to build His temple. David told Solomon to get up and go to work building the temple and God would be with him. These are word we all need to listen to today.

Do you have a hard time getting out of bed when you have a hard day of work ahead? Maybe you have a paper or project for school that you have put off for as long as you can, or perhaps its yard work for your Dad or cleaning for your Mom? Then as the verse teaches, get up. It's time to start working.

The second part of the verse is also important. It says that the Lord will be with you when you do His work. This should help you have a good attitude about your work. Do you have an attitude of, "I HATE this but I've got to do it because I can't put it off any longer." Or, "Maybe I can get out of this for one more day. I'll do it tomorrow." This is not the right attitude to have. Pray that God will give you a new attitude about your duties and then dive in. It doesn't mean that you will automatically start liking every job you have to do, but your attitude will change and you will be able to complete your task, "as unto the Lord".

QUESTIONS TO THINK ABOUT

1. Should you try to wait as long as possible to do the jobs you don't like?
2. What attitude should we have while doing the "not fun" jobs?

May 4

But the Lord said to Samuel, "Do not look at his appearance or at his physical stature, because I have refused him. For the Lord does not see as man sees: for man looks at the outward appearance, but the Lord looks at the heart."
I Samuel 16:7

The Lord gave Samuel some very good advice in this verse. Samuel was looking for someone to replace Saul as king of Israel. This advice is still important for us today. The world has influenced us so much in this area that we are tempted to judge people based on the way they look. Because of this influence, we sometimes don't want to be friends or associate with kids who are overweight, too skinny, "nerds", poor kids who don't wear "name brand" clothing, or kids of a different nationality. This is a shame because we might miss out on some friendships that could really be fun and strong.

When we base how we feel about someone strictly on the way they "look" on the outside, we are being PRIDEFUL. Some of my very best friends would not have been on anyone's "pretty-people" list. The point is that we should be attracted to people because of their inward beauty. Often, the kids that "have it all" are not friendly and are too busy thinking about themselves to GIVE anything to a friendship. They are only friendly to those who can help their image or get them what they want. This doesn't mean that if someone is pretty or handsome they are automatically bad—don't make that mistake either.

The Bible tells us that Jesus was not "comely" or pleasant to look at, so this should give us a big clue about how God views outward beauty. What we need to learn today is that we should be kind to everyone no matter what they look like. And remember, a true friend LOVES AT ALL TIMES.

Questions To Think About

1. Do you make friends based on their inward or outward beauty?

May 5

. . . Weeping may endure for a night, but joy comes in the morning. Psalm 30:5

Have you ever had an experience that seemed too much for you to bear? At the time you felt that your whole world had fallen apart and you couldn't go on any longer? You felt like nothing could ever be good again and there was no one who could make it better. All you could do was cry. You are not alone in this experience. Many people have had the same feelings, but things are never as bad as they seem at the time of our trouble.

Christians have a distinct advantage when troubles come into their lives because they KNOW that Jesus will see them through the crisis. Jesus will be there through the hard times and the sad times and the times when it hurts terribly. He knows what it's like to have hard times. When He was here on earth, people treated Him very badly. Jesus has suffered much more than you will ever have to suffer so He can relate to your pain. When you have troubles, go to Him and find comfort in His arms.

QUESTIONS TO THINK ABOUT

1. Have you sought out Jesus when you are sad, depressed, or have troubles in your life? If you have, you know the peace He brings. If you haven't do so today.

May 6

"But let all those rejoice who put their trust in You; Let them ever shout for joy, because You defend them; Let those also who love Your name be joyful in You." Psalm 5:11

Occasionally we should ask ourselves, "Are we happy people? Do we have a joy about us that others can see?" We should have that kind of joy.

If we trust in Jesus we should always be joyful. That doesn't mean we won't ever be sad. But when we are sad we know that joy is waiting when the sorrow has passed. In fact, we can even have joy through our sorrow.

If we trust in Jesus we can also shout for joy because he defends us. I can't think of anything more wonderful than having the Creator of the universe watching out for us and defending us. We can also be joyful because we love Jesus' name. This means that we are comforted when we hear His name, when we are in danger we speak His name, and when we give thanks we give thanks in His name.

We should have joy at all times, BECAUSE OF WHAT JESUS HAS DONE AND IS CONTINUING TO DO FOR US.

Questions To Think About

1. Why should we have joy?
2. How can we express our joy?

May 7

The Lord is my Shepherd; I shall not want. Psalm 23:1

Do you know what all a shepherd has to do? I didn't until I studied it. I found out that being a shepherd is hard work and a big responsibility. It takes a very special person to be a shepherd. So what does a shepherd do? First of all, a shepherd is very closely connected to his sheep. His sheep know his voice and will respond only to their shepherd. Secondly, the shepherd must watch over his flock very closely. He must know if even one sheep is missing, or is sick, or in danger. He must fight off any wild animals that might wound or kill them. In addition, the shepherd has to lead his flock to the best pasture where they have plenty of grass and cool, slow flowing water. At night the shepherd makes sure that his sheep are all in the fold and he lies down across the entrance so no sheep can get out and nothing harmful can get in. Wow! This is a really big job. You can see why David who was a shepherd himself said that the Lord was his Shepherd. He knew that a good shepherd would take care of all the needs of his sheep.

Today, we know that Jesus is our Good Shepherd. How do we know? First of all, Jesus is very closely connected to us—his sheep. He knows us by name and we know His voice. His voice is the Bible and when we study it we will know the TRUTH and not be fooled by false teachers. So we will only listen to Jesus' voice. Secondly, Jesus watches over us ALWAYS. He never leaves us and is with us every second of every day. Next, He promises that we will have everything that we need. He also keeps us faithful; we can never fall away from His salvation. Jesus will never loose one of His children. Wow! What a GOOD SHEPHERD WE HAVE!

QUESTIONS TO THINK ABOUT

1. Who is the Good Shepherd? Is He your Shepherd?
2. How does Jesus fulfill the role of our shepherd?

May 8

Blessed is he who considers the poor. The Lord will deliver him in time of trouble. The Lord will preserve him and keep him alive, and he will be blessed on the earth; You will not deliver him to the will of his enemies; The Lord will strengthen him on his bed of illness; You will sustain him on his sickbed.
Psalm 41:1-3

JUST LOOK what the LORD does for those who HELP THE POOR. First of all, if we help the poor He will help us when we are in trouble. Second, He will sustain us through out trouble and keeps us alive. Third, He blesses us. Fourth, He delivers us from our enemies. Fifth, He helps us when we are sick. The Lord will do all of these things for us just because we help the poor.

We may not be rich in the eyes of the world but we can always find someone who has less than we do. This verse doesn't necessarily mean that we have to give hundreds of dollars to the poor. Just giving a pencil to a classmate who can't afford a new one is helping the poor. Think of other things we can do. It may be something as simple as giving clothes that we've outgrown to someone in need. OR it could involve saving a certain percentage of our allowance to put together with our friends' allowances and then sending the money to a missionary who is working in a third world country. We just need to keep our eyes and ears open and to be sensitive to the people around us and we will soon find ways to help the poor. Remember that God does so much for us and has blessed us with so much that we should give back to Him. One way to do it is by helping the poor. Even then God says He will give us more because we give back a small portion of what He has given us.

Questions To Think About

1. List about ten things that God has given you. Then list ten more.
2. Are you rich then?
3. What do you plan to do with some of your riches?

May 9

Let my mouth be filled with Your praise and with Your glory all the day. Psalm 71:8

Have you ever stopped to think about what comes out of your mouth in a single day—EVERYTHING that comes out of your mouth? This Scripture is a good one to remember as you look back at some of the things you have said on any given day. Did you make a mental note of the time today when you talked back to your Mother, or had a fight with your best friend and said horrible things to her, or said mean, ugly, bad things about someone else? We need to realize that things that come out of our mouths can be more deadly than a knife, a gun, or even a bomb. Jesus tells us over and over that we should only have good thoughts and if we do, then good things will come out of our mouths. We can always find something to complain about and if we are not careful it will become a habit and then a way of life.

So if we are not to have bad, mean things coming out of our mouths what are we supposed to do? We are to do as this verse says and fill our mouths with praise and glorify God. If we do this, we will be much happier and fulfilled and God's peace will reign in us.

Questions To Think About

1. What has come out of your mouth today? Do you need to repent?

May 10

Teach me Your way, O lord; I will walk in your truth . . .
Psalm 86:11

Sometimes we don't think about the fact that we never have to be taught how to be BAD, but we always have to be taught how to be GOOD. Some people don't believe this, but the Bible teaches this fact. The Bible tells us that there is no one who is righteous, not even one. This brings us to a very important truth we need to learn today—GOD'S WORD is ALWAYS RIGHT. So if the Bible tells us something we can rely on the fact that it is TRUE. So we have learned two things so far. We know that we have to learn how to be GOOD and live God's way. And we also know where to go to find the TRUTH about how we should live a GOOD life—God's Word.

What about the second part of the verse? We can acknowledge that we have to be taught how to be good and we can even know where to go for answers, but if we don't put what we learn into PRACTICE, how have we benefited from knowing the TRUTH? So as the second part of the verse says, we must PRACTICE the TRUTH we learn from GOD'S WORD. No one ever makes us sin. It is always our decision to sin or not to sin. That is why we need to be studying God's Word daily. We need to know what is right and then ask God to help us practice what we learn. He will honor our prayer.

Questions To Think About

1. Where do we go to learn how to be good?

May 11

Revive me, O Lord, for Your name's sake, For Your righteousness sake bring my soul out of trouble.
Psalm 143:11

When we do bad things, whether we consider it a SMALL thing or get into really BIG trouble, we can always go to the Lord and ask Him to help us. The key is we need to go to the Lord with a repentant heart. This means that when we need to tell our brother or sister we are sorry for hurting them, we need to really BE SORRY for hurting them. We shouldn't just go through the motions because Mom and Dad say we have to apologize. Going through the motions is not having a repentant heart. So if we don't really feel sorry we can go to the Lord and ask him to revive us and put a soft heart in us that will hate sin and be open to repentance and correction.

Why do we need to do this? For the sake of Jesus' name, because we are bought with His blood and we bear His name. We never want to do anything to bring shame on the name of Christ. When we don't have a heart that is sensitive toward God and His instruction and correction, we bring shame on the name of Jesus. But when we OBEY and REPENT when we mess up and sin, we bring GLORY to Christ's name. Let's remember that the world is watching us.

Questions To Think About

1. *How do we bring shame on the name of Christ?*
2. *How do we bring glory to Christ's name?*

May 12

He shall be like a tree planted by the rivers of water. That brings forth its fruit in its season, whose leaf also shall not wither, and whatever he does shall prosper. Psalm 1:3

Can you guess whom this verse is talking about? Who is "He"? We learn from Psalm 1:2 that the "He" is a Christian who is walking in the way of righteousness. But why will "He" (or "We") be planted like a tree by rivers of water? This means that we—the tree—will always be by the LIVING WATER, that Jesus will always be with us to feed and water our spirit. He will help us to grow and know how to live as Christians should. Then, because we are planted and rooted deep in the LIVING WATER, we will produce fruit. The fruit is all the good works that God planned for us to accomplish before the foundation of the world. On top of that, we will have eternal life because we are rooted in Jesus. And, whatever we do will prosper. All of our good works that God planned for us will be successful. WE WILL NOT FAIL. Wow, there could never be a better guarantee.

Questions To Think About

1. *Who is the tree?*
2. *What does it mean to be rooted in Christ?*

May 13

For I was envious of the boastful, when I saw the prosperity of the wicked. Psalm 73:3

Why would a verse like this be in the Bible? Well, a few verses later, God tells us what becomes of the boastful and the wicked and it isn't good. However, it is sometimes hard not to envy others and all that they have. We see others with the latest new toy or computer game or clothes. Or maybe they are always going to really exciting places for vacations. But if they are not saved, if they don't have Jesus in their hearts, they really have nothing.

Our lives here on earth are short, even if we live to be 100, but as Christians we have an ETERNITY in Heaven with Jesus to look forward to. What do the boastful and the wicked have to look forward to? So we should really be praying for the boastful and the wicked to turn from their sin and repent and be saved. So be happy and content with what you have and remember that the BEST IS YET TO COME.

Questions To Think About

1. What should we do about the boastful and wicked?
2. Where will you spend eternity?

May 14

The Lord will give grace and glory; no good thing will He withhold from those who walk uprightly. Psalm 84:11

Our Scripture today tells us that some wonderful things are going to happen to those who WALK UPRIGHTLY. What does that mean? That means that those who have Jesus as their Savior and Lord and are living their lives according to God's Word will be blessed. And, not only will God bless us if we walk uprightly, he will give us the grace or the strength we need to do it. So the Lord not only blesses us when we do what is right and according to His plan, He also gives us the ability to accomplish the tasks he gives us. Then after we accomplish the tasks he gives us the ability to do, He gives us glory. What a great God we serve!

Questions To Think About

1. What does it mean to walk uprightly?
2. What do we receive when we walk uprightly?

May 15

Let the words of my mouth and the meditation of my heart be acceptable in Your sight. O Lord, my strength and my Redeemer. Psalm 19:14

STICKS AND STONES MAY BREAK MY BONES BUT WORDS CAN NEVER HURT ME. Did you ever say this to someone who was saying mean things to you? Actually this saying is NOT true. Words can hurt. And sometimes they can hurt even more than sticks or stones. This is what the verse today is getting at. You should always pray that the words that come from your mouth and the things that you think about and dwell on in your heart are good. You should strive to never say anything that is hurtful or mean. What should you think about? You should only think about things that you would be happy to share with Jesus. He already knows what you're thinking anyway. So you should PRACTICE being VERY CAREFUL about what you say and what you think. If you do this you will be much happier because you will be pleasing your Lord.

Questions To Think About

1. Do words hurt?
2. What type of things should you think about? Not think about?

May 16

"If I regard iniquity in my heart, the Lord will not hear."
Psalm 66:18

In the dictionary the word iniquity means "sin or wickedness". If we look up wickedness we find that it means "morally bad, evil, vicious, disposed to mischief, disgustingly unpleasant". That pretty well covers anything bad that we might have in our hearts. Sin is anything that separates us from God and if we have unconfessed sin in our lives we are separated from Him.

We probably don't do all the things listed under sin in the dictionary but any one of them is bad enough. Take anger for instance. I have to admit that in anger, I have done some pretty vicious things to people. It seems that we think all the rules and regulations go out the window when we are angry and we can do whatever we want. This is not the right perception to have. Reacting to things in anger is sin.

When we sin we need to pray and ask God to change us and help us not to "regard iniquity" in our hearts. We never want to break our fellowship with the Father and if it is broken by sin we want to connect with Him immediately by repenting and confessing our sin.

Questions To Think About

1. What is iniquity? How should we deal with it?

May 17

"I said to the boastful, do not deal boastfully . . . do not speak with a stiff neck." Psalm 75: 4, 5

Sometimes it's really hard not to brag. When everyone else is telling about how great they are and all the things they can do and we know that we can do them better it is really hard not to tell them. But the Bible tells us we aren't supposed to brag about ourselves. We are supposed to let other people brag about us. If no one ever brags about us we shouldn't be upset. We should remember that every perfect gift comes from God, including our ability to do things well. After all WHO really deserves the credit for the good things we do? God does. That is why it is important for us to recognize the good things God does in other people and brag about them. Even if no one ever recognizes the good things we do we should remember that we aren't doing them for glory or honor from men, we are doing them to bring glory and honor to God.

Questions To Think About

1. Who gives us our abilities? Who deserves the credit for them?
2. Have you recognized someone else's ability lately?

May 18

"I will sing to the Lord as long as I live; I will sing praise to my God while I have my being. May my meditation be sweet to Him; I will be glad in the Lord." Psalm 104: 33, 34

Do you cheer up other people around you? Do you laugh a lot? Do you say "thank you" often? If you answered yes to these questions, you are living out Psalm 104: 33, 34. The only way you can live out this Psalm is by "being glad in the Lord". You should always be glad because of the wonderful things Jesus has done for you.

Unfortunately we often THINK OF OURSELVES instead of THINKING OF JESUS. If we are not happy, and if we don't bring cheer to others around us then we are thinking of ourselves instead of Jesus. When we are sad or "down" or when we cry, it is often because we are feeling sorry for ourselves. If we are feeling sad and thinking about ourselves we need to ask God to forgive us and help us to live out Psalm 104:33, 34.

Questions To Think About

1. How can we bring cheer to those around us?

May 19

"Open my eyes, that I may see wondrous things from Your law."
Psalm 119:18

I remember going on a trip with my parents when I was little and falling asleep in the car on the way back. When we finally got home my parents told me to wake up and go to bed. I could hardly open my eyes and I stumbled out of the car and felt my way to my room and into bed. That is what it is like in life if we don't know God's law. If we don't know God's law it's like trying to feel our way through life with our eyes shut. We stumble and fall over and over again. This is why the Psalmist asked God to open his eyes, and why we should ask God to open our eyes too.

Sometimes when we read the Bible it doesn't seem to make sense, because our eyes are not open. The Holy Spirit has to come and open our eyes and then we will understand what we are reading. Only then will we know and understand how God wants us to live.

Questions To Think About

1. Ask God to open your eyes to His law.
2. THANK HIM for the wondrous things He shows you.

May 20

"The wicked have laid a snare for me. Yet I have not strayed from Your precepts." Psalm 119:110

Sometimes we think that because we are Christians that nothing bad will ever happen to us, but the Bible tells us that this is not true. Remember that Jesus was crucified because of sinful people. What's more, while He was teaching the Pharisees were constantly trying to trick Him and laying "snares" for Him. In spite of all this, Jesus never failed. He never strayed from God's plan.

Unfortunately we aren't perfect like Jesus and sometimes we fail. There will always be evil people around us who would like nothing more than to see us fail, so they can mock us and mock God. These wicked people will even "lay snares" for us when we least expect it. For instance, someone might ask us to do something bad just once since, "No one will ever find out." Or because, "It wont hurt anyone." But even if no one does find out, which is rarely the case, God still sees us. When we are being tempted we need to remember that God ALWAYS knows about it and He WILL ALWAYS GIVE US A WAY OUT.

But before we get to the point that we need an escape hatch in order not to sin, we should obey God's command and flee the temptation. This means that we are not to put ourselves into situations where we know we will be tempted. But even when we don't run at the first sign of temptation, God will hear us and help us if we ask Him to. He will save us from the wicked who try to trap us. And He will save us from our own evil desires if we ASK.

Questions To Think About

1. Why do wicked people want to see Christians fail?
2. How can we escape temptation and sin?

May 21

"I was glad when they said to me, 'Let us go into the house of the Lord'." Psalm 122:1

Do you enjoy going to church on Sunday? Can you hardly wait to get out of bed and get ready on Sunday morning so you can learn more about Jesus? Are you excited about worshiping God? Can you say with the Psalmist, *I WAS GLAD WHEN THEY SAID TO ME; LET US GO INTO THE HOUSE OF THE LORD."*

I have always enjoyed going to church. I like to think that it wasn't just because we got to dress up and drive in the car, but that I really felt something special at church. Maybe we don't always feel like going to church and we need to be reminded of why it is important. First of all, if we love God then we should want to be around Him and learn more about Him whenever we can. We can do this at church. Secondly, we get to see all of our Christian friends. It is very important to fellowship with other Christians. They can make us happy and help us when we are sad. We can ask our Christian brothers and sisters to pray for us when we are struggling and we can pray for them when they need help. But we can't do any of these things if we don't see them on a regular basis. So next Sunday, rejoice and be glad that we can *GO INTO THE HOUSE OF THE LORD.*

Questions To Think About

1. Are you glad when you get to go to church? Why?
2. Ask God to help you be excited about going to church.

May 22

You have hedged me behind and before, and laid Your hand upon me. Psalm 139:5

Have you ever lived in a place that had a hedge around the yard? Hedges are wonderful things. They can mark the boundary of our property. They are attractive—some even have flowers on them. They also keep things out that we really don't want in our yard. Today's Scripture reminds us that this is what the Lord does for each of His children. He puts a hedge around us so that we are sure just where our boundaries are so we won't stray where we are not supposed to go. God also surrounds us with his beauty and it is there for us to enjoy. His hedge is also there for our protection so that evil can't get to us. This doesn't mean that we will never have to face evil, it means that when we do, we know that God's protection surrounds us.

This Scripture should comfort us when we face troubles. It has been a big comfort to me today because my grandson is in the military and his unit is being deployed to Iraq today. But no matter what my grandson has to face in Iraq, I know that God's hedge is all around him and God's hand is on him. What a loving a gracious God we serve. PRAISE HIM.

Questions To Think About

1. Can anything touch God's children?

May 23

Do not be like the horse or like the mule, which have no understanding. Which must be harnessed with bit and bridle, else they will not come near you. Psalm 32:9

We used to own horses and a miniature mule. Owning a mule is lots of fun but also lots of work. John was our mule's name and he was stubborn just like everyone says mules are. He wanted to do what he wanted and go where he wanted and if he didn't get to he would throw a fit. A "mule fit" consisted of John stomping the ground, kicking up his heels and "hee hawing" loud enough for the neighbors several miles away to hear him. When my kids would ride our horses they would usually take John along—he followed behind them like a dog. But if they didn't let him go he would throw his "fit" and then lie down and crawl under the fence. I always thought he had a look on his face that said, "Ha, ha! I got to go after all."

Our horses were well trained and would follow their rider's commands. They knew what it meant when the rider gave them a little kick on the sides or pulled back on the reins or laid the reins across their necks to the left or right. And when we wanted to make John mind we had to bridle him as well. Even then he wasn't the best-behaved mule in the world.

Today's Scripture is saying that the Lord should not have to treat us like a horse or a mule in order to get us to do what is right. The horses and mules have an excuse because they don't have understanding, but we do. So we should WILLINGLY and FREELY WANT to do what is right because we love the Lord and because through His Word we know the right things to do. So let's pray that we aren't stubborn like a mule but that we will delight to do all that God wants us to.

QUESTIONS TO THINK ABOUT

1. What is a bridle? A bit? How are they used in this verse?
2. As God's children should we need a bridle? Why or why not?

May 24

Set a guard, O Lord, over my mouth; keep watch over the door of my lips. Psalm 141:3

"I just can't stand him. He makes me sick. She sure doesn't look very good in that outfit. I hate you and I never want to see you again." We've all heard or said things like this before. And this is what the Psalmist is talking about. It would be great to have a guard standing right beside us to know what we were thinking, because we have to think it before we can say it. Then the guard could stop us before anything bad came out of our mouths. Guess what? As Christians we can have a guard over our mouths. We can ask Jesus to put a guard on our mouths and to keep us from saying anything that would hurt others or displease our Lord.

Besides praying, we should also be careful what we feed our minds through our eyes and ears. That means that we should not watch or read things that would make us think bad or hateful thoughts or listen to talk that is bad or hateful. Remember again that we have to think it before we can say it, so if we think good, pure thoughts good things will come out of our mouths. If we think hateful, bad thoughts that is what will come out of our mouths. "O be careful little eyes what you see . . . O be careful little ears what you hear . . . O be careful little mouth what you say . . ." Next time before we speak let's remember this song.

Questions To Think About

1. What does it mean to set a guard over our mouths?
2. What else do we need to guard besides our mouths?

May 25

Wait on the Lord; Be of good courage, And He shall strengthen your hear; Wait, I say, on the Lord! Psalm 27:14

I hate to wait and I know I'm not alone in this. We can all be pretty impatient at times. For example we are often impatient when we are in a hurry to do something and someone else makes us late, like the time we had to wait on our friends at the movie and missed the opening scene. Or we are impatient when we know something is going to happen but the day seems to take forever to get here, like the day we are going to get to go on our first campout. Any number of things can cause us to be impatient.

Sometimes the hardest thing to wait on is the Lord's timing. Let's say we've prayed about something that is really important to us. We wait a week and nothing happens. So we think, "Well, either the Lord didn't hear me, or the Lord isn't going to answer my prayer, or maybe I shouldn't have prayed about that in the first place." First of all, the Lord always hears His children. Secondly, He always answers His children. And, we can talk to the Lord about anything. The Lord wants us to learn patience so sometimes He wants us to WAIT. He is working all things out for our good, but it may not happen over night. But we can always be assured that EVERYTHING WORKS FOR OUR GOOD IN GOD'S TIME. So let's ask God to give us courage and strength to WAIT for His time. The results will be God's very best for us at the very best time.

QUESTIONS TO THINK ABOUT

1. *Why does God want us to be patient?*
2. *What can we learn from having to wait?*

May 26

Because He is your Lord, worship Him. Psalm 45:11

Let's look at each key word of today's Scripture and study what it means. The first key word is *because*. This *because* means that since it is true that Jesus is our Lord then something should happen or there is something that we should do. Next, let's look at the word *Lord*. What does it mean in this verse? *Lord* here means master, leader, one who rules over us and one to whom we give our allegiance. Then we come to the key word *worship*. *Worship* means to honor and glorify God by gratefully offering back to Him all the good gifts He has given us. When we worship Him we have JOY because we can PRAY to Him, SING PRAISES to Him, and READ HIS WORD. Last, but certainly not least we come to the key word *Him*. This tells us who should be the object of our worship and that is Our Lord.

We worship Him because He is our Lord and we love Him and are grateful for all the blessings He pours out on us. We can worship Him at church or when we are alone. Our worship can be long or short. Mostly we need to remember to worship Him often.

Questions To Think About

1. Why should we worship God? How should we worship God?

May 27

Then Adonijah the son of Hagith exalted himself, saying, "I will be King." I Kings 1:5

Adonijah was a son of David. Hagith was his mother. When he made the statement in today's verse David was very old and about to die. He didn't know that Adonijah had set himself up as the new king. Solomon was also a son of David and David had promised Solomon's mother that Solomon would be the next king. Adonijah didn't go through David to be declared king. The Bible says that he EXALTED himself. All of this was to no avail in the end because Adonijah's plan failed and Solomon did become king of Israel. The dictionary says that to exalt means to raise high, to raise in rank, power or character; to elevate by praise or in estimation.

We sometimes have the same problem as Adonijah. We have a tendency to want to EXALT ourselves by bragging about how great we are. We like to brag about how we won a race or a spelling bee or some other contest. We like to tell others about our talents and the honors we have received. The Bible says that we should HUMBLE ourselves. That is the exact opposite of EXALTING ourselves. We always need to remember that Jesus, Creator of the universe humbled Himself to come to earth as a man and die the death of a criminal for our sins. If Jesus would humble himself in this way, we certainly should be humble. Let others exalt us if we deserve praise. If we really deserve it people will find out and then they will honor and exalt us.

QUESTIONS TO THINK ABOUT

1. What does it mean to exalt yourself?
2. What does it mean to humble yourself?

May 28

Now the son of David was strengthened in his kingdom and the Lord his God was with him and exalted him exceedingly.
II Chronicles 1:1

Solomon was just a young man when he was made king. He was probably only about 20 years old, but he knew he was not wise enough or experienced enough to lead a great nation. When God asked him what he wanted, he asked for wisdom to lead the nation as God would want him to. This pleased God so much that he gave Solomon wisdom and everything else that anyone could want. God gave him riches and He exalted Solomon above any mortal who has ever lived. Solomon had it all because he was unselfish in his request.

We have a great lesson to learn from this. Remember the verse that says IF we seek God and His kingdom FIRST He will add all the other things. Solomon is an example of what that verse means. If we seek out God's principles and live our lives by God's principles, then God will supply all of our needs and more.

Questions To Think About

1. What should we be most concerned about in our lives—money or wisdom?
2. How do we get wisdom?

May 29

And the temple which I build will be great, for our God is greater than all gods. But who is able to build Him a temple, since heaven and the heaven of heavens cannot contain Him? Who am I then, that I should build Him a temple . . . II Chronicles 2:5, 6

We sometimes sing the beautiful song "How Great Thou Art". Even as we sing we may not really think about how great our God really is, but Solomon did. He realized that God is greater than anything we can ever even imagine. Sometimes, because God is so great and we are so small, we feel that we are not very important in God's sight. We might think He won't hear us if we pray. Maybe He only has time to deal with the GREAT people of the world. After all, kids aren't usually noticed. But none of these ideas are true. We are all precious in God's sight and He is so great, He can take care of all things and all people all at the same time and could still do more.

Besides just realizing God's greatness, Solomon knew that God's temple had to be special so he sent far and wide to find the best materials and workmen to build the temple. Now, we are the temple of God because the Holy Spirit lives in us when we become Christians. Just as Solomon wanted everything that went into the temple to be the best, we should make sure that everything we use to build ourselves up is the best. I'm not speaking of physical things, although we need to do what it takes to stay healthy, I'm talking about spiritually building ourselves up so that we can be the best temples possible for the Holy Spirit. Of course it is God's grace and the Holy Spirit who teach us and open our eyes to the truth. However, if we don't read our Bibles and pray and listen to our pastor, parents, and teachers, we are not providing quality materials for building our spiritual temples. So don't forget that we have work to do too. Just like Solomon, we may not feel worthy, but God has chosen US for his dwelling place be diligent in building it.

Questions To Think About

1. Why is it important to try and realize the greatness of God?
2. What part do we have in building a dwelling place for the Holy Spirit?

Notes

May 30

So he was seven years in building it [the Temple]. But Solomon took thirtee years to build his own house; . . .
I Kings 6:38b; 7:1

Solomon took almost twice as long to build his own house as he did the temple where God was to dwell. This doesn't seem right, does it? Well, we can't be too hard on Solomon because he may actually have spent more time on the things of God than we do. Let's stop and think about how much time we give our "personal pursuits" and "things" compared to the amount of time we spend reading and studying our Bibles, going to church and Sunday school, or praying.

Let's just take television for example. How much time do we spend a day watching those television programs that we just can't miss. Everything else stops while we watch an hour or two or maybe more of entertainment on the tube. We have to ask ourselves are we that dedicated to studying the Bible and praying? How many times have we said, "I can't talk on the phone right now, I'm in the middle of studying my Bible. I'll call you back in an hour or so."? If we are honest with ourselves we will probably have to say, "NEVER". But, we have no problem saying that about our favorite TV show.

We seem to put off the most important things of the day until the last minute and if we don't have enough time to do them, "Oh, well, I'll do it tomorrow." But as the old saying goes, "Tomorrow never comes." Remember the verse about SEEKING FIRST THE KINGDOM OF GOD. Let's ask Jesus to help us put Him first in our lives and not give Him the leftovers.

Questions To Think About

1. CHALLENGE: Write down how much time you spend this week watching television or riding bikes or talking on the phone to friends, anything that's an activity you do for entertainment. Then, write down how much time you spend studying your Bible, praying, attending church functions. BE HONEST. Now, compare notes. What did you learn about yourself?

May 31

Thus Solomon finished the house of the Lord and the King's house: and Solomon successfully accomplished all that came into his heart . . . II Chronicles 7:11

We've all dreamed about what we want to be or do when we grow up and it takes discipline to accomplish those dreams. When Solomon became king he was a young man and he knew that he couldn't rule the people alone. He knew he didn't have enough experience or knowledge to do a good job. However, God had put the desire in his heart to be a good king and Solomon was wise enough to ask God to help him. The key to Solomon's success and ours is in knowing that WE NEED HELP and knowing WHERE TO GET IT.

The Lord has made it very plain in His Word that He is always ready and willing to help us do what is right and good. His Word tells us what to do and our part is to OBEY it. We will make mistakes, but we shouldn't give up. God planned for our mistakes and that's why he sent Jesus to make a way for our forgiveness. So KEEP PRESSING FORWARD. God knows what is in our hearts and He wants us to accomplish and succeed in completing all the good works He has prepared for us.

Questions To Think About

1. What good works are in your heart? Have you done them?

June 1

. . . if My people who are called by My name will humble themselves, and pray and seek My face, and turn from their wicked ways, then I will hear from heaven, and will forgive their sin and heal their land. II Chronicles 7:14

We all want our land to be forgiven and healed, right? Are we to be part of the solution? Let's look at our Scripture and see what we have to do to accomplish this goal. First, the Scripture is addressed to the people called by His name. Who are they? The people called by His name—by the name of Christ—are CHRISTIANS. So the verse is addressed to Christians.

We now know WHOM the Scripture is talking to so let's see WHAT we must do. The verse says, we are to humble ourselves and pray and seek God's face and turn from our wicked ways. Let's take each thing separately. Our first step is to HUMBLE ourselves. HUMBLING ourselves means that we acknowledge our sin and the sin of our country—the sin of trying to kick God out of everything—things like not allowing prayer in schools or the Ten Commandments in public buildings, abortion, evolution, and the list could go on.

The next step is to PRAY. After we realize the sins that our nation is committing against God, we need to pray that the people of our nation will realize what they have done—that's HUMBLING—and we need to PRAY that we will all REPENT and stop doing the wrong things we have been doing—that's TURNING FROM OUR WICKED WAYS. In other words PRAY we will all acknowledge our national sins and be broken hearted that we have displeased and rebelled against God. And PRAY that we will repent and do whatever it takes to turn away from those sins—this might mean working to get new laws passed.

The very act of praying is SEEKING GOD'S FACE, but we must also study His Word—through study we know what God has told us is right and wrong. Then we know which direction to go based on what

God's Word tells us. Then we need to follow that direction and will for our nation's future.

There are four wonderful aspects to this verse. The first is that God doesn't require ALL the people in our nation to do these things—only HIS PEOPLE. The second is that if HIS PEOPLE do these things He promises to HEAR FROM HEAVEN. But more than that He promises to FORGIVE OUR NATION'S SINS and lastly, to HEAL OUR LAND. WOW! If we FOLLOW God's instructions JUST LOOK AT WHAT GOD PROMISES WILL HAPPEN. Let's get going!

Questions To Think About

1. What can you do to help our nation be forgiven for its sins and be healed?
2. Will you dedicate yourself to this task, doing what you are able to do?

Notes

June 2

And men shall be blessed in Him; All nations shall call Him blessed. Psalm 72:17

Our Scripture today lets us know that we have a job to do. What? Yes, take a second look at it—can you see what the job is? IF ALL NATIONS are going to call Him blessed and there are some people groups who still haven't heard about Jesus, what has to happen? SOMEONE has to GO and TELL these people about our Savior and Lord.

When we lived in the Marshall Islands for a time, I was really surprised to find that the natives were Christians and I realized this didn't just happen. Someone had to GO and TELL the Marshallese people about Jesus. Someone had to say, "I'LL GO. SEND ME." Because someone did GO AND TELL these native people about Jesus 100 years earlier, I had some wonderful Christian friends.

We don't have to wait until we're grown and go to a foreign country to tell others about Jesus. We can start today in our own backyard. Let's share Jesus with the people we meet this week. And who knows some day we may say, "I'LL GO TO . . . SEND ME."

Questions To Think About

1. Have you thought of becoming a missionary? Think about it.

June 3

A wise man will hear and increase learning, and a man of understanding will attain wise council. Proverbs 1:5

Have you ever noticed how much of your life is spent HEARING? Just think about that for a minute. Usually when you wake up in the morning it's to the sound of your parents' voice saying, "Time to get up." You roll out of bed and find your way to the breakfast table and HEAR from everyone there. Sometimes it's about what they're going to do that day and sometimes you hear about good times they had the day before. Often it's instructions for the day. On the way to school you talk and HEAR what your Dad and Mom have planned for after school. Once you're in school, you spend most of your time HEARING facts and figures you need to learn. Even after school when you are with your friends, you are HEARING what they have to say and they are HEARING you. Are you're beginning to see that you HEAR a lot of STUFF in a day, 365 days every year?

The Scripture today is addressing this issue. It says that a person who is wise, and by that it means a Christian, increases his learning by HEARING what the Bible has to say on every subject. This is where your parents, Sunday school teachers, pastor, and other Christians come in. They love you and will give you good, true information taken from the Bible to help you understand everything that goes on around you. And when you have a question you need to go to them for advice so they can share their knowledge of the Bible with you. This is what this Proverb means. So you see, you can be wise and have great understanding if you HEAR the Word of the Lord and LISTEN.

QUESTIONS TO THINK ABOUT

1. What does it mean to hear and increase learning?
2. What does it mean to attain wise counsel?

June 4

"How I have hated instruction, and my heart despised correction! I have not obeyed the voice of my teachers, nor inclined my ear to those who instructed me!" Proverbs 5:12, 13

The young person spoken of in this verse was in total rebellion. He HATED instruction, DESPISED correction, and WOULD NOT OBEY or LISTEN. This is as rebellious as it gets. It's easy for us to fall into this kind of attitude too. Like the person in our verse we can HATE and DESPISE any kind of discipline that comes from anyone in authority—Dad, Mom, teachers. Getting to the point of rebellion doesn't happen over night. It's a habit that begins small and as we walk in the way of rebellion our rebellious spirit gets stronger and stronger.

Rebellion starts with a BAD ATTITUDE and an UNREPENTANT HEART when someone tries to correct us. The more and the longer we refuse to listen to correction and REPENT, the worse our BAD ATTITUDE becomes until we reach the point of the young person described in our verse. Our BAD ATTITUDE is also strengthened when we refuse to acknowledge our wrongdoing and blame someone else for our sin. If we never take responsibility for our actions we begin to feel persecuted and engage in a giant "pity party" instead of REPENTING.

The next time we're corrected let's be mature and take responsibility for our actions, confess our sin, repent, and be forgiven. Let's remember to ask God to help us in all of this. HE WILL because He wants us to succeed in our OBEDIENCE. So let's not end up like the person in our verse. Let's check our attitude frequently. If we are resisting correction, we know it's not from GOD.

Questions To Think About

1. What does resisting correction lead to?
2. Why do we have no right to indulge in self pity?

June 5

The fear of the Lord is to hate evil; pride and arrogance and the evil way and perverse mouth I hate. Proverbs 8:13

When Solomon talks about "the fear of the Lord", he is talking to Christians. How can that be? This kind of fear—deep awe and respect born out of love—is a good thing. People who don't know the Lord don't fear His power. They aren't thinking about Him as their Lord and Master. They don't love Him. They THINK they can live the way they want and not have to answer to anyone but themselves—maybe the police or government here on earth but only if they get caught. As Christians, we know that God is in control and we know that He will reward those who are obedient and punish those who aren't. The "fear of the Lord" is like our relationship with our parents. We "fear" their displeasure or disappointment in us when we are caught in our sins. We "fear" it because we love them and want to please them.

Besides "fearing" or being in awe of our mighty Lord, Solomon is saying that we, as Christians, will hate evil, pride, and arrogance. Why? We will despise these things because our Heavenly Father hates these attitudes. So what attitudes will a child of God exhibit? He will exhibit the opposite of those attitudes that God hates. Instead of EVIL he will love GOOD. Instead of PRIDE he will exhibit HUMILITY. Instead of ARROGANCE he will walk in MEEKNESS. Instead of a PERVERSE mouth, out of his mouth will come PRAISE. Why?—Because he HATES EVIL and LOVES GOOD. We strive to live these attributes because we hate what God hates because we "fear" Him and LOVE Him.

QUESTIONS TO THINK ABOUT

1. What does it mean to "fear the Lord"?
2. How can we live in goodness, humility, meekness, and love?

June 6

. . . *He who restrains his lips is wise.* Proverbs 10:19b

Have you ever met someone who talked too much? If you haven't yet, you probably will. Do you ever feel like you talk too much? Maybe you don't say anything bad about anyone but you seem to take over every conversation? This may be part of what Solomon is saying here, and he may also be talking about gossip.

First of all, he may be talking about gossip—someone saying bad things about others. Gossip is a terrible thing and rates high on the list of sins God despises. It seems that people today just don't take this seriously. So what should you do if someone starts talking about someone else—even if it's true? WALK AWAY. Soon they will get the idea that you don't like to listen to gossip and you'll be surprised how they won't gossip—at least when you're around.

The other thing Solomon might have been talking about is someone who talks too much, someone who talks so much no one else has a chance to say anything. This is also something you should avoid for a number of reasons. First, you never learn anything new if you are the one who is always talking. Second, it is impolite. Third, others get the idea that you think you know everything—commonly called a KNOW—IT—ALL. People don't like to be around know-it-alls. This doesn't mean that you should never talk. It just means that you should be sure that everyone present is included in the conversation. If others don't speak on their own, ask them a question. By the way, there is nothing wrong with a few moments of silence in a conversation either. Remember that each person has something to contribute, so GIVE HIM A CHANCE.

Questions To Think About

1. Do you gossip? If so, what are you going to do about it?
2. Do you talk too much? If so, what are you going to do about it?

June 7

He who guards his mouth preserves his life, but he who opens wide his lips shall have destruction. Proverbs 13:3

When I read this Scripture again, I thought about my "toothbrush story". Once when I went to the dentist to have my teeth cleaned, the dental assistant taught me something that I will never forget. She told me that I had some plaque on the teeth at the very back of my mouth. She said a good way to get it off was to SHUT MY MOUTH a little and it would be easier to get the toothbrush back there. What she didn't know was that her words hit me like a ton of bricks. I really felt that the Lord had sent me a message via the dental assistant. It was like Jesus saying, "If you would keep your mouth shut a little more you could stop lots of the bad stuff that comes out of your mouth." WOW! I started thinking. Jesus means the hateful, hurtful things I say sometimes to other people, things I say and then wish I hadn't. When I prayed about all of this I knew that I had a lot more than my teeth cleaned that day.

As Christians we need to be careful to STOP and THINK about what we say. It's a good test to ask ourselves, "Would Jesus say what we are about to say to someone?" We especially need to do this when we are angry; we need to STOP and PRAY before we speak. We could stop so much HURT if we would just KEEP OUR MOUTHS SHUT A LOT MORE.

QUESTIONS TO THINK ABOUT

1. Have you hurt someone with your words?
2. Do you need to apologize? Will you?

June 8

There is a way that seems right to a man, but its end is the way of death. Proverbs 16:25

Recently I was in a toy store and I came across a puzzle maze—one of those games with a tiny marble in it. The object is to get the marble or ball to the center of the maze without falling off the path or ending up stuck in a dead-end. It's fun to maneuver the ball faster and faster toward the goal, racing against the clock. However, it can be frustrating as well, especially when the ball hits a dead end. Turning the ball around and getting back on the right track is not easy and slows things down or causes lots of extra work and stress.

Our lives can be much like the puzzle maze. As Christians, God has given us a path to follow to help us reach the goals He has planned for us, just like the marble in the maze. However, because we are sinful and live in a fallen world, there are lots of "dead-ends" we stray into along the way. Sometimes these "dead-ends" are things we didn't count on like the death of someone we love. Sometimes the "dead-ends" are brought about because of sin on our part or the sin of someone else. The point is that if we don't turn around and go a different direction, we will not be where God wants us to be.

Getting our lives back on track can definitely slow things down and cause us lots of extra work and stress. We'll need God's help to get us through these times in our lives. If sin caused the detour, we need to repent and ask God to help us not to repeat the same mistakes again. As today's Proverb says, the detour leads nowhere except death.

Questions To Think About

1. If your life is off the path right now, repent of any sin that might have caused it or kept you stuck in the dead-end.
2. What do you need to do to get your life back on the path? Ask your parents for Biblical advice to get back on track.

June 9

Even a child is known by his deeds, whether what he does is pure and right. Proverbs 20:11

Someone is watching you. Do you agree with that statement? You think that you're just a kid and no one notices you or notices what you do. For that matter, you may think that no one cares as long as you don't get into trouble. But that isn't what the Bible says. In this Proverb it says that people know whether you are a good kid or a delinquent because of how you act and live.

There are at least four groups of people who are WATCHING you and KNOW you for how you live. The first group is your younger sister, brother, or friend. Surely you've noticed them trying to be just like you—wearing things like you, playing games you like, and even acting like you. It is a big responsibility to have someone wanting to be JUST LIKE YOU.

Then there are adults who notice you. Adults like your teachers or Sunday school teachers notice you because you are always respectful to your elders. They think you are great because you behave well in class and everything you hand in is well done and on time.

Next, your peers are watching you. They notice if you are nice to everyone, help people out when they need it, and especially when you go out of your way to serve others.

The last people watching you are your parents. They know you better than anyone on earth. Even though they see you at your worst, they always remember you at your best and appreciate all the wonderful things you do for them and others. They see that you are just a "good kid". So you can see that it is important to be PURE and RIGHT because not just someone is watching you, lots of people are watching. Most importantly NEVER FORGET that Jesus is ALWAYS watching you.

Questions To Think About

1. Who is watching you?
2. Are you being pure and right in the way you live? If not what do you need to do to remedy the situation. If yes, what are you doing to maintain this situation?

Notes

June 10

He who has a generous eye will be blessed, for he gives of his bread to the poor. Proverbs 22:9

If you put two three year olds in a room with one toy you know what will happen? One of them will say "mine" and the fight is on. Part of your parents' job is to teach you to share. You and the rest of the world were born with a nature that says "mine". Yet, the Bible says if you GIVE you will be blessed. So why do you think that greed is such a big part of the world today? You have heard reports of kids killing other kids for their designer shoes. So how do you make a difference?

Since you are a Christian, the answer for you is easy even if doing it isn't. The Bible says over and over that if you GIVE you will be BLESSED but for some reason it's very hard to do. Remember, you don't have to give a great deal of money; your attitude about giving is what is important. God sees your cheerful heart. You can give other things as well—your time to a nursing home, your friendship to a lonely classmate, your helping hand to rake leaves for an elderly neighbor. So start being a giver today.

Questions To Think About

1. Why is there so much greed in the world today?
2. What are you going to do to be a giver?

June 11

Do not exalt yourself in the presence of the king, and do not stand in the place of the great; for it is better that he say to you, "Come up here," than that you should be put lower . . .
Proverbs 25:6, 7

We used to live in the Marshall Islands (in the Pacific Ocean between Hawaii and Japan). I never will forget one of the flights back to the islands after our vacation in the U.S. was over. The airline had overbooked the airplane and they ran out of seats in the coach section. Our tickets were guaranteed so they booked us in the first class section of the plane. This is where the important people usually sit and all four of our kids had a ticket so each one of them had a seat. Back then, out of kindness, the airline would let people with kids board the plane first.

So there sat all four kids buckled into their "first class" seats when a man, who thought he was very important, walked by and said disgustedly, "What are these kids doing in all these seats?"

What he didn't know was that the Captain of the airplane was walking in behind him. The Captain replied firmly, "Because they all bought tickets."

The man just muttered, "Oh," and sheepishly sat down.

This is an example of what today's Scripture is talking about. The man on the plane was "put down" by the Captain for thinking he was better than "those kids". We can fall into the same trap. Sometimes we start thinking more highly of ourselves than we should. This usually happens when we've been given some special honor or won a contest or made good grades or been voted "most popular". When this happens we need to stop and remember who we are and not exalt ourselves. We are children of the King but we are called, like Jesus, to be servants and to put others first. God will bless us for our humble hearts.

QUESTIONS TO THINK ABOUT

1. *What does it mean to exalt oneself?*
2. *What does it mean to be put lower?*

June 12

The rod and rebuke give wisdom, but a child left to himself brings shame to his mother. Proverbs 29:15

It's not a popular thing among today's "experts" to discipline children. Some kids might think, "That sounds good to me." But the Bible teaches something different and God who is the source of all wisdom knows what He is talking about.

I can remember being punished when I was a kid. I dreaded it. I didn't like it one bit. I would make all kinds of promises to never do whatever again if they just wouldn't punish me this one time. My pleas and promises never worked. Then my Dad or Mom would say, "This hurts me more than it does you." Of course, I didn't believe either of them one bit. However, now that I'm a parent I know exactly what they meant—but that's another lesson.

As I was growing up and being punished along the way, I knew a boy in town whose parents never corrected him at all. As he got older the "sins" or "crimes" he committed grew steadily worse. He got into trouble in school. Eventually he was expelled from school. Then he got into trouble with the police for stealing. Before long, he was standing in front of a judge. Because his parents had refused to punish him, the judge was going to have to. If the young man's parents had read the Bible and obeyed what it teaches, they would have saved themselves a lot of heartache and their son from prison.

So, remember, when we sin and our parents punish us it's because they LOVE us and want all that is good for us. The best way to escape punishment is not to sin, but when we do mess up we should be thankful that our parents love us enough to discipline us. They are carrying out God's command and we will be blessed because of their obedience.

QUESTIONS TO THINK ABOUT

1. What brings shame to a mother?
2. Are you bringing glory or shame to your mother?

June 13

Every word of God is pure; He is a shield to those who put their trust in Him. Proverbs 30:5

This Scripture tells us three important things. First, God and His Word are PURE. I know we've been bombarded with advertisements telling us that this and that thing is "pure"—pure orange juice, pure water, pure soap. We think of anything labeled "pure" as having nothing added to make it better—until the "new improved" version comes out. In reality the only "pure thing" is God. He needs nothing outside of Himself and He never changes. He is PURE so we can always BELIEVE Him and His Word. Second, we see that He is our SHIELD. What does the word shield bring to mind? I think of a windshield on a car or motorcycle that protects us from anything that might come flying at us as we race along the road. I also think of a shield that soldiers used in times past when they were in battle. It protected them from the blows the enemy threw, shot, or launched at them. The SHIELD whether a windshield or a soldier's shield is used for PROTECTION. So this Proverb is teaching us that we can always rely on God's pure Word and He says he will be a shield of protection to us. Third, the shield of God is in place for those who TRUST in Him. To trust means to believe in, put faith in, to acknowledge. If we trust our friends to meet us at a certain time on a certain day, we believe that they will come.

We have many things in our world that could harm us. We have many things in our world that could discourage us and make us want to quit. But, we have One who is always by our side and will never leave us. So, we must TRUST in Jesus to shield and protect us. HE WILL DO WHAT HE SAYS. Now we can go out into the world and live for Him because he is our shield.

Questions To Think About

1. Who is our shield? In what way?
2. What must we do to have God as our shield?

June 14

. . . *And his banner over me was love.* Song of Solomon 2:4

As I have said before, banners are mentioned throughout the Bible. They have always played an important role in societies. They were carried before warriors into battle as a representation of the nation or people they were fighting for. They were displayed in banquet halls as symbols of what a kingdom stood for. They were created for families as reminders of a proud heritage.

Flags are one kind of banner that we have today. Flags represent everything from a nation to a military unit to a school mascot. The most important banner is the one that represents the love God has for His children. We know God loves us because He sent His Son to die on the cross to save us from our sins. When we ask Jesus into our hearts we become Christ's followers or Christians. As Christians we carry a banner for all to see in our appearance, our words, and our actions. Our banner—the banner of Christ—represents who we are fighting for, what our kingdom stands for, and reminds us of our heritage.

We are soldiers of the cross and we must boldly fight the good fight against evil and spread the Gospel throughout the world. Our kingdom is not of this world but is in Heaven. Our kingdom stands for the truth and we must work to lay up treasure in our kingdom. In other words we must lay up heavenly treasure such as obedience to God's Word and spreading God's truth. We must never forget our heritage and share with others all that God has done for us. We must give God credit for everything that we have and that we are because all good and perfect gifts are from Him. So remember that God's banner over us is love and we are to wrap His banner around us and proudly "wear our colors"—proudly name the name of Christ and declare to the world through our appearance, actions and words that we belong to Jesus.

Questions To Think About

1. What is God's banner of love?
2. How can we proclaim God's love?

Notes

June 15

For God gives wisdom and knowledge and joy to a man who is good in His sight; . . . Ecclesiastes 2:26a

Isn't it great to get a present? It's always wonderful to receive gifts on our birthdays and for Christmas, but we kind of expect to get presents then and we sort of have an idea of what we will get. What's really exciting is when we get a present we aren't expecting. But the greatest gifts are those that come from God. Just look at what He gives us, wisdom, knowledge, and joy.

Wisdom is a very precious gift. As we grow we will need the wisdom that only comes from God to understand the Bible and be able to discern between truth and error. Knowledge is important too because only God's knowledge contained in His Word is truth. We will need His knowledge to combat the lies of the world and his wisdom to know how to apply His knowledge to our lives and the world around us. And the third gift discussed in this verse is joy. This is what everyone is searching for and so few know how to obtain it. This joy is greater than anything we can imagine and will sustain us through all sorts of ups and downs in our lives. Isn't it great that we can look forward to a lifetime of gifts from our Lord—gifts that are so unspeakably precious? Our part is obedience to the Lord.

QUESTIONS TO THINK ABOUT

1. *Who gives the greatest gifts?*
2. *Is there any good thing in our lives that doesn't come from God?*

June 16

To everything there is a season, a time for every purpose under heaven: . . . A time to plant, and a time to pluck what is planted; . . . Ecclesiastes 3:1, 2b

Raising a garden can be lots of fun. When I was a kid, my Dad and I planted a garden. I would go out every day to see if the plants had any ripe fruit that I could pick. When the plants finally began to produce we had more vegetables that we knew what to do with so I decided to take some of them to the grocery stores in town and see if they would buy them. I was kind of scared at first, but when the first man said he would buy my cabbage it was easy to go to the next place. That summer I sold all the extra vegetables I could raise. The long wait for the vegetables to ripen was well worth it.

I had to wait for my garden to grow, mature, and produce fruit. We all have to do the same thing as Christians. The seed—the Gospel—has to be planted in our hearts. This happens when we have Jesus in our hearts as our Savior and Lord. Our little sprout has to be fertilized to help it grow; this happens when we study and memorize Scripture. The plant must also be watered; this happens when we pray and worship and fellowship with other Christians. Before long, we are producing fruit. The fruit we will produce is love, joy, peace, longsuffering, kindness, goodness, faithfulness, gentleness, self-control. As the fruit ripens we apply it to the world around us. Love makes us less selfish and we are able to give to others. Joy helps us cheer our classmates when they are hurting. Peace gives us assurance so we can strengthen our friends who are afraid. Longsuffering produces patience with our brothers and sisters. Kindness starts us thinking of ways to help our Moms more. Goodness enables us to love our neighbors. Faithfulness causes others to trust in our word. Gentleness earns us a place in the hearts of others. Self-control generates a calm and persevering spirit in us to help us accomplish the tasks that God sets before us. Each season or age of our lives God will give us tasks to do that will need tending like my garden. Planting, nurturing, and harvesting is our calling as the children of God—let's go plant and reap the fruit!

QUESTIONS TO THINK ABOUT

1. Are you producing fruit? If not figure out why?
2. If you are producing fruit, is your "crop" of fruit increasing?

June 17

Remember now your Creator in the days of your youth, before the difficult days come, . . . Ecclesiastes 12:1

If all we ever think about when we are young is ourselves that's all we'll think about when we are old. If we remember Jesus our Creator and Lord when we are kids we will have our whole lives to enjoy His blessings. What would it be like if we could have anything in the world we wanted? If we wanted a horse we would get it. If we wanted a boat it would be ours. If we wanted to be a movie star it would happen. The list could go on and on. Believe it or not there are people in the world who can have anything they want. But guess what? THEY AREN'T HAPPY. We might think, "Well I sure would be." We need to stop for a minute and think about what really makes us happy. It isn't "things"—it's friends, family and knowing Jesus.

The Bible tells us this so we won't be fooled by what we think we need. Lots of kids out there still think of themselves first and others second and Jesus not at all. They are missing out on all of God's blessings and they don't even know it. Let's start praying for these kids, BEFORE THEIR DIFFICULT DAYS COME.

Questions To Think About

1. How can you remember your Creator in your youth?

June 18

Then King Rehoboam consulted the elders who stood before his father Solomon while he still lived, saying, "How do you advise me to answer these people?" And they spoke to him, saying, "If you are kind to these people, and please them, and speak good words to them, they will be your servants forever." But he rejected the advice which the elders had given him, and consulted the young men who had grown up with him, and stood before him. II Chronicles 10:6-8

This is such a sad story and it could have been a very happy one instead if Rehoboam had listened to the right people. He rejected the good advice of the elders and took the bad advice of his friends and peers. His foolishness divided the kingdom of Israel.

We have to be very careful which counselors we listen to. Sometimes we are tempted to listen to our friends because they are saying what we want to hear. We don't want to listen to the wise counsel of our parents because we don't like having all those rules and regulations put on us. But no matter how old we get, we will always find ourselves in situations where we need advice. We need to learn early on which people to go to for guidance.

The first place to go for advice is always God's Word. The answers to all our questions are there, if not directly, in principle. Sometimes we can't find what we need in God's Word or we don't understand what we read, so we go to our parents for help. God has put our parents in authority over us and we should always listen to what they say. When we follow the advice of God's Word we always come out on top.

QUESTIONS TO THINK ABOUT

1. Where should you go for advice?
2. Who put your Mom and Dad in charge? Should we question them?

June 19

He said to him, "I too am a prophet as you are, and an angel spoke to me by the word of the Lord saying, "Bring him back with you to your house, that he may eat bread and drink water." [He was lying to him.]
I Kings 13:18

Here is another sad story. The prophet in this verse had been so strong at first and had done everything that the Lord had told him to do. But then he listened to a man instead of God and he died on the road and was not buried by his family. The lesson to be learned here is the same as yesterday's lesson. Be sure to listen to the right people.

Again, the first place you must go is the Word of God. The answers for life are contained in it. Secondly, you must always, always, always listen to your parents because they have your best interest at heart unlike some of your friends. For example, let's say your parents tell you at breakfast to come straight home from school and finish all of your homework because the whole family is invited over to the Smith's for a cookout. You are really excited because the Smith's have a kid about your age and you always have lots of fun when you get together. You rush home after school and start in on your homework. Jarod, the kid next door comes over and asks you to come outside and shoot some hoops. You tell him you can't but you let him come in the house while you work on your math. He keeps bugging you and telling you that since you are almost finished it won't hurt to come outside for just a little while. He says you can always come back in and finish before your Dad gets home. You would much rather shoot hoops than do math homework so you agree. Suddenly you look up and your Dad is pulling into the driveway. At this point you only have two options. You can either lie and tell your Dad you have your homework done or you can tell the truth and miss the cookout.

You see if you ONLY listen to the people who have your best interests at heart, you won't get into trouble because they will want what is best for you, not what satisfies their own selfish desires. Don't be like the prophet in our verse. Be wise and listen to the right people.

QUESTIONS TO THINK ABOUT

1. Why should we listen to our parents?

NOTES

June 20

"LORD, it is nothing for You to help, whether with many or with those who have no power; help us, O LORD our God, for we rest on You and in Your name we go against this multitude. O LORD You are our God do not let man prevail against You!
II Chronicles 14:11

At one time or another, we have probably all felt that some little problem we were worried about was such a small thing that it would be silly to bother God with it. Some men even say that God won't bother with every little problem that comes along; He's only available for the BIG THINGS.

This made me think. I've only had a few BIG things happen in my life and if I only went to God with them, I wouldn't have had much contact with Him at all. Then I remembered the Lord's Prayer where we ask DAILY for our bread. And I recalled more verses that stressed going to God daily or praying without ceasing and I knew that all the people who said God isn't interested in the LITTLE things were wrong. I understood that the Lord wants a close relationship with each and every one of us. I realized that even though my problems are *nothing* before God, I could *rest on* Him because He is my *God.* God is interested in everything about us. Go to God with everything. Our God is a BIG GOD—He can handle it.

Questions To Think About

1. What kind of a relationship does God want with us? Are you close to Him?

June 21

For thus says the LORD God of Israel: "The bin of flour shall not be used up, nor shall the jar of oil run dry, until the day the LORD sends rain on the earth." I Kings 17:14

What a fantastic story! A drought had plagued the land for some time and a poor widow had only enough oil and flour to make one more cake for her son and herself and then she thought she would die. But the Lord had a plan, like he always does for each of us. He sent Elijah to her house. When he arrived Elijah made a strange request of the poor starving widow. He told her to use up the oil and flour that she had left to make HIM a cake.

If we had been there would we have said, "I'm sorry but this is all I have left between me and starvation so go somewhere else to get a cake." Or maybe we would have been even more cruel and said, "Get out of here. Who do you think you are asking me to give up my last bit of food? And don't come back. I've got my own troubles."

If the widow had replied in this way she probably would have died after she had eaten her last cake. But she did what Elijah asked and a WONDERFUL MIRACLE happened. Every time she got oil and flour there was enough to make a cake for both her and her son.

God's plan and the means to accomplish that plan are perfect. However, sometimes we think we know better than God and decide to do things our way. That's when we get into trouble. So let's obey God and see his perfect plan for us unfold.

Questions To Think About

1. Are you being obedient to God's plan?
2. Are you obeying your parents? That is God's plan for you now.

June 22

And Elijah came to all the people, and said, "How long will you falter between two opinions? If the LORD is God, follow Him; but if Baal, follow him." I Kings 18:21

Elijah was a prophet of God and he was very disheartened by the people of Israel because they wouldn't follow the Lord the way they should. Some of them realized that God was the Creator of all and was the only true God, but they didn't want to give up their idols and their sin. So these people wavered back and forth between worshipping God and worshipping Baal—a false god.

There are still people like that today who think they can get to Heaven some way other than through Jesus. They may even go to church on Sunday or at least be on a church role, and they will tell you that Jesus is ONE way to get to heaven but not the ONLY way. When we run into people like this if we are truly committed Christians we make them feel uncomfortable. So they begin to say and do little things that cast doubt on what we believe. They want us to change and be like them so they won't have to admit that Jesus is the ONLY WAY. Most of what they say may be really close to the truth. But something close to the truth is not truth. We must be very careful not to get away from the teachings of Jesus.

In order to stay close we need to spend time learning His teachings. We need to stand firm in the fact that Jesus is God and that the only way to Heaven is through HIM. Jesus says in His Word, *I am the way, the truth, and the life. No one comes to the Father except through Me.* BELIEVE GOD AND LIVE!

Questions To Think About

1. How do we get to Heaven?
2. Is there more than one way to get there?

June 23

Let not the one who puts on his armor boast like the one who takes it off. I Kings 20:11

Ahab, King of Israel said this to Ben-Hadad, King of Syria, when they were about to go into battle. Ben Hadad boasted that there would not be anyone left when he got through with the Israelites. Even though King Ahab was an evil king what he said to Ben Hadad was true. The outcome of the battle was in God's hands and God would deliver the victory to whichever side He pleased. On this day it was God's plan to give victory to the Israelites and the Syrians fled from the field of battle after loosing many men.

This is an important thing to remember. Sometimes we come up against an enemy or task that seems overwhelming. But with God all things are possible. Let's ask God to help us see things through His eyes. Let's ask Him to give us courage to persevere to the end. Our job is to obey God and do the right thing. The outcome is up to God. As someone once said, "I don't know WHAT is in the future, but I know WHO holds it in His hand."

Questions To Think About

1. Who holds the future?
2. Should we try to predict the future?

June 24

So the king of Israel said to Jehoshaphat, "There is still one man by whom we may inquire of the LORD; but I hate him, because he never prophesies good concerning me, but always evil."
II Chronicles 18:7

Jehoshaphat, King of Judah, was trying to decide whether or not to go with King Ahab, King of Israel, to do battle against Ramoth Gilead. King Ahab had called his prophets and they said what Ahab wanted to hear, that if they went into battle they would be victorious. Jehoshaphat, on the other hand wanted a man of God to give him instructions so he sent for Micaiah, one of God's prophets. Ahab, being evil, didn't want to call Micaiah. He said that every time Micaiah prophesied the prophecy went against what Ahab wanted and, of course, it always came true.

When Micaiah arrived, he told the kings that if they went into battle the soldiers of Israel would be scattered as sheep without a shepherd and that Ahab would die. Ahab was so arrogant that he thought he could outsmart God, so instead of dressing as the king he wore the clothes of a common soldier. During the battle a certain man drew a bow at random, and struck the king of Israel between the joints of his armor. *Thus Ahab died at the battle Ramoth Gilead, just as Micaiah had prophesied.*

Sometimes we are just like Ahab. We know what is right but we refuse to listen to it and we do what we want anyway. We should pay attention to what happened to Ahab because rebellion against God leads to death. Let's pray that the Holy Spirit will teach us how to listen to the Word of God, understand the Word of God, and then obey the Word of God.

QUESTIONS TO THINK ABOUT

1. *Have you been willfully ignoring God's Word?*
2. *If you have ignored God's Word, what can you do to remedy the situation?*

June 25

"O our God, will You not judge them? For we have no power against this great multitude that is coming against us; nor do we know what to do, but our eyes are upon You."
II Chronicles 20:12

Jehoshaphat, who was a good king of Judah, prayed this prayer just after he received news that a great army was coming to attack his people. This is a prayer we can pray daily as we go about our lives. There are always those who come against us to hurt us, even if we can't see them and they are hurting us behind our backs. Jehoshaphat knew and we should learn that we can't stand against our enemies without God to protect us.

We may think that God doesn't have time for us, since he is taking care of whole countries and protecting them from powerful armies, but this is not true. We need to remember that no matter how small the problem the Lord has an answer for it and IF we just ask Him He will help us. Sometimes we think that we can handle the "little" problems we have and so we don't ask God for help. We need to learn from Jehoshaphat who looked to God for help and advice.

We need to remember to ask God for help all the time, even when we aren't in trouble. We need to ask him to give us wisdom to make the right decisions. Remember the song that says, "Look into his wonderful face."? As a Christian this is our privilege and our duty. SO NOW WE KNOW WHERE TO LOOK and we do this through prayer. We should always keep a prayer right on the tip of our tongues; we never know when we might need to call on God for help.

QUESTIONS TO THINK ABOUT

1. Where did Jehoshaphat go for advice?
2. Where do we need to go when we are in trouble or need advice?

June 26

A certain woman of the wives of the sons of the prophets cried out to Elisha, saying, "Your servant my husband is dead, and you know that your servant feared the LORD. And the creditor is coming to take my two sons to be his slaves."
II Kings 4:1

The good woman in this verse had a problem. Her husband had died and now a creditor was coming to make her sons slaves to settle her debt. The prophet Elisha asked her what she had of value and she said, "I have nothing but a jar of oil." So Elisha told her to send her boys to all the neighbors and collect empty jars. When they brought back the jars, Elisha had the woman pour oil into the empty jar from her one full jar. She poured and poured but her jar never ran out of oil. Eventually she filled all the jars with oil and Elisha told her to sell them and pay off her debt.

This is an amazing miracle that saved the woman from loosing her sons. However, the miracle was only possible because the godly woman went to God for help. First of all, she went to God's Word in the form of the prophet Elisha. Secondly, she listened to what Elisha said and acted on it. The woman was saved because she went to the right place to get help, she believed that God had the answer, and she acted on the instructions she received from God through Elisha.

This is exactly how we should deal with problems. We should first go to God's Word and see what it says about our problem. Secondly, we should listen to what the Bible says. Lastly, we should act on what the Bible teaches. This is why God gave us the Bible, to teach us how to deal with our problems, and live according to His will. If we obey God and study His word He will show us what to do, just like the woman in the story.

Questions To Think About

1. What steps did the woman take when she had a problem?

June 27

And Elisha sent a messenger to him, saying, "Go and wash in the Jordan seven times, and your flesh shall be restored to you, and you shall be clean." II Kings 5:10

This is a story of Naaman. He was commander of the Syrian army and he had an incurable disease called leprosy which would eventually kill him. Naaman's wife had a servant girl and she told her mistress that in her homeland lived a prophet who could cure Naaman's leprosy. Now, the King of Syria loved Naaman. So when Naaman told him about the prophet the King of Syria wrote a letter to the King of Israel telling him to find the prophet Elisha and have him cure Naaman. Naaman took the letter and set out for Israel.

When Naaman arrived in Israel he assumed there would be a big ceremony with the King of Israel and the prophet standing by to heal him. But Elisha didn't even come to see him. Elisha sent his servant to tell Naaman what to do. Naaman was furious. He had not been properly received and now this prophet wanted him to wash in the Jordan River—one of the dirtiest rivers around. No! Naaman wouldn't even consider it. He stormed off toward Syria, probably saying some pretty bad things about the whole situation. But one of his servants said to him. "If the prophet had wanted you to do something GREAT, you would have done it. So why not do this simple thing he asks?" Naaman was a great man and he was also pretty smart—at least smart enough to listen to his servant. So Naaman, HUMBLED himself and washed in the Jordan River seven times as instructed and he was healed. He became a believer after this and was truly grateful. What if he hadn't listened to his servant?

Like Naaman, we are sometimes disappointed with the way things happen in our life, as a result, we go off mad and miss out on a great blessing. So think twice before you dismiss things that don't go the way you want them to. Be like Naaman. Humble yourself and be obedient to those in authority whether a teacher, a club leader, or parent. It will pay off in the long run.

Things To Think About

1. Why did God make Naaman wash in the Jordan River before He healed him?

Notes

June 28

He [Elisha] went up therefore, shut the door behind the two of them, and prayed to the Lord. And he called Gehazi and said, "Call this Shunammite woman." So he called her, and when she came in to him, he said, "Pick up your son." So she went in, fell at his feet, and bowed to the ground; then she picked up her son and went out. II Kings 4:33, 36, 37

Elisha was a prophet who traveled all over the land of Israel. The Shunammite woman and her husband had been very kind to Elisha and had even built a room on top of their house for him to stay in when he came to town. Elisha wanted to repay her for her kindness and found out that she couldn't have a child. So Elisha asked God to give her a son and He did. Once when Elisha was away, her son grew sick and died. The woman had such faith that she went after Elisha because she believed he could heal her son. And he did. It's a wonderful story.

I want to talk a little bit about the Shunammite woman. We don't know much about her except that by her actions we can tell that she was kind, unselfish, put other people's wants and needs before her own, went out of her way to help a spiritual leader, and she had a lot of faith. Even though she had to go through a bad time, she knew God was in control and her faith didn't waver. She is a great example of just how a Christian should act.

FIRST LESSON: BE KIND. In this world it seems like we come into contact with more people who are rude and hateful than nice. Be kind to each other. SECOND LESSON: DON'T BE SELFISH. Don't always want to be first. Think about others before yourself. THIRD LESSON: GO OUT OF YOUR WAY TO HELP. Most of the time, we don't do things for others unless they ask us to. Isn't it great when someone does something for us just to make us happy? FOURTH LESSON: SHE

HAD FAITH. Faith is a gift from God, but it is something that we can ask God for as well. So ask the Lord to increase your faith. Believe and trust that Jesus will do what He promises in His Word. And just like the Shunammite woman YOU WILL BE REWARDED.

Things To Think About

1. What lessons can we learn from the Shunammite woman?
2. Why do you think God included this story in the Bible?

Notes

June 29

So the Levites and all Judah did according to all that Jehoiada the priest commanded. II Chronicles 23:8a

The people of Judah were tired of the wicked Queen Athaliah and Baal worship and all the sinning in the land. They had not lived up to the covenant that God made with them, but they were ready to act. After Jehoiada, the priest, commanded them to get with it they did. They finally listened to their spiritual leader and did what they were told.

Just think of all the people in the world today who go to church every Sunday and listen to the preacher and then go about their business the rest of the week not really caring about the covenant we make with the Lord when He saves us. Wouldn't it be wonderful if we all did what we are supposed to do?

We are quick to say, "I'd live a true Christian life if they would." Or, "I'd live a true Christian life, but THEY won't." It's not about "they" or "anyone else", it's about YOU. One person can make a great difference if he is willing to stand up and be heard for the Lord. Being young doesn't exempt us from standing up for our beliefs. The younger we start the more practice we have standing on our beliefs. So let's be like the Levites and ALL of Judah and live up to our commitment to the Lord.

Questions To Think About

1. Are you living up to your commitment to the Lord?

June 30

The Lord also will roar from Zion, and utter His voice from Jerusalem; the heavens and earth will shake; but the Lord will be a shelter for His people, . . . Joel 3:16

While Joel is prophesying about the future in this verse, there is one phrase that caught my eye that will not only be true in the future but is true today as well. The idea that "the Lord will be a shelter for His people" is a wonderful comfort. It should make us feel good as we go about our everyday lives KNOWING the GOD OF THE UNIVERSE will SHELTER us if we believe in Him. Being a shelter means that God will protect us and whatever happens to us, his children, is for our good. Only He knows the beginning from the end. That's why sometimes we don't think what is happening to us is good; but, we must remember that we don't see the entire picture so we can't really make that judgment. This doesn't mean that we won't have to go through some pretty bad stuff. It does mean that we can TRUST THE LORD to watch over us.

We need to listen to what the Bible tells us through our study time and through our parents, pastors, and teachers rather than turning to movie stars, sports' figures, or famous musicians, in the world for our advice and direction. We don't have to be afraid of what the future holds if we believe what Joel says. The Lord WILL take care of us. When it seems that no one else CARES, we KNOW that JESUS DOES.

Questions To Think About

1. Where are you getting your advice, the Word or the World?

July 1

Joash did what was right in the sight of the Lord all the days of Jehoiada the priest. II Chronicles 24:2

It's so sad that in the Old Testament the Kings of Judah start out great doing what the Lord requires, but as time passes, they become corrupt and usually end up being killed by their own people. Joash the boy king fits this mold. He was only seven years old when he became King. We remember him because he restored the temple. But the real hero in the story is not Joash, but Jehoiada the priest. As long as Jehoiada was alive, Joash "did what was right in the sight of the Lord", but minute the priest died, Joash started worshipping wooden idols and getting into trouble. We can learn three very important things from this account.

First, we should do what is right early in our lives and persevere in doing what is right. It is especially helpful if we have Christian parents and they are guiding us along the right way, but if we don't, we are not excused from doing what is right. Second, we need to listen to our spiritual leaders—parents, Sunday school teachers, and pastors—and do what they tell us just as Joash listened to Jehoiada and then acted on what he said. Third, Joash looked up to his earthly spiritual leader, but when Jehoiada died, Joash began to listen to the secular leaders who eventually led him astray.

This is where we should differ from Joash. Our greatest spiritual leader, the Lord God, will never die and we will always have Him to look to for guidance. Isn't it wonderful to live on this side of the cross—to know that God sent Jesus to die on the cross to pay for our sins, that He rose from the dead and is now seated at the right hand of the Father? Though Jesus is no longer with us on earth, we have the Holy Spirit. We need to be thankful that God has provides us with earthly spiritual advisors, but more importantly that He gave us the Holy Spirit to direct us, teach us, and open our hearts and minds to His TRUTH.

Questions To Think About

1. Have you thanked God lately for sending Jesus?
2. Have you thanked God for our earthly spiritual leaders?
3. Have you thanked God for the Holy Spirit?

Notes

July 2

Now the word of the Lord came to Jonah the son of Amittai, saying, "Arise, go to Nineveh," . . . Now the word of the Lord came to Jonah the SECOND TIME, saying, "Arise go to Nineveh,." . . . Jonah 1:1 and 3:1

We all know the story of Jonah and how he didn't obey the Lord the first time He spoke to him. He tried to run from the Lord, but that didn't work out so well either. The Lord, who is always in control, had Jonah thrown overboard and had a big fish swallow him. Finally, when Jonah was ready to obey, the fish spit him out and Jonah went to Nineveh. I am so glad this story is in the Bible. I know it isn't there to show us how a miracle was performed by God (even though it was miraculous) and it isn't there to show us how many times people will do anything to get their way (even though that is what happened). The story of Jonah shows us that God has great patience with us and that He is the Lord of the SECOND CHANCE (and many more).

For example, let's say your Mom tells you to hurry home from school to watch your little sister or brother because she has an important meeting. After school, your friend Felix invites you to his house to play his new X-Box game. You decide to stop by and stay for just a few minutes to check out the new game. When you finally get home, your mom rushes out to her meeting. She doesn't say anything to you then, but when she gets home she explains that she didn't accomplish what she wanted at her meeting because you were late getting home. When your dad comes home, he breaks the bad news, you are grounded; but, your mom has another meeting next week and you have a second chance to obey. If you do, your grounding will be lifted. Aren't you glad you get a second chance?

The Lord is so patient with us and wants us to be obedient, not because he wants to show us that he is in control, but because He wants what is BEST FOR US!!!! (By the way, in the above scenario, your mom's goal was to get new tables and chairs for the school cafeteria and a new—better—menu.) Let's praise God for that SECOND CHANCE.

Questions To Think About

1. Do you need a second chance to put something right? Ask your parents to give you that chance. When they do, be sure you obey.

July 3

". . . But Me she forgot," says the Lord. Hosea 2:13

Hosea is one of the shorter books in the Old Testament. It was written by Hosea a prophet of God. The nation of Israel had forgotten God and all He had done for them. So God sent Hosea to preach to Israel calling them to repent and telling them what would happen if they didn't. Even though the book was written to the Israelites many hundreds of years ago, it is still the Word of God and therefore, it is just as true today as it was then. It warns us what will happen to us if we don't OBEY God's commands. It also tells us how easily we are misled because we don't have the KNOWLEDGE about God that we should. Why don't we have this knowledge—because we don't study the Bible like we should?

What can we do to remedy this situation? The Bible is the source of all TRUE KNOWLEDGE so we need to go to the Bible first. In it the Lord has given us all the information we need to follow Him and life a good life. After we learn what we are supposed to do, we need to JUST DO IT. If we don't use what we learn it has no value. It's sort of like learning that two plus two equals four. What good does it do to learn that fact if we never apply it to anything practical? But of course we apply this knowledge to lots of things including playing games, baking cookies, or dividing things among our friends. Knowing the facts meant nothing. It only became real when we put it to use. The knowledge we gain from Bible study is the same way. God gives us the knowledge so we can USE IT. We never want the Lord to say about us what the He said of Hosea's wife—the saddest four words I can think of—*BUT ME SHE FORGOT.*

QUESTIONS TO THINK ABOUT

1. Are you studying the Bible as you should—often and diligently?
2. Are you putting what you learn to use—often and diligently?

July 4

Who is wise? Let him understand these things. Who is prudent? Let him know them. For the ways of the Lord are right: The righteous walk in them, but transgressors stumble in them.
Hosea 14:9

If we look up wise in the dictionary it says that a wise person is marked by deep understanding. When we look up prudent it tells us that a prudent person is marked by wisdom. So, if we really understand the ways of the Lord then we have wisdom and are prudent as well. But that's not all. Our Scripture goes on to say that if we walk in what we have learned from God's Word, we are righteous. We also see that sinners stumble on what the Lord tells us in His Word.

Now we know from the Bible and also from experience, that we all stumble and do wrong things sometimes. However, the Lord helps us get back on track when we repent. God promises that if we REPENT He will be FAITHFUL AND JUST TO FORGIVE US. Let's ask God to keep our hearts tender toward Him and when we do something wrong we will run to Him in repentance and confess our sins and He will forgive us. Then we will again be ready to walk in the wise and prudent ways of the Lord.

QUESTIONS TO THINK ABOUT

1. 1. Do you have unconfessed sin in your life? What can you do about it?

July 5

. . . *Yet you have not returned to Me says the Lord.* Amos 4:6

This book is another one of what scholars call the "Minor Prophets". It doesn't mean that it is less important; it just means it doesn't deal with as many problems as some of the other prophets in the Old Testament. Amos tells us that the Lord had sent bad times on the people of Israel to wake them up to their sin and call them to repentance, but nothing worked. All of the physical calamities that were happening to them did not change their hearts. They continued to make all the wrong choices.

We also need to be very careful what choices we make. If we want something so badly that we adopt an attitude of doing WHATEVER IT TAKES to get it, we can easily end up in trouble just like the people of Amos' day. Sometimes we know that the thing we desire is not really what's best for us, but we still want it. So we say, "I don't care if this isn't good for me, I want it anyway." If we get what we want what usually happens? We end up in trouble and then we are miserable. What we wanted was not really what we needed to make us happy.

To prevent things like this from happening we should always go to the Lord first. Then we should "listen" to what He tells us. The Holy Spirit will either convict us, usually by bringing to mind Scripture that shows us something isn't right, or He will withhold the thing that isn't good for us. In other words, IF WE GO TO GOD FIRST, He will let us know if something we want to do is wrong by pricking our conscience. He will not give us what we ask for if it is bad for us. This is why we always pray, "YOUR WILL BE DONE, NOT MINE."

Questions To Think About

1. Are you involved in something that pricks your conscience? Repent and turn away from it.
2. Are you asking for something that God hasn't given you? Could it be he doesn't want you to have it?

July 6

Then Amaziah said to Amos, "Go you seer! Flee to the land of Judah. There eat bread, and prophesy. But never again prophesy at Bethel, for it is the King's sanctuary, and it is the royal residence." Amos 7:12, 13

When I was little and I got into trouble, my parents would start talking to me about what I had done. I knew what I had done was wrong but I would say, "I don't want to talk about it." Well, needless to say we did talk about it! Like the people Amos prophesied to, I didn't want to hear the truth. Many of us are like this. We don't like to hear what will happen to us if we keep doing bad things; we don't want to talk about it. Just like in Bible days there are pastors today who don't talk about what the congregation needs to hear. They "tickle our ears" as the Bible puts it because they want to be popular with the people.

Hopefully the churches we attend are not this way. But if they are we need to remember that it is always our responsibility to study the Bible and learn the truths of God. Let's read our Bibles every day and we will know the truth. When we know the truth we will be able to discern when someone is saying something that is false. So STUDY DILIGENTLY!

Questions To Think About

1. Have you studied your Bible today?

July 7

Say to the righteous that it shall be well with them, for they shall eat the fruit of their doings. Woe to the wicked! It shall be ill with him, for the reward of his hands shall be given him.
Isaiah 3:10, 11

In this Scripture Isaiah is giving the people a great message. This message is also important for us today, especially Christian young people. It is so important for us to realize when we are still young that we REAP WHAT WE SOW. The righteous will be blessed and they will benefit from their good works. Jesus makes us righteous and helps us to sow good works that we will reap as blessings later. If we know this and live like this from the time we are young, it will save us so much pain, suffering, and heartache.

The wicked, on the other hand, will be punished for what they do. Remember that God HATES EVIL and evil has its reward just as righteousness does. Of course, we realize that we still sin even though we have been made righteous in Christ. God will correct us when we sin because He loves us and wants us to do good rather than evil so that we will live happy, productive lives. We should be grateful to God that he corrects us when we sin and forgives us when we repent. His love is so GREAT!

Questions To Think About

1. What does "you reap what you sow" mean?

July 8

Also I hear the voice of the Lord, saying: "Whom shall I send, and who will go for Us?" Then I said, "Here am I! Send me." And He said, "Go and tell the people." Isaiah 6:8

The Lord wants to use us to further His kingdom. He doesn't NEED us but He has chosen to work through us to accomplish His will here on earth. Our part is to answer the call and obey the will of our Lord. Isaiah answered the call by saying, "Here am I! Send me." This should always be our answer too.

Let's look at what the Lord told Isaiah to do. He said TELL THE PEOPLE. That doesn't seem very hard. What was Isaiah to tell the people? He was to tell them WHO God is. He was to tell them how to SERVE, OBEY, LOVE, and WORSHIP Him. That is the same message we are to deliver today. We might wonder how we can tell others about God but we really don't even need to worry about that. If we are praying for an opportunity to proclaim the GOOD NEWS to others, God will make sure that we get an opportunity. Usually a person we are talking to will bring up a topic that will naturally lead into a discussion about these things. God makes it so easy for us to obey.

But remember that some people won't want to listen when we start talking about the things of God. If they don't want to listen we can think back about the Disciples. The same thing happened to them and the Lord told them not to worry about the results. The important thing is that we are being obedient to our calling. We are not responsible for the other person's reaction or response. God will bring in the Harvest in His own time.

Questions To Think About

1. What should our response be to God's call to share the things of God with others?
2. Are you sharing with others?

July 9

He has shown you, O man, what is good: and what does the Lord require of you. But to do justly, to love mercy, and to walk humbly with your God. Micah 6:8

This is a short list isn't it? Just three things that the Lord requires of us: 1. To do justly. 2. To love mercy. 3. To walk humbly with our God. Let's see what each of these things requires. To be JUST means to always obey God's commands. We are JUST if we follow the Ten Commandments. Following the commandments is more than going through the motions; we must heed the commandments in our hearts as well. So when it says, "Thou shalt not steal," we should not be jealous of someone who has something we don't have. We should be happy for him. This is observing the commandments in our hearts.

The second part of the verse requires us to love MERCY. This helps us to temper our justice. Requiring justice in ourselves tends to make us want everyone else to observe all the commandments to the letter also. But God in his wisdom has told us that we must have mercy as well. Why? Because God showed us great MERCY when He let His JUSTICE fall on Jesus. Remember that we deserve death as the price of our sin. God couldn't just do away with the price, someone had to pay it or God would no longer be JUST. Because of His MERCY, God sent His Son to pay for OUR SIN and declared that we are PAID UP. We no longer owe anything for our debt of sin, JESUS PAID IT ALL. As a result God says that we should show mercy to others because He has shown greater mercy to us. So forgive others when they wrong you, take up for those who are younger, and protect those who are weaker.

The third thing is to walk humbly with our God. This means that we ALWAYS put GOD FIRST. We believe it, say it to others, and live like He is the most important thing in our lives. *THIS IS GOOD*!

Questions To Think About

1. Are you being just? How are you living out God's justice?
2. Do you love mercy? How are you living out God's mercy?
3. Are you walking humbly with your God? How?

Notes

July 10

. . . If they do not speak according to this word, it is because there is no light in them. Isaiah 8:20

Isaiah is speaking a great truth in this verse. If something is not "in us" it is impossible for it to "come out" of us. For example, if we go to school and the math teacher hands us a test and all the problems are algebra problems and we haven't even taken algebra yet, we won't be able to answer any of the questions. Algebra is not "in us" because we haven't learned it so it can't "come out of us" as answers on a test. This is what Isaiah was saying about the people of his day. They could not talk or walk as believers because the LIGHT OF THE WORLD was not in them.

Let's go back to algebra for a minute. Let's say that we tell others that we know how to do algebra. We really don't know anything about algebra, we just thought it sounded cool or was politically correct to SAY we knew algebra. When the test comes what happens? We fail because we lied. We were trying to "fake it". There are those among us who "fake" being a Christian. We will find out who is real or who is "fake" when the tests come. Maybe some friend of ours says he's a Christian because the church youth group goes on cool trips or because they have fun parties or they get "recognition for their good works" in the community. But when it is no longer cool or popular or politically correct to be a Christian, they will "fall away" because the TRUTH is not in them, but the real Christians who have the LIGHT of JESUS in them will persevere.

QUESTIONS TO THINK ABOUT

1. Is the LIGHT OF THE WORLD in you? If yes, are you persevering in God's commands?
2. If no, do you want to know the LIGHT OF THE WORLD? Ask your parents to help you.

July 11

For unto us a Child is born, unto us a Son is given; and the government will be upon His shoulder. And His name will be called Wonderful, Counselor, Mighty God, Everlasting Father, Prince of Peace. Isaiah 9:6

In times past the names people gave to their children were very important and told something about them or their family or the times in which they lived. This is the case with Jesus too. His names tell us about who He is. He is given five names in this verse. Let's look at them individually.

First Jesus is called WONDERFUL. There has never been and never will be anyone who lived a perfect life except for Jesus. That causes us to be full of wonder at the perfection of our Lord. JESUS IS WONDERFUL. Next, He is called COUNSELOR. This is a very important name because Jesus is a counselor to all who know Him. He has all the right answers and can help and comfort us in all situations. JESUS IS THE GREATEST COUNSELOR. He is also called MIGHTY GOD. Not only is Jesus God, He is also mighty. The gospel of John says, "In the beginning was the Word [Jesus], and the Word was with God and the Word was God . . . All things were made through Him, and without Him nothing was made that was made." JESUS IS MIGHTY GOD. The verse also calls Him EVERLASTING FATHER. Jesus said, "I and the Father are ONE." He is one with God and IS GOD. In Isaiah 63: 16b the prophet says, "You, O LORD are our Father; Our Redeemer from Everlasting is Your name." So we see here in another place that the Bible declares JESUS IS OUR EVERLASTING FATHER. The last name Isaiah gives Jesus in this verse is PRINCE OF PEACE. This name means that Jesus is the only one who can really give us peace. In the Hebrew language "peace" means, "the possession of adequate resources". This tells us that Jesus possesses and then gives to us everything that we need. JESUS IS THE PRINCE OF PEACE. WOW! WHAT A SAVIOR!!

QUESTIONS TO THINK ABOUT

1. Do you personally know the Wonderful, Counselor, Mighty God, Everlasting Father, Prince of Peace? If not talk to your parents about asking Jesus to be your Savior.

NOTES

July 12

I will punish the world for its evil, and the wicked for their iniquity; Isaiah 13:14

In this Scripture, God is telling Israel through the prophet Isaiah that even though He has been longsuffering and given them lots of chances to repent and it may seem like they have gotten away with their sin, THEIR SIN WOULD NOT GO UNPUNISHED. What the people in Isaiah's day had forgotten is that GOD IS JUST. That means that He must ALWAYS punish sin or He will cease to be JUST. However, God is longsuffering—that means He is patient and gives us lots of chances to repent and turn away from our sin. But in the end, GOD ALWAYS PUNISHES SIN. Even the sins of God's children have to be punished, but instead of punishing us God punished Jesus in our place. If we are Christians, Jesus has already paid for all of our sins so God will never PUNISH us, BUT he does CORRECT us.

The difference between CORRECTION and PUNISHMENT is that when God punishes someone He is fulfilling the just requirements of His law and His wrath falls on that person—God's wrath is a terrible thing. However, when He corrects His children, He is teaching us not to commit that sin anymore. It's like our parents correcting us. Sometimes it might seem like they are punishing us, but what they are really doing is trying to teach us a lesson that helps us remember not to do that same sin again.

So even though God does promise to forgive us when we repent, He still uses the consequences of our sin to correct us. This doesn't mean that every bad thing that happens to us is God correcting us for sin in our lives, but sometimes it does. We also need to remember that God's laws are for our good so we should delight in following them.

Questions To Think About

1. Is there a sin in your life that you know about? Repent early so it doesn't harden your heart.

July 13

. . . *Let us eat and drink for tomorrow we die!* Isaiah 22:13

This is how most of the people of Isaiah's day were living. Some people today believe that we should do whatever we want because we are just going to die. They tell us to live it up and not to worry about what will happen to us later. This is very foolish thinking. First, if everyone did what he wanted it would conflict with what someone else wanted to do which would lead to a great deal of fighting which would eventually lead to complete chaos. We see that if we really put this philosophy into practice it would be impossible for any of us to live even a halfway "normal" life. The truth of the matter is that what we do does have an effect on other people even if we don't always see it. Through our influence we can cause others to want to be good or we can cause them to want to be bad. SO WHAT WE DO IS VERY IMPORTANT.

Remember that little saying God first, others second, and me last. That is the way we are to live. We are not to live only for ourselves. This advice, as is illustrated in the verse above, is contrary to what the world will tell us. The world says, ME FIRST and let the chips fall where they may. But we are to be like Christ so we need to see how he lived His life. He certainly didn't put Himself first or He would never have willingly died a horrible death on the cross for people who didn't care anything about Him.

The second part of the verse is another lie. It implies that we just die and are buried and turn back into dirt. We know this isn't true. Our soul will live forever. If we believe in Jesus we will spend eternity with Him and it won't be the end of our life. It will be just the beginning.

QUESTIONS TO THINK ABOUT

1. Where will you spend eternity?

July 14

O Lord, You are my God, I will exalt You, I will praise Your name, for You have done wonderful things; Your counsels of old are faithfulness and truth. Isaiah 25:1

Our Scripture today is a statement of faith for everyone who is a believer in Jesus. That means that this verse explains what Christians believe and do. First, we state that the Lord is our God and because He is our God what naturally follows is that we will EXALT Him or put Him first. We WORSHIP Him because we know He is God by all the WONDERFUL THINGS He has done. He created all things, Jesus died for us, He forgives us when we sin, He has let us take part in His work, and He is preparing an awesome place for us to live with Him forever.

So if anyone ever wants to know "Why do you believe in all that stuff and go to church?" We can say, "I believe in Jesus because He has said all the things I believe and He has always done what He said He would do in the past so I trust Him with the future.

Questions To Think About

1. Are you trusting Jesus with your future?

July 15

The humble also shall increase their joy in the Lord . . . Woe to the rebellious children says the Lord who takes counsel, but not of Me . . . Isaiah 29:19; 30:1

HUMBLE has gotten a bad rap. Most people today think of a humble person as someone who is a doormat for other people, who won't speak, and just sits in the corner of the room trying not to be seen by others. But a humble person is actually someone who puts his trust in the Lord rather than in himself. When we realize who is really in control and that God wants the very best for us then we will have JOY. Some people have the mistaken idea that it is a sign of weakness to rely on Jesus. It is not a sing of weakness it is a sign of WISDOM.

The second part of our Scripture is just the opposite and it doesn't paint a very pretty picture. It seems like that more and more children are being rebellious. They don't want to obey anyone in authority let alone the Lord. These rebellious children take their advice and counsel from people who are evil—people who do not love the Lord. This verse tells us that if we are not obedient but instead are rebellious we will suffer greatly. That is what WOE means. It is used to express a condition of deep suffering due to misfortune, affliction or grief, trouble, and calamity.

We have before us two choices. We can be humble and obedient before the Lord and have JOY. OR, we can be rebellious and SUFFER the consequences. Choose today.

Questions To Think About

1. Which will you choose?

July 16

He who walks righteously and speaks uprightly . . .
He will dwell on high . . . Isaiah 33: 15, 16

MORE GOOD NEWS from the Lord. There are two words for us to look at in today's Scripture and they are both very important. The first word is "walks". Too often we SAY we are followers of Jesus but when we start looking at how we act, it doesn't match up. If we are FOLLOWING Jesus we are WALKING the walk. This means there is ACTION involved. I don't mean just going to church and sitting there for an hour or two. When we follow someone it means that we do what he does. As Christians we are FOLLOWERS OF CHRIST, so that means we will do what He does. To learn what Jesus did we need to read the Bible, especially the New Testament books of Mathew, Mark, Luke and John. Then we need to "WALK" LIKE JESUS.

The next word is SPEAK. Part of walking like Jesus is speaking like Jesus. This is where most of us have trouble. Too much of the time we speak like those around us instead of speaking like a Christian. For example, when we are with our friends do we talk about others who aren't in "our" group and maybe even tell things that aren't really true? We are not speaking uprightly. Then we wonder why we don't have the JOY in our lives that we talked about in the last lesson.

So what should we learn from this? We should learn to be VERY CAREFUL how we walk and how we talk. We need to call on the Lord when we pray to strengthen us and help us to walk and talk consistently as a Christian should. If we ask for strength God will give it to us.

Questions To Think About

1. Are you walking the walk?
2. Are you talking the talk?

July 17

He [King Hezekiah] broke in pieces the bronze serpent that Moses had made: for until those days the children of Israel burned incense to it . . . He trusted in the Lord God of Israel . . .
II Kings 18: 4, 5

Hezekiah was a very great King of Judah because he TRUSTED THE LORD. When Moses made this bronze serpent the verse speaks of, the Israelites were on their way to the Promised Land and God was leading them in a roundabout way to the land to teach them some things. But they became discouraged and began to complain against Moses. Because of their complaining, God sent snakes among the people to bite them and many of them died. So they cried out to Moses to do something and Moses went to the Lord. God told him to make a bronze serpent and lift it up on a pole and anyone who looked on the serpent would get well. The descendants of these Israelites had taken this incident and created a ritual of burning incense to this snake statue as a way of worshipping it.

The first commandment says that we are to have no other gods but the one true God and the second commandment says not to worship idols. But no king in Israel had enough courage to put a stop to this evil practice until Hezekiah came along. Because he trusted in the Lord, he was not afraid to TAKE A STAND for what was right.

Today Christians seem to let lots of things get in the way of standing up for what's right. Sometimes we let groups at school who are more vocal than we are intimidate us into remaining silent. They go on doing what is evil and we just keep quiet. We RATIONALIZE our silence by convincing ourselves that what they are doing won't really hurt anyone or by saying it isn't my job to stop them. But if we remember Hezekiah and we TRUST IN THE LORD like he did, God will strengthen us to STAND UP FOR WHAT'S RIGHT.

QUESTIONS TO THINK ABOUT

1. Are you standing for what's right?

July 18

Be strong and courageous; do not be afraid or dismayed before the king of Assyria, nor before all the multitude that is with him; for there are more with us than with him. With him is an arm of flesh; but with us it the Lord our God, to help us and to fight our battles. II Chronicles 32:7, 8

WOW! What a great verse and a great thing to know. Our Scripture is one we should memorize and repeat any time we feel like the "world" is getting the best of us and we can't make a difference. This reminds me of times in the Bible when one kid did make a difference. Think about David and Goliath, Daniel and the king's table, and the boy King Josiah.

The world wants Christians to believe that we are small, insignificant, and few in numbers. But even if we are, which I don't really believe, that still shouldn't deter us from our calling. God says in this verse that we need to be strong and courageous and not fear the world no matter how many people they say they have on their side, because their help is only flesh and ours is the Lord our God. WE HAVE GOD ON OUR SIDE. We don't need anything or anyone else. Remember this and be ready for any job He has for you.

Questions To Think About

1. With God on our side is there any reason to fear?
2. Are you facing your battles against evil remembering this truth?

July 19

O Lord, I am oppressed; Undertake for me! Isaiah 38:14

I know many people have the mistaken idea that when we become Christians we won't have any problems and that every day will be wonderful and filled with fun and easy times. But God's Word never tells us that. In fact it tells us the opposite. So what are we to do when our friends want us to go with them and our parents have told us not to go? If we don't go our friends will mock us and call us a baby. Besides what they are going to do will be fun and we would like to go. On the other hand we know that we should obey our parents and they trust us to do so. If we go in spite of them, we will break their trust and disappoint them. THIS DECISION IS OPRESSING US. It's time for us to go to the Lord and ask Him to help—undertake for—us.

In the above case there really is no decision. We are ALWAYS TO OBEY our parents. The struggle is between doing what we have an inclination to do and what is right. Our old sin nature is tempting us to sin and the struggle is weighing us down. But God can lift us up and give us strength of will to do what is right and HE WILL if we ask Him to. We will probably even be surprised how our friends respect us for OBEYING our parents—at least if they are good friends they will. They may still tease us a little, but deep down they respect us. So when we feel oppressed by circumstances or decisions we have to make let's remember to PRAY and ask God to *undertake for us.*

Questions To Think About

1. Do you feel weighed down with decisions? Go to the Lord for help.

July 20

. . . take root downward, and bear fruit upward.
II Kings 19:30

This is a picture the Israelites would have understood very well. They were farmers and they knew that a fruit tree which has deep roots in fertile soil that is fertilized, watered, cultivated, and pruned bears beautiful, delicious fruit. This picture tells us what we are to do.

As Christians, our roots are to be planted deep in the Word of God. We know this is fertile ground because the Word is God inspired TRUTH. As we are cultivated through the reading of His Word, praying, and having times of fellowship with other Christians, we grow in the Lord. We don't let ungodly "weeds" creep into our lives to steal the nourishment from us. The weeds are things that take time away from our consistent study of God's Word, prayer, or Christian fellowship. God and the truth of His Word protect us from the storms of life. Because we are deeply rooted in Him, when the storms come we may bend in the blast and loose a few leaves, but we will not be broken. We begin to bear fruit as God prunes us of unproductive limbs—things in our lives that we don't need or things that take our time away from God's plan for us. What a beautiful tree—Christian—we have become. With our faith rooted deep in Jesus, our Lord and Savior, we will become more and more like Him. ALL HEAVEN REJOICES.

Questions To Think About

1. Are you rooted in Jesus?
2. Have you let "weeds" come into your life? Be Honest! If so what do you plan to do about them?

July 21

But those who wait on the Lord shall renew their strength. They shall mount up with wings like eagles. They shall run and not be weary. They shall walk and not faint. Isaiah 40:31

None of us likes to wait, yet it seems that we spend lots of time waiting. We wait for the weekend, we wait for our birthday, we wait for our friends to come over, and we wait for our favorite movie to come out on DVD. We wait and wait and wait. But often we don't wait the way we should. This verse tells us that if we wait on the Lord our strength will be renewed. The word wait in this Scripture means to wait patiently but with the expectation that something will happen. It's more like watching than waiting. In other words when we "wait on the Lord" it means that we talk to Him about what we need or problems we have or whatever, and then we watch for His answer. We wait knowing that the answer will come. If we wait correctly then the Lord will renew our strength. He will give us the strength to wait patiently while we watch for His answer.

QUESTIONS TO THINK ABOUT

1. Are you waiting and watching for an answer from God?

July 22

Everyone helped his neighbor, and said to his brother: "Be of good courage!" Isaiah 41:6

Wouldn't it be wonderful if everyone DID help his neighbor? Think about it. There would be no wars. Instead, the rulers of the different countries wouldn't be greedy for power and they would always have in mind what was best for the citizens of that nation. Instead of different ethnic groups quarreling with each other they could build friendships. Instead of the rich lording over the poor they could show them a better way to live. Instead of one church trying to outdo another church, they could come together at the foot of the cross and win more people to the Lord. Instead of fighting with the kid next door who doesn't see thing our way, we could be a true friend and work out any little differences we have.

We often wonder why there are wars but if we bring it down to a personal level we can see that we often don't help our neighbor. Instead we want things our way no matter how it affects others. We need to pray and ask God to help us LOVE OUR NEIGHBORS AS OURSELVES.

Questions To Think About

1. Do you love your neighbor? How do you show it?
2. Have you encouraged someone today?

July 23

. . . *And there is no other God besides Me, a just God and a Savior; there is none besides Me.* Isaiah 45:21

We can learn a number of things from today's Scripture. First, we learn that the Scripture teaches that there is only ONE God. We've talked about this before but it is always good to think about it again. We will always find those around us who say, "Oh sure following Jesus is one way to get to heaven but there are other ways too." Of course, this is a lie and if we KNOW that there is only one God we won't be tempted to accept this false teaching. Then there is the truth that God is a JUST God. The word JUST means to be righteous or holy. This means that God and sin don't mix. So God must punish sin. The next truth we learn is that He is a SAVIOR. If God is a savior then it stands to reason that we need saving from something. That something is sin. The Bible tells us that we have ALL SINNED. Now, since God is JUST and must punish sin and we have ALL SINNED, then God must punish us. This is true. But we can't leave out that he is a SAVIOR. Because He loved us, God sent Jesus to pay for our sin. So He SAVED us from having to pay the price of God's JUSTICE which would have required us to pay for our own sin and the WAGES OF SIN IS DEATH!

The ONE TRUE GOD who is wholly JUST acted as our SAVIOR to satisfy God's justice and save us from DEATH. As the verse says *There is none besides* Him. What a GREAT and MERCIFUL God we serve.

QUESTIONS TO ANSWER

1. Has Jesus saved you from death?
2. Do you thank God for all He has done for you?

July 24

"Listen to Me, you who know righteousness, you people in whose heart is My law; Do not fear the reproach of men, nor be afraid of their insults. Isaiah 51:7

The dictionary definition of "reproach" is, "to blame someone." We live in the age of the BLAME GAME. This means that when anyone is questioned about anything the first thing he does is try to blame someone else. For example, when something doesn't work or when something is misplaced we tend to jump in and say, "Well, I didn't do it. He must have done it. It sure wasn't me. I'll bet she did it."

This Scripture tells us that we are not to fear anyone who blames us for something we didn't do, or tries to make us look bad in front of other people. I'll always remember when I went to a new school in fourth grade and the other kids made fun of the way I dressed—it happened to be cowboy boots with a dress. This girl who of course is now a grandmother still brings up what I wore to school that first day whenever I see her. At first this really hurt my feeling, but now it has become a joke.

Throughout our lives we will have people who will insult us and mock us but we are not to be concerned about them or what they say. Treat them with genuine kindness and they may just turn out to be a new friend. If not, we have nothing to be ashamed of in our actions.

Questions To Think About

1. Do you pray for those who insult you and mock you? Are you kind to them?

July 25

All we like sheep have gone astray; We have turned, everyone, to his own way . . . Isaiah 53:6

Not many people have sheep for pets but I would guess that most of us have had a dog at some time in our lives. Dogs may not wander away accidentally like sheep, but they do sometimes RUN away. When I was in grade school my Dad was very sick so my parents, my sister and I had to pack up and leave our hometown and move to another state. We planned to live there for a while hoping that my Dad's health would improve. Because of all this upheaval in our lives my parents promised us that we could each have a small dog. My sister and I started looking in the newspaper right away. We passed up German shepherds, collies, and boxers. We knew those were too big. We began to get discouraged when finally we found an ad for some Pekingese puppies for sale. We were really excited but the ad didn't say how many puppies were available. We went to the address in the paper and sure enough there were two puppies for sale. We bought the dogs and pampered and petted them from puppies into adulthood. Now, the only bad thing about this particular breed is that these dogs had to be on a leash at all times or they would run off and it was a terrible job to try and find them. We tried letting them off the leash while we were sitting right there watching them but they would run off. They wanted to do their own thing and we were really cramping their style.

Like the sheep in our Scripture, those Pekingese dogs are another perfect picture of US. Yes, US. We think we know what is best for us or at least we know what WE WANT. Just like the sheep in the Scripture and our dogs, we want to RUN OFF every chance we get and DO OUR OWN THING. I don't mean run off literally, but we want to be in charge of our lives and do things our way. Jesus has a better way for us and if we listen, learn from His Word, and then act accordingly, we will be so much happier and so much better off. REMEMBER—Flee youthful temptations.

Questions To Think About

1. *Do you flee temptation?*
2. *Who's in charge of your life?*

Notes

July 26

. . . So the Lord God will cause righteousness and praise to spring forth before all the nations. Isaiah 61:11

I am so glad that GOD IS IN CONTROL. He has such great things planned for all of us. He has plans for some of us to be missionaries in foreign countries. We need missionaries or evangelists to go to these places and TELL the people about Jesus so that they will know and praise God. There is a need for Christians to SHOW these people by helping them how we love God and others for His sake. God's Word will go throughout the world and into all nations. He could accomplish this through many different means, but He has chosen to accomplish this task through people. Perhaps he will call one of us to go into a foreign land as a missionary.

God also evangelizes foreign people in reverse. By that I mean that He has sent many foreign people to America either to get an education or for a job or some other reason. He has placed these people from foreign nations right on our doorstep. We need to think about being a "foreign missionary" in America too. In other words we have thousands of people from foreign nations here in America and we can evangelize them without even leaving our country. There is always a great deal we can do for the kingdom of God. TELLING people from different lands about Jesus and SHOWING them God's love can happen across the oceans or right here at home. Let's pray that God will lift up workers for the harvest.

Questions To Think About

1. Pray that God's Word will saturate the whole earth.

July 27

I looked, but there was no one to help, . . . Isaiah 63:5

In the last lesson we talked about becoming a missionary to foreign peoples either in their native land or right here at home. Now let's just talk about our own Christian community. WE DON'T HAVE ENOUGH WORKERS. That's a terrible thing. Right before Jesus ascended into Heaven, He told the Disciples to go into all the world and THEY DID. But Christians today seem to think that Church workers are here to SERVE THEM. Many think or act like Christians are not expected to do anything but ENJOY the efforts of the few Christians who are using their gifts and talents to glorify God.

Christians are not to sit around DOING NOTHING—that includes kids—they are to HELP OTHERS. How? AT HOME: OBEY! Cheerfully do chores, ask permission before going places, find little things that need to be done and do them, play with younger brothers and sisters, just to name a few. AT CHURCH: OBEY! Be polite, kind, helpful, invite others to join the groups, work during clean-up days. IN THE COMMUNITY: OBEY! Pick up trash in the neighborhood, start an after-school Bible club, help out an elderly neighbor, respect the neighbor's property. We can always find plenty to do if we just open our eyes and look around for about two minutes. So think of lots more ways to help others and then GO and DO.

Questions To Think About

1. Have you helped your Mom or Dad today?
2. Have you helped your neighbor today?

July 28

And it shall come to pass at that time that I will search Jerusalem with lamps, and punish the men who are settled in complacency, who say in their heart, the Lord will not do good, nor will He do evil. Zephaniah 1:12

Do you know what it means to be complacent? The dictionary says it means, "to be self-satisfied." The people in Jerusalem had become so self-satisfied with the way things were that they didn't think God would do anything to them—good or bad. Then God told Zephaniah the prophet what He was going to do to the people. He said He was going to PUNISH them.

Are you satisfied with your spiritual growth over the last year? Have you even given it any thought? If not, you may be complacent. Think back to when you first became a Christian or when you first started studying and memorizing the Bible. Do you have that same enthusiasm and drive today?

You know that God is longsuffering. But you also know that there is a day of reckoning just like in our Scripture. Don't be fooled into thinking that it doesn't matter to God whether or not you study His Word or memorize Scripture or go to church. It does matter whether or not you have grown spiritually. So if you have neglected these things, REPENT and ask God to help you get back on track.

QUESTIONS TO THINK ABOUT

1. Ask yourself all the questions from the lesson once more.

July 29

Then said I, "Ah Lord God! Behold, I cannot speak, for I am a youth." But the Lord said to me, "Do not say, 'I am a youth,' for you shall go to all to whom I send you, and whatever I command you, you shall speak. Do not be afraid of their faces, for I am with you to deliver you," says the Lord. Jeremiah 1:6

This Scripture shows that if age wasn't a problem between God and Jeremiah, it won't be a problem between God and YOU. Sure you've had people tell you to keep quiet because you were just a kid. Perhaps you had a chance to speak but what you said was discounted because of your age. BUT—the good news is that GOD CAN USE YOU no matter how old you are. AND—He wants to use you. All you have to do is to be ready. You know, it isn't so much your ABILITY as your AVAILABILITY.

Questions To Think About

1. Are you available?
2. Are you listening to what God has for you to do?

August 1

Hear and give ear: Do not be proud, for the Lord has spoken. Jeremiah 13:15

Since we were small children we have heard our parents and others say, "Take pride in what you do." Then, we read in Scripture that we are not to be proud. Is this a contradiction? Let's see. When our parents tell us to take pride in our work, they mean that they want us to do the very best we can. God wants us to work hard and do our best too. He has given each of us special talents and He wants us to use them for HIS GLORY. What does this mean? It means that when we do something well and receive recognition for it we give God the credit for our talent and for helping us to develop it. When we keep all the recognition for ourselves because we like the attention and the praise we become the kind of proud this verse is talking about. We begin to think more highly of ourselves that we ought.

This is one way we can be the wrong kind of proud, but there is another way too. When we know that we have done something wrong and we refuse to admit it because we are too proud, this is bad. This kind of pride keeps us from admitting to anyone, and especially to God, that we are sinners. If we suffer from this kind of pride—and we all do at least some of the time—we will not be forgiven because we won't ask. For unbelievers, this pride keeps them out of heaven because if they won't admit they are sinners they can never believe they need a Savior. If this kind of pride keeps us as Christians from confessing our sins, our fellowship with God will be broken. Only repentance can restore us to a right relationship with our Savior. So the wrong kind of pride is thinking too highly of oneself and being too stubborn to admit our sins. As we can see, these two kinds of pride are not the same as "taking pride in our work".

Questions To Think About

1. Do you take pride in your work?
2. Do you give God the glory for your talent?
3. Are you quick to admit your sin or are you stubborn about it?

Notes

August 2

. . . each one follows the dictates of his own evil heart, so that no one listens to Me. Jeremiah 16:12

It is so easy to do what you want to do, isn't it? It seems like you have this little voice inside you commanding you to do whatever pleases you and let the rest of the world look out for itself. Today's Scripture says that you are not to get your orders from selfish desires but from God. For example, you see something in a store that you want. You don't need it, you can do without it, but the more you think about it the more YOU HAVE TO HAVE IT. You've been saving your allowance for a long time to go on a mission trip with the church. It's been hard. You have done without a lot of things. You really need to go on this trip because you think you might want to be a missionary when you grow up. That was before you saw IT. Then you start thinking, maybe it would be better to have IT than to go off and serve someone else. Besides the trip is only for two weeks and you wouldn't be able to do very much good in that short time anyway. This is called rationalizing. You start trying to convince yourself that your selfish desire is what God really wants for you.

This is what God is saying in Jeremiah. You put your wants ahead of His plan for your life. You follow the dictates of your own heart and don't listen to God. Pray that God will guard your heart and keep it tender toward His Word and what He says.

QUESTIONS TO THINK ABOUT

1. Is your heart tender toward God and His Word?

August 3

I, the Lord search the heart, test the mind, even to give every man according to his ways. According to the fruit of his doings.
Jeremiah 17:10

In this passage God tells us that He knows our hearts and minds even better than we do ourselves. This means that we cannot hide anything from God. He knows everything we do, think, and feel. Some people are obedient outwardly thinking they can fool God into believing that they are good enough to get into Heaven. Some people are obedient because they want other people to think well of them, but in their hearts they don't really love God. Sometimes these people will even fool the church for a while. They may even be honored and respected, but in Jeremiah we learn that even if these people fool the world, they don't fool God. Some day God will judge them for their unbelief and hypocrisy and all the praise and honor they got on earth won't matter because God will give them justice "according to their ways".

Questions To Think About

1. Do you really love God or are you just "going through the motions"?

August 4

And he made all who were present in Jerusalem and Benjamin take a stand. So the inhabitants of Jerusalem did according to the covenant of God, the God of their fathers.
II Chronicles 34:32

I recently heard a lady tell about her little grandson who was just seven years old. His mother picked up two other children who were on his soccer team to take them to a match. When they were settled in the car one of them said, "Isn't it funny that we came from monkeys?" Her little grandson spoke up and said, "Well I didn't come from a monkey. I came from Adam." That little seven-year-old boy took a stand. He took a stand for what he had been taught from the Bible and what he believed.

Our Scripture today talks about Josiah. He restored the true worship of God to the temple. No king of Israel or Judah had been interested in truly worshipping God for so long that they had even lost the Scriptures. When they were found, Josiah had them read to the people. They believed what the Scriptures taught and began once again to truly worship God. Josiah took a stand for God and we should too, every chance we get.

Questions To Think About

1. Are you standing up for God and His Word?

August 5

And the Lord God of their fathers sent warnings to them by His messengers, rising up early and sending them, because he had compassion on His people and on His dwelling place. But they mocked the messengers of God, despised His words, and scoffed at His prophets, until the wrath of the Lord arose against His people, till there was no remedy. II Chronicles 36: 15, 16

This Scripture tells about a time when God's messengers were mocked and hated. Have you ever heard anyone today make fun of God's Word or His messengers? They may say things like, "Do you believe that fairy tale? You must be dumber than I thought." Or, "Why should I go to church, the Bible is just a story book about a bunch of junk that happened a long time ago. I'll have more fun going to the beach." Or, "I don't like your preacher, he's boring. I'd rather watch TV."

There are people today who are just like the ones described in this Scripture. These people in Jerusalem and Judah were given many chances to repent but they rejected God's mercy. God was very patient with them but finally God said NO MORE and they were conquered by another nation and taken into slavery. They could have been free but they would not listen to the Word of the Lord so they lost their freedom. Wouldn't it be terrible to lose our freedom because we wouldn't listen to what Jesus says in His Word?

I've talked to women in jail and they all say they wish they had listened. They wish they had done what is right instead of committing a crime and ending up in jail. Remember the Lord sends us warnings through His Word, our parents, the pastor, and other teachers—SO LISTEN AND OBEY.

Questions To Think About

1. How do you feel about God's Word? Do you think it's TRUE?
2. Do you LISTEN? Do you OBEY?

August 6

Behold the proud, his soul is not upright in him; but the just shall live by his faith. Habakkuk 24

Have you ever noticed how easy it is to say the right thing and do the right thing when you are around "right" people? When you are with your church buddies it's easy to be bold and tell others what you believe. It's easy to be kind and do what is right because the rest of the gang expects you to. BUT what about when you end up in a group of people you don't know very well and you are the only Christian in the bunch. This will happen at some point in your life no matter how hard you try to avoid it. Is it as easy for you to be uncompromising in your faith in front of these people? Habakkuk is saying that no matter what situation you find yourself in, who you are with, or how terrible things get, you should remember your faith and act accordingly.

This Scripture changed the course of the ENTIRE CHRISTIAN CHURCH when a priest named Martin Luther read it. When he read it Luther realized for the first time in his life that it wasn't what rituals he went through or what he did in his own strength, it was WHO HE HAD FAITH IN that mattered.

If your faith is in Jesus and what He did for you it doesn't really matter where you are or who is around. You will act the same way in all situations because you know that Jesus is right there with you and your trust is in Him. You have no reason to be afraid; He will see you through.

QUESTIONS TO THINK ABOUT

1. Are you living by faith?
2. In whom do you place your faith or trust?

August 7

. . . But although I have spoken to you, rising early and speaking, you did not obey Me. Jeremiah 35:14

There is that word again—OBEY. It is so important for us to realize that obedience is more than "not doing something bad". Obedience is also taking advantage of any opportunity that comes our way to "do good". I've often heard someone say, "I'm bored." As Christians we should never be bored. There is always something for us to do. We might say, "What can I do, I'm just a kid." Or, "How can I help, I can't drive." WHAT ABOUT AT HOME! Our Moms can always use a helping hand. If we offer to help it will mean so much to her. What about Dad, with all those little jobs he's always going to do but never has time to get done? How about jumping in and doing one of those?

When I was a kid and knew that I should help with the dishes, I used to "lay low" until they were done. Even though I knew I should help, if I could get by without drying the dishes I would. But when I did that, inside I always felt like I had cheated. That's because I didn't have the attitude that Jesus had—a SERVANT'S HEART. He was always available to help at any time; He was always ready to serve others. As we can see, OBEYING is much more than not acting bad and breaking the rules—OBEYING ncludes SERVING OTHERS and DOING GOOD.

Questions To Think About

1. Are you REALLY OBEYING?

August 8

It may be that the house of Judah will hear all the adversities which I purpose to bring upon them, that everyone may turn from his evil way, that I may forgive their iniquity and their sin.
Jeremiah 36:3

Several lessons are evident in this verse. First, of all, God tells us through Jeremiah that we are required to follow His laws. He makes it easy for us to know His laws because they are all contained in His Word. They are also summed up in the TEN COMMANDMENTS. That means if we take what the Ten Commandments say and apply them to our lives today, we have a perfect outline of how we should live. But, as we all know we will never live them perfectly. Sometimes we sin and we need to be forgiven. The good news is if we repent and turn from our sin, God will forgive us!

Isn't it wonderful that God WANTS to forgive us of our sins and when we repent He does! Then we don't have to go around with guilt weighing us down and keeping us from serving God. We need to remember that feelings of guilt do not come from God. By that I mean that God convicts us of our sin for the purpose of prompting us to REPENT. Satan accuses us before God—and in our minds—and brings the weight of guilt down on our heads. His idea is to make us feel guilty and unworthy without thinking of repenting and then we are paralyzed. Without forgiveness we feel worthless and we can't live as God intended us to live—for His glory.

Questions To Think About

1. Do you have unconfessed sin in your life? Repent and ask God to forgive you.
2. Has Satan weighed you down with a burden of guilt? Confess your sin and God will forgive you and forget your sin FOREVER!
3. Have you repented, asked for forgiveness, and you still feel guilty? If so remember God has forgiven you so you must forgive yourself. Learn from your mistakes but when you are forgiven LET THEM GO.

August 9

But Daniel purposed in his heart that he would not defile himself. Daniel 1:8

"Purposed in his heart," means that Daniel made a decision. We make a bunch of decisions every day. It starts before we even get out of bed in the morning. When our Mom calls us to get up, we have to decide between staying in bed and obeying her. It's our decision but whichever choice we make there will be consequences. If we choose to stay in bed, we DID NOT OBEY. If we stay in bed we won't have as much time to get ready. We will have to rush around and that puts us in a bad mood because we feel pressured to hurry. On the other hand, if we choose to go ahead and get up, even though we may still be sleepy, we DID OBEY. Plus, we have plenty of time to get ready and we won't feel all that pressure.

Hopefully we all see that the decisions and choices we make determine what happens to us. Just like Daniel, we can make the decision to do what is right, like Jesus wants us to, or we can do what WE WANT to do. However, we will have to deal with what happens when we go our own way instead of the way Jesus would have us go. Let's DARE TO BE A DANIEL and make the wisest choices early in life by doing things GOD'S WAY. We will be so blessed if we do.

QUESTIONS TO THINK ABOUT

1. Are you making WISE CHOICES in your life?
2. Are you being obedient to God's Word?

August 10

O earth, earth, earth, Hear the word of the Lord!
Jeremiah 22:29

God was disappointed that His people continued to sin and that he would have to punish them. He even told them repeatedly through the prophets what would happen if they didn't repent and turn from their sin, but they just wouldn't listen. This is true in our day as well. So much of the time instead of really listening to what God has to say in His Word, we just go about our day and do pretty much whatever we want. We don't stop to look in His Word for direction or if we do read His Word we often don't put into practice what it says.

It's sort of like going out into the woods and thinking in our minds that we know the way back. Suddenly it hits us that we are LOST. This is not a good feeling. This happened to me once and I'll never forget how I started running first one way and then another, but no matter which way I ran it didn't seem to lead out of the trees. Then I realized that if I looked at the SUN peaking through the pines, I could figure out the directions. I knew I had come into the forest from the north, so all I had to do was head north. By doing this I quickly found my way out and boy was I ever relieved.

Without the SON—Jesus—we have no direction. We are just running about first in one direction and then another. Just as God cried out to Judah in Jeremiah's day, today He cries out to us through His Word. Of course, this means that we must pick up our Bibles and study them and ask the Holy Spirit to help us understand His Word. All we need is right there but we have to OPEN the WORD OF GOD and apply it to our lives. Let's read His Word TODAY and HEAR THE WORD OF THE LORD.

Questions To Think About

1. Do you read God's Word consistently?
2. Do you apply what you read to your life?

August 11

"Can anyone hide himself in secret places, so I shall not see him?" says the Lord; "Do I not fill heaven and earth?" says the Lord.
Jeremiah 23:24

It's great fun to play hide and seek. The GAME is great fun, but what the Lord is telling Jeremiah in this verse is that He is OMNIPRESENT. That's a big word meaning that God is everywhere all at the same time. So when we learn that God is OMNIPRESENT we realized that no matter how we try to leave God out of what we do He is always present and hears and sees all. Even when we mutter things under out breath—like the time our feelings were hurt and we just wanted to hit someone—God hears us. Or sometimes when we may not understand why our parents forbid us to do something and we THINK bad things about them—God knows our thoughts.

This truth is very important for us to learn. We need to know that God is always with us—when we are being obedient and when we are being disobedient, when we are in danger or when we are safe, when we are happy or when we are sad, when we are in a crowd of friends or when we are alone. GOD IS ALWAYS WITH US—HE IS OMINIPRESENT. We should be thankful that God is always with us—even when we sin. Why should we be glad about that? We should be glad because when we sin God, knowing all, immediately convicts us of our sin and if we listen to that conviction we will repent immediately. Besides, when we know that God is always with us we might just think twice before we sin in the first place which of course is always good. We should thank God daily for HIS OMNIPRESENCE.

Questions To Think About

1. Do you understand what omnipresent means?
2. Are you thankful that God sees everything and is always with you? Tell Him.

August 12

He has mad the earth by His power; He has established the world by His wisdom, and stretched out the heaven by His understanding. Jeremiah 51:15

Maybe you have seen some of the movies lately with a hero who has tons of special powers. He logically should be killed many times throughout the movie, but he always comes out on top—always the most powerful. Well what is power in the first place? The dictionary says that power is the ability to do something effectively, to have strength, or to control something or someone. These are all aspects of power, but when we talk about God's power it means so much more. God is all-powerful. That means He can do anything and has done so many great things that it is hard to even imagine it all.

In the verse today, Jeremiah talks about how God created the earth with His POWER. Think of everything in nature that has been formed out of nothing by God. You know some kids have the mistaken idea that God is like an old, old man sitting up in heaven somewhere and He isn't doing anything He's just sitting there filling our requests, kind of like Santa Claus. This doesn't paint the picture of anyone who is ALL-POWERFUL does it? It may be hard for you to understand all the power God possesses. So when you watch a thunderstorm and hear the loud crashes and see the long jagged flashes of light and know that He is in control of that storm and everything else that is going on at that exact moment in the entire world, it might help you understand God's power a little better. God is ALL-POWERFUL, yet He loves you and wants you to love Him too. Isn't it awesome that God is so powerful yet He has time for you?

Questions To Think About

1. Do you understand that God is ALL POWERFUL?
2. Have you thanked Him for his Power?

August 13

Moreover He said to me: "Son of man, receive into your heart all My words that I speak to you, and hear with your ears. And go, get to the captives, to the children of your people, and speak to them and tell them, 'Thus says the Lord God,' whether they hear, or whether they refuse." Ezekiel 3:10, 11

Have you ever tried to tell someone about Jesus being your Savior but you couldn't seem to make the other person understand? Or maybe the Lord has done something really special for you and you can't seem to make your friends understand that it didn't "just happen". They don't understand that Jesus has His hand on your life. Well, in today's verse God told Ezekiel to tell rebellious Israel what He would do for them if they would OBEY and what He would do to them if they continued in sin. God told Ezekiel to KNOW His Word and then to speak His Word to them. He told him to do this and that's all that he had to do. Ezekiel was not responsible for the people's belief or unbelief. He was just responsible for telling the people what GOD TOLD HIM TO.

You need to remember this today. You can get really excited when you see Jesus working in your life and you want to tell others about it. And you should. But some of your "friends" may not share in your excitement because the Lord doesn't mean anything to them. If this is the case what should you do? Should you get discouraged and quit telling people about Jesus? NO. You should remember that you must do what is right—in this case that is to give Jesus credit for what He has done for you—and then don't worry about what happens next. It's not your job to MAKE someone respect and love Jesus. It's not your job to MAKE someone ask Jesus into his heart. You are to tell him why he should love and respect Jesus or what Jesus has done for you. You are to tell him how to ask Jesus to be his Savior. BUT THEN YOUR WORK IS DONE. It is in God's hands what happens next. So don't get discouraged. God is taking care of the "results" and you don't have to worry.

Questions To Think About

1. Are you giving God credit and telling others about Jesus but getting discouraged when they don't respond? What should you do about it?

Notes

August 14

Their silver and their gold will not be able to deliver them.
Ezekiel 7:19

In this verse Ezekiel is telling the children of Israel that it doesn't matter how rich they are, their money will not save them when God's judgment falls on them. God's judgment was going to fall because they would not repent and turn from their sin. See, they were rich and they felt like they didn't need God. They thought that all of their silver and all of their gold came from smart business practices. They would not acknowledge that God had given them everything.

We are the same way today. Everything we have comes from God and our nation is very rich like Israel was during Ezekiel's time. However, very few of us really act like we believe that God has given us all we have. When we pray and thank God for our food do we really mean what we say and really understand? If we really did understand wouldn't we be more humble and more grateful and more generous to others who don't have what we have. After all, it ALL BELONGS TO GOD AND COMES FROM HIS HAND. When we get new video games, DVD's, books, or clothes do we REALLY BELIEVE all of the stuff BELONGS TO GOD AND COMES FROM HIS HAND?

Then there is the issue of what we are trusting in. The Israelites were trusting in their silver and gold to buy a big enough army to save them from their enemy. Who are we trusting in to save us from our enemies? Nothing delivers us and gives us victory from our enemies EXCEPT GOD. Having better clothes or shoe or toys or whatever will never deliver us from the enemy of discontentment. When we get these "things" it seems we always want more and getting more doesn't satisfy us. This is because only trusting in Jesus will really satisfy us. Remember, joy comes, not from silver and gold, but from trusting in JESUS.

Questions To Think About

1. Are you truly thankful for everything you have or are you discontent?
2. What are you trusting in?

Notes

August 15

Then I will give them one heart, and I will put a new spirit within them and take the stony heart out of their flesh and give them a heart of flesh. That they may walk in My statutes and keep My judgments and do them; and they shall be My people and I shall be their God. Ezekiel 11:19-20

Do you ever get discouraged and think, "I just can't do this. I can't be good enough for Jesus. I've tried but then I always mess up." I'm sure if you haven't said this out loud, you've thought it in your heart, but that's why these verses are so wonderful. The truth is, YOU CAN'T DO IT. But the Good News is that Jesus can. By this I mean that Jesus can give you a new heart. He also gives you the Holy Spirit to teach you and help you to WALK in His way and KEEP His commandments.

Because you have a new heart you are now ABLE to choose to do what is right every time. But you and I both know from experience that we don't always do what is right. Why? Well, when Jesus put a new heart in you he made you ABLE to do what is right but he didn't make you a puppet. You have a choice. You can choose to do what is right or you can choose to do what is wrong. The Holy Spirit is always with you, telling you what is right, but sometimes you choose not to listen. Each time you choose to ignore God's Word and what is right you "harden your heart" or become less sensitive to God's Word. But when you mess up and you know it—REPENT. God will forgive you.

God promises that when He gives you a new heart he has made it possible for you to choose good over evil. That is what the Scripture is talking about. So now that you have been given a new heart—choose righteousness.

Questions To Think About

1. What does it mean when the Scripture says, "I will . . . take the stony heart out of their flesh and give them a heart of flesh"?
2. Whose fault is it when you sin?

Notes

August 16

Because with lies you have made the heart of the righteous sad, whom I have not made sad; . . . Ezekiel 13:22

I often have a hard time telling if someone is lying. I knew a person who could look me straight in the eye and tell me something that was just not true. LIES ARE TERRIBLE THINGS! In recent years we have found out that some very important people, even some church leaders, have lied about things. So how do we know if someone is telling a lie?

We can become more discerning by praying and by studying God's Word. First, we need to pray for the person who might be lying. Ask God to make the person who lied repent and admit he lied, or if he won't repent that he would be caught in his lie. Second, turn to God's Word. God's Word is TRUTH, so if anything the person says goes against what God's Word says then "he is a liar and the truth is not in him". In addition to this we need to pray for wisdom for ourselves. We need wisdom to know and understand what the Bible says and to recall to our minds what we have learned from God's Word. With wisdom we will probably be able to "see through" what a liar says or we will notice little inconsistencies in his story. Most importantly, if we encounter someone who might be lying to us, we need to go to our parents and tell them all about the situation and ask them for guidance.

Today's Scripture tells us that God's people will encounter false teachers and they need to be wary of them. God tells us another way to know if someone is a false teacher. False teacher's lies make our hearts sad; God's teachings do not. We need to also be careful not to lie ourselves. We must ALWAYS TELL THE TRUTH even if we get in trouble for something we did. Lying just makes things worse and gets us into more trouble.

Questions To Think About

1. How can we become more discerning?
2. Are you careful not to tell lies?

August 17

Your fame went out among the nations because of your beauty, for it was perfect through My splendor which I had bestowed on you," says the Lord God. "But you trusted in your own beauty . . . Ezekiel 15:14-15

In today's Scripture, God reprimands Israel for relying on its beauty rather than on Him. God had blessed Israel and made it prosperous. With this wealth, Israel had been transformed into a beautiful nation with glorious buildings and palaces, a magnificent temple, and gorgeous gardens and fields. God had also blessed the people with beauty and gold and silver to purchase splendid robes and jewelry. So Israel was a beautiful place filled with beautiful people. But God's Word also tells us that God doesn't look at the outside He looks at the heart. What did God see when he looked at Israel's heart? God saw that the Israelites didn't love Him, they weren't grateful for what He had given them, and they thought that all of the wealth and beauty came from the work of their own hands. They were "trusting in their own beauty". God goes on to tell them through Ezekiel that their beauty would not save them from their enemies.

So what can we learn from this Scripture? We can learn the same lesson that Israel should have learned, and that is: What someone looks like on the outside doesn't matter. What matters is his heart. Why is this any big deal—because we need to look at people's hearts too and not just at their outsides. We need to see if the "pretty, popular" person is really nice and good on the inside—or is he/she self-centered and demanding. And maybe the "not-so-pretty" boy or girl is kind and giving. We need to base our decisions about others, and especially our friends, on their "heart" not on what they look like, the clothes they wear, and how much money they have to spend. We also need to remember that we all have the ability to be beautiful if we follow Jesus. So choose friends that are beautiful on the inside and who are trusting in Jesus, not in their own "beauty".

QUESTIONS TO THINK ABOUT

1. Are you trusting in Jesus for your beauty?
2. Have you chosen friends based on inward or outward beauty?

NOTES

August 18

Cast away from you all the transgressions which you have committed, and get yourselves a new heart and a new spirit.
Ezekiel 18:31

This is some really good advice, but the people of Israel wouldn't listen. Ezekiel told the Israelites to repent and ask God to change their proud hearts by giving them a new spirit of humility and thankfulness. This is good advice for us today, but what does it mean?

First of all, casting away our transgressions means to repent of our sins. In other words we need to be truly sorry for the sins we have committed and then ask God to forgive us of those sins. We also need to turn away from those sins and ask God to help us not commit them again.

Then, we need to ask God to put a new attitude in us. What new attitude? We need a humble attitude—the opposite of a self-centered, prideful attitude. We need an attitude of gratitude. We need to be thankful for our salvation through Jesus and for EVERYTHING that God gives us daily. We need to realize that without Jesus we would be and have nothing. So let's ask God to FORGIVE us and GIVE us a NEW HEART and NEW SPIRIT and DON'T PUT IT OFF as the Israelites did.

Questions To Think About

1. Are you forgiven? Do you have a new heart and new spirit?

August 19

Thus says the Lord God: "Exalt the humble, and humble the exalted. Ezekiel 21:26

Have you ever known someone who continually bragged on himself, telling everyone how great he was at something or everything? Have you known someone who thought she was better than everyone else and snubbed everyone except those she ALLOWED to be her friends? These people are not what you would call HUMBLE. So what is humility? Being humble DOES NOT mean that you go around putting yourself down and acting like you can't do anything well and letting people "run over" you. So what is humility?

Being humble means that you don't think of yourself at all. You see when you are putting yourself down or saying things like, "I'm not really very good at this," it is still all about YOU. You are still focused on yourself. You are still saying "I" can or can't. This is "false" humility. Truly humble people are those who don't think about themselves because they are continually thinking about others or about God's righteousness.

For example, when David was a "youth", he came to the army camp of King Saul. While he was there he heard Goliath mocking God. He also saw how all the men of Israel were afraid to go out and fight the giant because they were all afraid they would be killed. They were all thinking about themselves—this is NOT HUMILITY. But David rose up in righteous anger and said, " . . . who is this uncircumcised Philistine, that he should defy the armies of the living God?" David wasn't afraid because he wasn't thinking about himself, he was thinking about God's honor and glory that were being mocked. You know the rest of the story. So you get the picture, being humble is not being a doormat or being timid or being weak. Being humble is thinking, "What would God or Jesus think or do in this situation" and then doing it. It's focusing on Jesus or others and not on yourself. So if we HUMBLE ourselves God will exalt or use us like he did David—in a mighty way.

Questions To Think About

1. What does it mean to be humble?
2. Are you humble?

Notes

August 20

And the Lord God of their fathers sent warnings to them by His messengers, rising up early and sending them, because He had compassion on His people and on His dwelling place. But they mocked the messengers of God, despised His words, and scoffed at His prophets . . . II Chronicles 36:15-16

Let's look at three of the verbs in today's Scripture: MOCKED, DESPISED, and SCOFFED. These verbs tell what the people of Jerusalem did to God's prophets. God sent the prophets to warn the people that if they didn't REPENT and turn from their wicked ways He would JUDGE them. God sent the prophets because he was compassionate and He loved the people even though they MOCKED, DESPISED, and SCOFFED at His messengers, which is really mocking, despising, and scoffing at God.

We still have mockers and despisers and scoffers today. In fact, we have probably all encountered them. They are kids or adults who say things like, "Look at those Christian kids. They all think they're so good, always going to church and talking about Jesus. I hate those Jesus freaks." Or "I hate the way they won't do anything "fun" (they mean wrong)." Or "Those idiots keep cramming that 'God created the world' crud down our throats. They know it's all a big hoax. Science proved that man evolved. I don't know what their problem is, I mean they're living in the Dark Ages."

When we encounter these people as we are witnessing in word or deed, we need to remember that the prophets of old endured the same thing. In fact, Jesus himself endured being MOCKED, DESPISED, and SCOFFED at. So HANG in there and remember, we are doing what God's prophets and Jesus himself did—fighting the good fight. So BOLDLY share the GOOD NEWS.

Questions To Think About

1. Have you been mocked, despised, or scoffed at because of your faith?
2. How did you handle the situation? Would you do the same thing again?

Notes

August 21

Praise the Lord of hosts, for the Lord is good, for His mercy endures forever. Jeremiah 33:11

I can remember waiting on my Mom and Dad to come pick me up after school and sometimes it took them longer than I thought it should. I thought, "Man, it's taking them FOREVER." We say FOREVER frequently, but do we really know how long forever is? Let's think about it for just a moment. FOREVER means from now on and that's a long, long time. What we often don't realize is that it doesn't just mean the future. Forever means the past as well. It means all the way back when it was only God, Jesus, and the Holy Spirit. Now let's think again about how long FOREVER is. The reason it's important for us to know that FOREVER is more than we can comprehend is because the Lord is GOOD and MERCIFUL FOREVER.

God's Word tells us that He is GOOD and MERCIFUL FOREVER, so we never have to worry about His goodness and mercy running out just when it gets to us. We can ALWAYS depend on Jesus and know that all His promises in the Bible are there for US even though we live some 2000 years after He was here on earth. This should make us thankful! Let's praise Him as Jeremiah says—our Lord is GREAT and MIGHTY.

QUESTIONS TO THINK ABOUT

1. How long is forever? Why is it important?
2. Are you praising God for all He has done for you?

August 22

. . . then you shall know that I am the Lord. Ezekiel 25:5

Have you ever been introduced to someone at school or church or maybe on vacation? You know his name but not much more. He is just a slight acquaintance, not really a friend. Now if you come into contact with that person a number of times, write him letters, or see him every day at school, you become a little more familiar with him. You learn his likes and dislikes and maybe even information about his family. But if you really get to KNOW him and he becomes a close friend of yours it might prove to be a relationship that will last forever.

In today's Scripture the Lord is telling the Israelites that this is the type of relationship He wants to have with them—an intimate, close friendship. He says that He knows they have heard of Him, after all they have the Scriptures—the Pentateuch. He knows they have seen and read about miracles that He has performed for them like crossing the Red Sea, the fall of Jericho, and many more. They know more about Him than just His name so He is more than just a passing acquaintance. However, He also knows that they do not have that close friendship that He wants to have with them. What's more they really don't want that friendship which involves worshiping and serving Him alone. They have been disobedient people going against everything that the Lord has commanded them to do or not to do and He is getting ready to punish them. This is why God says over and over again through Ezekiel, "Then you shall know that I am the Lord."

Isn't it too bad that they will not acknowledge Him as their Lord after He has been so good to them? Because of their rebellion God is going to have to judge and punish them. Let's pray that we will not be like the Israelites who ignored God and His Word even though they had easy access to it. Let's pray that our relationship with the Lord is close and strong, one of joy, obedience, worship, and that we will KNOW THAT HE IS LORD all the days of our lives.

QUESTIONS TO THINK ABOUT

1. Do you have a close friendship with the Lord?
2. What can you do to make that relationship even better?

NOTES

August 23

. . . What city is like Tyre, destroyed in the midst of the sea?
Ezekiel 26:32

Tyre was a great city in Ezekiel's day. It had great wealth and a busy trading business with Israel and other nations. But Tyre was a pagan city that worshiped a heathen god—Baal. Ezekiel said that the Lord would destroy the city. The people made fun of Ezekiel and called him crazy because no one though that anything bad could ever happen to the great and wealthy city of Tyre. However, Tyre was eventually conquered and it never amounted to much again.

The Bible tells us that God will not be mocked. This means that any nation, state, city, or person who trusts in anything except the Lord, will eventually fall. The Good News is that when we put our trust in Jesus and He lives in our hearts He will never ever leave us. Things on this earth come and go—look at all the mighty nations down through history that have ruled the whole world and have fallen. The only thing that is FOREVER, as we talked about a few lessons back, is GOD. So let's PUT OUR TRUST IN JESUS WHERE WE KNOW IT IS SAFE.

Questions To Think About

1. What or whom are you trusting in?

August 24

Thus says the Lord. Do not deceive yourselves. Jeremiah 37:9

Have you ever wanted to believe something so badly that even when you really knew it wasn't true you tried to convince yourself it was. Sort of like the time you planned for two months to go to an amusement park on a certain day. About a week before the departure date arrive the weatherman started predicting that it would rain the day you were to go. You refused to believe it. You had planned and looked forward to this trip for so long you just wouldn't accept the idea that it was going to rain out your trip. Every day that week the weatherman kept saying that it would rain on YOUR DAY but you still said to yourself, "It isn't going to rain, it isn't going to rain." The day finally arrived. You jumped out of bed, threw back the curtains and saw a torrent of water rushing down the window. A giant lightning bolt lit up the sky and that horrendous crack of thunder followed. The trip was off.

This is exactly what Jeremiah was trying to tell the king of Judah. Jeremiah said that the King DECEIVED himself. Because he didn't want the Chaldeans to destroy Jerusalem and he kept saying it wouldn't happen, the King had convinced himself that Jerusalem would not be destroyed. BUT GUESS WHAT! The Chaldeans did destroy Jerusalem and the people of Judah were carried off into captivity.

We probably all know people who say, "Jesus isn't the ONLY way to get to heaven. You just have to be as good as you can and God will understand. He knows that we aren't perfect. Besides, I'm pretty good." These people are DECEIVING themselves because being "good" has nothing to do with us getting into Heaven. I can hear it now, "You're saying we don't have to be good?" "NO." I'm saying that being good has nothing to do with our salvation. We are saved because we TRUST in JESUS; we trust in His death to pay for our sins. HE IS THE ONLY

WAY TO THE FATHER. We are "good" after we are saved because we love Jesus and want to do the good works He has set before us to do. What a blessing we know the TRUTH and are not DECEIVED. Pray for those who don't know the truth. Ask God to open their eyes and their hearts to His Good News.

Questions To Think About

1. What is the Good News?
2. Are you deceived or do you know that JESUS IS THE ONLY WAY?
3. Are you praying for those who don't know about Jesus?

Notes

August 25

The Lord is good to those who wait for Him,
to the soul who seeks Him. Lamentations 3:25

We live in a world where we always seem to be in a hurry for something to happen—we can hardly wait for anything. We can hardly wait to get a new bike, we can hardly wait for whatever holiday, we can hardly wait for our friend to get to spend the night, we can hardly wait to become a teen-ager, and when we become a teenager we can hardly wait until we're "on our own". We all have a tendency to want everything RIGHT NOW! Let's STOP for a minute. Remember that God has a plan for each of our lives? Remember that he wants us to be still and wait on Him—on His plan? Why?—because His plan is the very BEST PLAN for us.

As our Scripture tells us today, if we go to the Lord and ask Him to lead us, He will honor our request. He will be *good to those who wait for Him, to the soul who seeks Him.* I'm SOOOO glad He loves us and wants to watch over us. So let's STOP rushing and wishing our lives away and BE STILL and WAIT UPON THE LORD.

QUESTIONS TO THINK ABOUT

1. Are you rushing through life or waiting on the Lord?

August 26

. . . *He will uncover your sins!* Lamentations 4:22

We know from Scripture that we have all sinned and fallen short of the glory of God, so let's talk a little bit about sin today. Isn't it strange that when we sin we always want to hide it or deny that we did it? Even though we KNOW that Jesus sees everything we do and knows every thought that we think we STILL TRY TO HIDE OUR SIN. Usually when we try to hide our sin we have to lie so no one will find out about it.

For example, let's say your Mom just told you not to eat any more candy before supper. Those luscious rich chocolate pieces are just sitting there tempting you. Chocolate is your favorite thing in the whole world, or that's what you tell yourself at the moment. Then you think, "Mom won't know if I have just one more piece." So you decide to take the candy. You run into the bedroom and open your treasure and stuff the smooth creamy chocolate into your mouth just as Mom calls you to supper. You quickly hide the wrapper under the other papers in your trashcan and smugly head for the dining room. However, because you stuffed the whole piece of candy into your mouth and it didn't quite fit a little bit of chocolate flaked off and landed right on your chin. You know the rest of the story before I even tell it. Your Mom sees the chocolate on your chin and confronts you about it. You're bewildered—"How can she know?"—You deny everything—Your Mom points out the chocolate on your chin—your "crime" is uncovered.

God has given all Christians a very special and important gift—the gift of the Holy Spirit. The Holy Spirit lives in our hearts and teaches us the truths we find in God's Word and convicts us when we sin. Thanks to the Holy Spirit convicting us we know when we have done something wrong and we can never hide our sin from Him, HE WILL UNCOVER OUR SINS. This conviction is a great blessing because when we sin we break our perfect fellowship with the Lord, but when the Holy Spirit uncovers our sin we know we need to REPENT and ask God to forgive us and restore us to a right relationship with Him. So let's PRAISE GOD that *He will uncover our sins.*

Questions To Think About

1. Do you have any known sin in your life? Have you asked God to forgive you?
2. What does God say will happen when we try to cover up our sins? What should this truth teach us?

Notes

August 27

We will obey the voice of the Lord our God to whom we send you, that it may be well with us when we obey the voice of the Lord our God. Jeremiah 42:6

Will we ever learn? Time after time in the Bible, the Lord tells us that if we obey, good things will happen to us. It seems that after hearing this over and over we would be more obedient, but . . . We can all remember a time when we did something we shouldn't have and got into trouble. Being disciplined is a terrible feeling. I can remember saying, "If I ever get out of this mess, I will NEVER do that again." But the truth is, I disobeyed again and again and that terrible feeling was back again.

On the other hand, when we are walking in obedience we have PEACE. It feels so wonderful. It seems we would obey for no other reason than that, but our flesh is weak. That is why we need to do everything we can to place ourselves in a position to make it easier to obey. What does that mean? First, we can surround ourselves with friends who are also trying to be obedient to Christ. The support that we get when we have a close friend who is following the Lord can help us stay on target. Next, we should not be slack in reading our Bible, praying and regularly attending worship services. These things help us to remember what we are aiming for. Then we must act out our faith. This means, once we learn what the Bible teaches us to do and pray for faith and grace to accomplish those things, we ACT. Knowing we are DOING what is good and right is a wonderful feeling. Keep up the good work.

Questions To Think About

1. Are you feeling at peace today? If not, why?
2. What can you do to improve your obedience?

August 28

So they come to you as people do, they sit before you as My people, and they hear your words, but they do not do them: for with their mouth they show much love, but their hearts pursue their own gain. Ezekiel 33:31

Do you go to church every time the doors are open? That's great if you do, but there is more to the Christian life than just going and sitting in church and having a good time. There is even more to the Christian life than saying how much you love the Lord. This is what Ezekiel was trying to get across to the people of Judah. He said the people would come and listen and would even say they loved the Lord with their mouths, BUT THEY DID NOT DO what Ezekiel told them to do; in their hearts they pursued their own plans.

Everyone needs to take this Scripture seriously. Have you thought about how you act outside of church? Do you act like Jesus would want you to act ALL THE TIME? Do you only hear with your ears the words the pastor or Sunday school teachers say but never take them to heart? Or do you HEAR THE WORD, LISTEN TO IT, AND APPLY IT TO EVERYTHING IN YOUR LIFE? If you do HEAR, LISTEN, and APPLY, you will act the same when you are in or out of church, you will act the same when your parents are present or not present, you will act the same in every situation—you will do what Jesus would want you to do. Remember that if you claim to know Jesus but do not ACT LIKE YOU KNOW JESUS, then you are not being honest with others or yourself. You won't be perfect, but Jesus living in your heart will change the way you act.

Questions To Think About

1. Have you checked to see how you act in church and out of church? Is it the same?
2. Have you asked yourself if you act the same in front of your parents or when they are not present? Is it the same?
3. If you don't act the same way all the time what will you do about it?

August 29

. . . and I will not let them profane My holy name anymore.
Ezekiel 39:7

The dictionary defines profane as, "to put to an improper, unworthy, or degrading use; to abuse." Have you ever noticed how many times a day you hear people use God's name as a curse word? You hear it on TV, on the playground, on the bus, at the movies, and just walking down the street. You never hear anyone say, "Oh Buddha!" Or "Oh Allah!" Have you ever wondered why people say "God" or "Jesus" when they are angry, excited, or surprised? It is because the name of God is HOLY and the world wants to profane anything that has any authority over it. In order to "bring God down", the world tries to debase His holy name. This means that the people of the world think they can make God seem insignificant and unimportant if they use God's name in an unholy way.

So, the next time you hear a person using God's name in a profane or unholy way, ask the Holy Spirit to help you confront the person in a loving and godly manner. Pray that the person will repent of this sin and turn away from using God's name in an unholy way. And remember, you must always be an example to others, especially in this area.

Questions To Think About

1. What does it mean to "profane" God's holy name?
2. Do you use God's name in vain? If you do, what are you going to do about it?

August 30

. . . and they saw these men on whose bodies the fire had no power; the hair of their head was not singed nor were their garments affected, and the smell of fire was not on them.
Daniel 3:27

We have all heard the account of Shadrach, Meshach, and Abed-Nego the young Hebrew men who would not bow down and worship an idol the King of Babylon had made. Their refusal made the King so angry that he put them in a furnace heated seven times hotter than usual. They told the King that they believed God would protect them, but even if He didn't, they still wouldn't bow down and worship anyone or anything but God. This story is awesome not only because God protected these young men from death, but because when the guards took them out of the fire, they didn't even smell like smoke.

In today's Scripture we learn that if we are God's child He will never forsake us or abandon us no matter how impossible our circumstances seem at the time. In addition, God will not only walk with us through the "fires of life", He will even keep our clothes from smelling like smoke. In other words, we will come through our trials and tests as glorious victors. We will not "smell of fire" but will be more like Jesus. We will not be joyless lumps of burned out clay, we will "shine" with the light of Jesus in our lives.

When gold is found in rocks it has many impurities in it, sort of like us. In order to remove the impurities, the gold must be heated to high temperatures to "burn off" all the worthless junk in it. After going through the fire, the gold is beautiful and pure, reflecting a golden light in every direction. This is exactly what God is doing with us when we go through life's "fires"—He is burning off the junk in our lives to make us beautiful and pure, reflecting the light of Jesus to those all around us.

Questions To Think About

1. What is the significance of the young men not even smelling like fire when they were removed from the furnace?
2. When you go through a trial do you come out of it "smelling like fire" or do you look more like Jesus?

Notes

August 31

The Spirit lifted me up and brought me into the inner court; and behold the glory of the Lord filled the temple. Ezekiel 43:5

In this Scripture God showed Ezekiel the temple of the Lord in a vision. Ezekiel describes what he saw in detail in the next several chapters, but what we want to look at today is the last part of this verse—"behold the glory of the Lord filled the temple." Things have changed since Ezekiel saw this vision. Now, the temple of the Lord is not a building, it is WITHIN US. The Bible tells us that believers' bodies are the temple of the Holy Spirit. I know this is hard to imagine, but what we need to focus on here is that even when the temple was a building, God's glory was in it and as believers; God, in the person of the Holy Spirit actually lives in us.

Jesus sent the Holy Spirit after His resurrection, to comfort us and to open our minds and hearts so we could understand what the Scriptures teach. What a glorious truth! Let's praise God for His loving care, for sending His Son to pay for our sin, and for sending us His Holy Spirit to indwell us.

Questions To Think About

1. Do you praise God frequently for His blessings?
2. Spend time in prayer today just thanking God for all He has done for us.

September 1

. . . *and they shall hallow My Sabbaths.* Ezekiel 44:24b

In this Scripture, God is teaching His people the laws for their new temple. He tells them to "hallow" My Sabbaths. The word "hallow" means to make holy and set apart as holy. So God is reminding the Israelites of the Fourth Commandment, "Remember the Sabbath to keep it holy."

Back in the days when God gave the Israelites the Ten Commandments, they worshipped on the seventh day of the week because that is the day that God rested when he finished creating the earth and everything in it. God rested, which means he stopped creating new things out of nothing, He "hallowed" the seventh day, and then He commanded men to keep the day holy. After Jesus our Savior came to earth, died on the cross, and rose from the dead, the Christian church changed the day of rest and worship to Sunday. As Christians we celebrate Jesus' victory over sin and death by worshipping Him on the first day of the week—the day he arose—Sunday.

Some people call Sunday the Christian Sabbath. By this they mean that we need to take Sunday and set it aside as a day to worship and glorify God, and rest from our work. Sunday should be the highlight of our week because it is the day we get to spend worshipping God with our fellow believers. We should prepare ourselves for Sunday by getting a good night's sleep Saturday night. When we stay up too late on Saturday it is hard to drag ourselves out of bed on Sunday morning and we are tempted not to go to church at all. In addition, when we are sleepy and tired, we can't pay attention to the pastor and we can't participate in worship with all our mind and heart. There are times when we can't go to church on Sunday, but when that happens we should still try to set aside the day to worship and glorify our Lord. We will be so blessed when we "hallow" the Sabbath.

Questions To Think About

1. What does hallow mean?
2. What is the Sabbath?
3. Do you keep the Sabbath?

September 2

. . . *The sanctuary of the lord shall be in the center.*
Ezekiel 48:10

In today's Scripture, the Lord is describing the plan for the new Temple, its boundaries, and allotment of land. He instructs the people to put the sanctuary of the Lord in the CENTER of the building and the building in the center of Jerusalem. We might think, "That's nice, but what does that have to do with US?" It has lots to do with us because it is a picture that still applies to us today.

The sanctuary of the Lord was where the worship of God took place. God told the people to build it in the CENTER to remind them that the worship of God was to be CENTRAL to their lives—everything else in their lives was to revolve around this center. This means that God and our worship of Him should be at the center of our lives today. When we push aside our time of worship and neglect to praise the Lord, pray to Him, and live for Him, we are taking God from the CENTER of our lives and putting our own selfish desires in the CENTER. It is so easy to get off track just like the people of the Old Testament. We need to stay on track by keeping the Lord at the CENTER of all we do, say, and think. We can do this by studying our Bibles, praying, listening to our parents, pastors, and Sunday school teachers. And when we mess up, we need to repent and ask God to forgive us. He will. Let's remember the Temple and keep Jesus at the center of our lives.

QUESTIONS TO THINK ABOUT

1. Is Jesus at the CENTER of your world?

September 3

But at last Daniel came before me, in him is the Spirit of the Holy God and I told the dream before him, saying . . . I know that the Spirit of the Holy God is in you and no secret troubles you, explain to me the visions of my dream that I have seen, and its interpretation. Daniel 4:8

This Scripture is talking about Daniel who interpreted Nebuchadnezzar's dream, and it reveals a great deal about Daniel. This verse tells us what Nebuchadnezzar thought about Daniel. He knew that the Holy Spirit lived in Daniel because of the way he acted. He was different from other men. Nebuchadnezzar knew that nothing bothered Daniel because Daniel always turned everything over to God and trusted Him to take care of it. Wouldn't it be great to trust God so much that we wouldn't worry about anything? We all say we want to trust in this way but then worry creeps into our lives without us even realizing it. God doesn't want us to worry about things—that means He doesn't want us to be concerned about things that we can't control. For example, when we move to a new neighborhood we shouldn't worry about whether or not the kids will like us. If we are Christians and act like it, whether the kids like us or not is beyond our control. We shouldn't worry—we should pray and trust the Lord to work out the situation for our good. We need to learn from Daniel's example—obey God and then trust Him to take care of us.

Questions To Think About

1. Are you worried? How can you become more like Daniel?

September 4

So we, Your people and sheep of Your pasture, will give You thanks forever; We will show forth Your praise to all generations.
Psalm 79:13

This Scripture has two important points we need to look at. First, it says that if we are Christians we will GIVE THANKS. Like most people, we feel good when someone says THANK YOU for something we have done. God enjoys hearing our THANKS too. He does so many things for us each and every day, from bringing the sun up each morning to seeing us safely in bed at night and everything between. We have a limitless number of things we could and should thank God for daily.

The second thing we need to see in this Scripture is—if we are Christians we will PRAISE God. We can praise God by singing, praying, and proclaiming the truths of His Word. There are many ways to PRAISE GOD FROM WHOM ALL BLESSINGS FLOW. So lets THANK God for His gifts to us and PRAISE Him for His many blessings.

QUESTIONS TO THINK ABOUT

1. Can you sing The Doxology (Praise God from Whom all blessings flow)?
2. Can you read Psalm 150 aloud and mean each word?

September 5

But they mingled with the Gentiles and learned their works.
Psalm 106:35

The dictionary definition of "mingled" is, "to mix or bring together in close association; to combine." The Israelites were not supposed to "mingle" with the Gentiles, but as this Scripture says, they didn't obey God. They went right ahead and mingled with the Gentiles. The Gentiles were pagan people who worshipped all kinds of things and for the most part didn't know or even want to know anything about the TRUE GOD. This is why God didn't want his people to mingle with them. He knew that if they did associate with the Gentiles they would start acting like them and they would forget God, and of course, this is exactly what they did.

Have you ever noticed that when you hang around someone who has a certain mannerism or way of talking that before long you are doing the same thing or talking the same way? Let's take the High Five for example. Someone started that whole craze and before long EVERYBODY was "High Fiving". Or maybe you remember hearing someone say, "Make my day." At one time this was a common phrase—EVERYBODY was saying it. People have a tendency to do and say what the people around them are doing and saying, this is why God didn't want His people hanging out with "gentiles" or pagans.

This doesn't mean that you are supposed to stay away from unsaved people or isolate yourself from everyone in the world who isn't a Christian. Jesus said you are to be IN the world but not OF the world. In other words you don't spend lots of time with unsaved people and you don't have non-Christians as close friends. You need to be witnessing to the non-Christians and if they become a Christian, then you befriend them and help them grow. So be sure the kids you hang around with are living for Christ like you are and then help the non-Christians meet Jesus too.

Questions To Think About

1. What does it mean to be IN the world but not OF the world?

September 6

TEKEL: You have been weighed in the balances and found wanting; . . . Daniel 5:27

This verse tells about Belshazzar the evil king of Babylonia. He reigned about 42 years after Nebuchadnezzar's death when Daniel was still a captive of Babylon. He was having a party and he called for all the gold and silver cups and vessels that Nebuchadnezzar had taken from the Temple in Jerusalem to be brought from the storehouse so he and his family and guests could drink from them. While they were drinking a hand suddenly appeared and wrote on the wall: *MENE, MENE, TEKEL UPHARSIN.* No one at the party, including the king, could interpret the meaning of the words. Eventually Daniel was called in and asked to interpret the message from the "hand of God". He did interpret—THE HANDWRITING ON THE WALL—and it was BAD NEWS for the king. Daniel told the king that he had been judged by God and had not measured up; he would be overthrown and his kingdom would be divided between the Medes and the Persians. That very night the Medes conquered Babylon, Belshazzar was killed, and Darius the Mede took over.

Wouldn't it be terrible to wake up some morning as the sun's rays peeked through the blinds in the room and realize that the rays formed a word on the wall across from the window? "TEKEL: You have been weighed in the balances, and found wanting!" This is exactly what shines on the walls of our hearts without Jesus. The Bible says that ALL of us have been checked out and there is NOT ONE of us that can make the grade. No matter what we do on OUR OWN, nothing is GOOD ENOUGH to earn us a place in Heaven. Until Jesus gives us a new heart and His righteousness, we are weighed and "found wanting". Jesus took all of His children's sins on Himself and paid for every single one. What a relief to know that we don't have to pay for our sins because Jesus already did.

But some kids still think they can be GOOD ENOUGH to get to Heaven on their own. They think because they never killed anyone they are okay. Help them out! Show them in the Bible that we have all been in the same boat—NONE of us can be good enough. We can only get to Heaven to live with Jesus forever by trusting in Him and His death on the cross and His righteousness. Just think, we can live with the KING OF THE UNIVERSE and call Him FATHER. Now that's GOOD NEWS—Spread it!

Questions To Think About

1. What does it mean to be "weighed in the balances and found wanting"? To whom does this refer? Does it apply to us today? How?
2. Are you spreading the GOOD NEWS?

Notes

September 7

And I prayed to the Lord my God and made confession, and said, "O Lord, great and awesome God who keeps His covenant and mercy with those who love Him and with those who keep His commandments, we have sinned." . . . Daniel 9:4

Probably one of the hardest things we ever have to do is to ADMIT WE HAVE SINNED. How many times have we found ourselves telling a LIE because we didn't want to "fess up" to something we did that was wrong? But we also know that not going to God and confessing our sins makes things even worse. It's sort of like being on a hill when the grass is slick with dew or snow and no matter how hard we try to get up the hill we can't make it—with each step we loose our footing and slide back to the bottom. This is what it's like to have sin in our lives.

So how do we take care of our sin? First, we recognize that we have sinned and confess that sin to God. Then, we repent or turn away from that sin. After this, we ask God and anyone who might have been hurt by our sin to forgive us. Yes, if our sin hurts someone else we must ask him to forgive us too. In addition, if we can make restitution for the sin we must. Restitution means fixing the sin or repairing the damage done by the sin. Sometimes there is nothing we can do to repair our sin, but much of the time there is something we can do. For example, a cashier hands us too much change when we buy something, if we don't give back the extra money she will not balance at the end of the day and will have to make up the difference herself. If it is a big mistake she might even loose her job, all because we think we are "lucky" to get to keep money that isn't ours. What should we do? If we give the extra change back immediately we haven't sinned at all. Or, if we don't think about the amount until later and then realize it is too much and take it back, that's not a sin either. But, if we know all along that we got back extra money and we keep the change we have actually taken something that isn't ours. We must repent by giving back the extra change and confess that we sinned. Remember that Jesus said, "If you love Me, keep My commandments."

Questions To Think About

1. What happens to us when we have unconfessed sin in our lives? What can we do about it?
2. What does it mean to "make restitution"?

Notes

September 8

Then He said to me: "Son of man, go to the house of Israel and speak with My words to them. Ezekiel 3:4

Do you get nervous and tongue tied when you try to tell someone about Jesus? In today's Scripture, God tells us what to do to overcome these problems. God told Ezekiel to speak "My Words". This is still the best advice today.

If we want to let our friends know that everyone needs Jesus, we need to show them Romans 3:23, "For all have sinned and fall short of the glory of God." Explain that we are all in the same boat just like the verse says—ALL have sinned against God. Next, let's look at Romans 6:23, "For the wages of sin is death, but the gift of God is eternal life in Christ Jesus our Lord." This verse means that sin equals death. Move on to John 3:16, "For God so loved the world that He gave His only Son that whoever believes in Him should not perish but have everlasting life." Jesus gives us life for death. Next, let's read Romans 10:9, "That if you confess with your mouth the Lord Jesus and believe in your heart that God has raised Him from the dead, you will be saved." So, we must confess and believe. Lastly, find John 10:28, "And I give them eternal life, and they shall never perish; neither shall anyone snatch them out of My hand." This verse says that whoever belongs to Jesus can never be lost again.

This isn't so hard, is it? There are many other verses we can use in place of or in addition to these. The point is the Word of God is LIVING and can work in people's hearts. We don't have to be nervous or worry about saying the wrong thing. LET GOD'S WORD SPEAK FOR ITSELF. It worked in Old Testament days and it will work for us today.

Questions To Think About

1. Do you have a plan for sharing Jesus with others? If so, are you using God's Word when you share?
2. Can you learn the verses or references you need to share the Good News with others?

September 9

And he said, "O man greatly beloved, fear not! Peace be to you; be strong, yes, be strong!" *Daniel 10:19*

This is great advice and we can learn a few things from this Scripture. The first thing we learn from this verse is that as a believer in Jesus we are GREATLY LOVED. Wow! Isn't it wonderful to be GREATLY LOVED by Jesus? Then we learn that we don't have to be afraid. Most of us spend way too much time being afraid of things that never happen. God says that we don't have to worry or be afraid of things because He is in control of everything. So, the next time we're afraid we need to call on God to strengthen us and give us the blessings of courage and peace like Daniel. (Think of Daniel in the lion's den!) When we pray, we need to REALLY BELIEVE that Jesus will take care of us; He promises that He will and He always keeps his promises.

Daniel was told twice to "be strong". Maybe this means to be strong in both our physical and spiritual lives. It's good to discipline ourselves in every area of our lives. It seems that being disciplined in one area helps make us strong in other areas as well. In other words we need to be strong enough to discipline ourselves to study our Bibles so that we know what we believe and why. We need to be strong enough to stand up and speak the truth even if all those around us are opposed to what we are saying. So, "Stand strong. Yes, be strong," and the blessing of PEACE will be ours.

Questions To Think About

1. What does it mean to us to be GREATLY LOVED by Jesus?
2. What is it worth to have PEACE?
3. How can we grow in strength?

September 10

Yet now be strong, Zerubbabel, says the Lord: and be strong, Joshua, son of Jehozadak, the high priest; and be strong, all you people of the land, says the Lord and work; for I am with you, says the Lord of hosts. Haggai 2:4

In our last lesson we read about being strong, and today, God is repeating the same message in this Scripture. He is including ALL the people of the land, which means kids too. Besides being strong, this Scripture goes on to tell the people to WORK. The working part also means all the people of the land. The children of Israel are in the process of rebuilding the walls of Jerusalem and they must be strong—as in courageous—and WORK.

Sometimes kids think that what they are doing right now is not WORK. They imagine what line of work they will go into WHEN THEY GROW UP. But work is not just going to a job. Work is accomplishing the task set before us and when we do everything "as unto the Lord"; we are obeying and bringing glory to God. For example when we do our homework we have accomplished something so we have worked. When we bake cookies or take out the trash we have accomplished something so we have worked. When we study our Bible and memorize Scripture we have accomplished something so we have worked. Even when we are kind and help our neighbor we have accomplished something so we have worked. By working with a good attitude and diligently we bring glory and honor to our Lord. And, the most terrific part of this Scripture is that God PROMISES that HE IS WITH US. Jesus will help us to bring honor and glory to the Father and Himself by helping us be obedient.

QUESTIONS TO THINK ABOUT

1. What is work?
2. How do we bring honor and glory to God through our work?

September 11

And this shall come to pass if you diligently obey the Lord your God. Zechariah 6:15

What a wonderful promise. But there are three things that we need to see in this Scripture that are very important to its meaning. First, the key word in the verse is OBEY. We have talked repeatedly about this word because it is in the Bible so much and obedience is not something that comes naturally to people. We sometimes feel that obedience ties us down and hinders us from pursuing what we want. But this word is not only the key word in this verse it is the key to a happy rewarding life. Obedience is not something God commands in His Word to keep us under His thumb; it is what is best for us. Everything that God requires of us is for our own good.

This verse also says *THIS SHALL COME TO PASS*. What does THIS mean? In the context of the Scripture it is a promise from the Lord to His people who are rebuilding the temple in Jerusalem. Remember that Solomon's Temple was destroyed when Nebuchadnezzar conquered Judah and most of the people were carried off into exile in Babylon. When the Medes conquered Babylon they agreed to let the Israelites return to Jerusalem and their land. The first thing they were instructed by God to do was to rebuild the Temple and the city walls around Jerusalem. In this verse God is promising them that if they *diligently OBEY* Him, they will accomplish the task of rebuilding the city walls and the temple. So what does THIS mean for us today? First let's talk about the third element we need to examine in this verse.

The verse has a very little word that makes ALL the difference in the world—IF. It says *IF you diligently OBEY the LORD YOUR GOD.* This is definitely tied with what THIS means to us today just as it was back in the Old Testament. The verse is saying that IF we OBEY God's commands then any task He sets before us we will accomplish. So any time we set out to do anything for God's glory and in obedience to His Word, we WILL SUCCEED. WOW! What a glorious promise.

QUESTIONS TO THINK ABOUT

1. Why does God want us to obey Him?
2. What glorious promise is contained in this Scripture?
3. Are you walking in obedience to God's Word?

NOTES

September 12

. . . show mercy and compassion everyone to his brother.
Zechariah 7:9

As Christians we have been shown incomprehensible mercy from the Lord. I am so thankful that God has shown mercy to us instead of giving us what we deserve, which is eternal death. Even though we have been shown incredible mercy, too often we cannot show mercy ourselves. It takes a BIG person to forgive someone for wronging him and it seems almost impossible to forget the wrong. But God commands His children to show mercy and compassion to their brothers as the verse says.

If this is a "big deal" to God, then we need to do it, so how do we show mercy and compassion? One way to show mercy is for us to truly forgive others who have wronged us by forgetting the wrong and never bringing it up again. Compassion is caring about others—the golden rule in action. Too many times we don't try to understand how other people feel because we are too concerned about ourselves. So let's get our focus off of US and focus on someone in need. And, let's forget all those things we have stored in the back of our minds even though we told our friends and family we have forgiven them. Remember, God has forgiven us infinitely more.

Questions To Think About

1. Do you have "stored-up" wrongs in the back of your head? Will you forget them? Ask God to help you.

September 13

This is the day the LORD has made: We will rejoice and be glad in it. Psalm 118:24

How are you feeling this morning? Are you saying to yourself, "Whoa, I don't even want to get up today. I have all that homework that I didn't do last night and if I go to school I know my teacher's just going to pick on me like she always does—I can't seem to do anything right in her eyes. Oh yah, and there are those kids that don't like me and are always saying bad stuff about me—nobody likes me. I wish I lived some place far away from here and went to a different school, then things would be better."

If you really feel this way you need to look UP instead of AROUND. The Lord Himself made this day and there is a reason you are experiencing all of these things. Perhaps it's partially your own fault. Whatever the reason—and you may not know for a long time and maybe never—you need to quit seeing only the bad and ask the Lord to show you the good in the day. Maybe you can pray a prayer something like this, "Father, show me what I am to learn from this experience and help me to take my eyes off of myself and my feelings and help someone else who is worse off than me. Lord, thank you for this day that you have made." Remember, as a Christian you are to give thanks in every circumstance. So go forth, rejoice, and be glad today no matter what happens, because joy is not a "feeling", it is a choice.

QUESTIONS TO THINK ABOUT

1. Are you feeling "down" this morning?
2. How should a Christian respond?
3. Is there any sin in your life that might be causing some of your troubles? If so, repent and ask God to forgive you. If not, choose to be joyful today.

September 14

As the mountains surround Jerusalem, so the Lord surrounds His people . . . Psalm 125:2

Mountains surround the city of Jerusalem. That is one of the reasons the people originally decided to build a city there—built in defenses. The mountains protected the city and this verse tells us that God protects His people.

When God tells us that he will protect us He means it and nothing can hurt us. We might ask, "Then why do bad things happen to good people sometimes." Well, first of all, we don't know the person's heart and they may not actually be one of God's children. They might be going through the motions of being good because that is the way they were brought up, but they might never have been saved.

However, sometimes what we think of as "bad things" do happen to people who are truly Christians—think about Job for example. But the Bible promises us that everything we encounter *works together for good to those who love God, to those who are the called according to His purpose.* Remember what happened to Job after God restored him? He had more than he did before all of his troubles. So when something that we think is bad happens to us, if we are a child of God, we can rest assured that God will work it out for our good according to His purposes. This doesn't mean things will turn out like we want them to or think they should. It means that God will do what is best for us in His purpose for our lives. We don't have to worry about the future and what might happen, because come what may, God is always in control and He always does what is best for us.

Questions To Think About

1. Since God is in control of everything, how should we feel about the future? Should we worry or be afraid?
2. What does the Bible promise us concerning any troubles that we may have to go through?

September 15

... *They shall fight because the Lord is with them* ...
Zechariah 10:5

In this verse the children of Israel were in a war with the enemies of God and they knew that the Lord was with them. We don't often think of ourselves as being in a war, but we are. We are battling the enemies of God today just as His people were long ago and we fight because Jesus is our Lord.

But who is the enemy and how do we fight against him? The enemy is really no different today than he was during the battle discussed in our Scripture. The enemy is anyone who doesn't put his faith in Jesus—the enemy is anyone who rebels against God. We have encountered this enemy in the past, he is the scoffer who makes fun of us because we are Christians and proclaim the Gospel; he is the liar who distorts or maliciously misrepresents the truths of God; he is the deceiver who calls evil good and good evil; and he is the pretender who subtly tries to destroy our faith.

Although sometimes battles with the Lord's enemies are fought against real people, more often for us it is a spiritual battle. This enemy's tools or weapons are all around us in our textbooks, movies, magazines, fads, traditions, laws, and many other things. The enemy uses these tools to tempt us to rebel against our Lord.

So what is the battle plan? We have the plan outlined for us in God's Word. It is up to us to study our Bibles and listen to our spiritual leaders—our parents and pastors—to help us to learn and understand the Lord's battle plan. We need to put on the whole armor of God: truth, righteousness, faith, salvation, preparation of the gospel of peace, all of which are explained in Ephesians 6:11-17. One of our most important weapons besides God's Word and prayer is our "feet". What?

Yes, the Bible tells us to "flee temptation", so our "feet", whether literal or spiritual, help us to flee or run from sin right to God and He will give us strength and understanding to do what is right in every situation. And remember, when God is for us no one can stand against us.

Questions To Think About

1. Who are God's enemies discussed in this lesson? Can you give an example of each one?
2. What are the weapons used by God's enemies? Can you give real life examples of these weapons?
3. Have you been "putting on" the whole armor of God and "fleeing temptation"?

Notes

September 16

. . . Who know whether you have come to the kingdom for such a time as this. Esther 4:14

In this Scripture Esther was married to King Xerxes of Persia. He was one of the most powerful people on the earth at that time. Esther, a Jew, had been told that evil men were plotting to convince the king to sign a law that would allow all the Jews to be killed. Esther had a choice. She could keep quiet and remain safe, because these men would not dare to kill the Queen, or she could risk displeasing the king, which meant instant death, by pleading for her people. In this verse she is reminded that she has been raised by God to the position of Queen for a purpose. She listened to this advice, courageously chose to do what was right, and both she and her people were spared.

Have you ever wondered why you were born into your specific family in your specific town, state, country and in your specific time period? Well, God has a plan for each and every person and it is not an accident that you are who you are, living where you live, in this day and time. Isn't it wonderful that God who is the creator of all things would see fit to take time to plan each person's life? So—there are no accidents in your life! This is why it is so important to listen to what God says in His Word and to fellowship with Him through prayer. By doing this you keep your mind and heart close to God and His instruction and you gain strength to obey what God's Word commands.

Just like Esther you have many choices every day. Just like Esther you have been placed where you are for a specific purpose in God's plan. Will you choose God's way or the way of the world?

QUESTIONS TO THINK ABOUT

1. Why were you born? Does God have a specific plan for your life?
2. Will you follow God's plan?

September 17

. . . if I perish, I perish. Esther 4:16

In the last lesson we talked about Queen Esther and the fact that if she displeased the king it meant instant death. We know that the story turned out well, but when Esther had to live the "story" she didn't know for sure whether she would live or die. However, in this verse she said she would do what was right even if it cost her life.

Esther's decision took lots of courage—the courage to do what is right no matter what. It is so easy to compromise and our culture today makes it seem so right. In fact, the world says that if we don't compromise we are "close minded" or "narrow minded" or "fanatics". For example, when our "buddy" in school asks us to let him copy our math homework or asks for an answer on a spelling test we have the choice to do the right thing or to compromise. We talk ourselves into believing, "it's okay to cheat for our buddy because we're just trying to help him and it really doesn't hurt anything", but this is compromising. We are taking the cowardly way out of the situation. We don't have the courage to say "no" because we're afraid he might not like us any more.

By compromising even in this situation we are setting up two things to happen in the future. First of all, we are not really helping our buddy—we are setting him up to fail. If he doesn't know how to do the math problems or how to spell correctly he will suffer when he tries to get into college or when he tries to get a good job. In addition, his laziness and ignorance are not good qualities to cultivate. If we are his friends we will help him nip these bad habits in the bud.

Secondly, if we compromise in this "little" thing, what will we do when we need all of our courage to face a big test like Esther? Let's say we get a great job as an engineer. Perhaps we are building a bridge. What will we do when our boss says, "Fudge the numbers a little and don't use as much steel and use a lower grade of concrete. You know our company is way over budge on this project. I mean we won't have a job if the company goes under and besides those standards are really higher than they need to be. It won't hurt anything." What will we do? Will we be courageous and refuse to compromise or will we give in repeating a pattern that started many years ago with cheating on homework in 6th grade? How will we feel if that bridge collapses?

We need to start right now developing a pattern of doing what is right no matter what because God commands us to be holy and because the consequences of our decisions are too important to mess around with.

Questons To Think About

1. Are you living with an ATTITUDE of compromise or courage? Will you ask God to change your attitude?
2. Are you ACTING out of courage or compromise?

Notes

September 18

For Ezra had prepared his heart to seek the Law of the Lord and to do it, and to teach . . . Ezra 7:10

We can learn a great deal from Ezra, a scribe from the priestly line of Israel. He led a group of his people back to their homeland from Babylonian captivity. This verse tells us three things that Ezra did which we should do today. First, Ezra prepared his heart by seeking the Law of the Lord. We prepare our hearts by studying God's Word, talking with Him in prayer, and worshiping Him daily both personally and in family worship, as well as on Sundays with fellow believers. Secondly, we should follow Ezra's example of keeping God's Law. After we study to know and understand what God commands in His Word, we are to live it with unwavering courage. Yes, we will fail sometimes, but when we repent and ask God to forgive us we know He will. Then we continue on doing the right thing asking for God's strength and guidance. Thirdly, Ezra prepared his heart to teach. This is also our responsibility, even as a child. We can teach others by the way we live—by example either good or bad; and, we can teach others by our words—proclaiming God's truths. Either way we must teach others God's ways boldly and without compromise.

God will give us these abilities if we just ask Him. So, let's ask God to prepare our hearts with the wisdom of His Word, with the discipline to live His Law, and with the courage to teach by our actions and our testimony.

Questions To Think About

1. How are you preparing your heart? Are you studying God's Word? Are you keeping His law? Are you teaching others?
2. How can you improve in these areas?

September 19

... *they have not separated themselves* ... Ezra 9:1

In this verse, the Levites or priests of Israel had not separated themselves form the people living in the land of Canaan and their pagan practices. They had married these pagans and were now worshiping their gods. They thought since they were priests they could "handle it" but sadly we see that they couldn't.

God has always called His people to separate themselves from people who are not Christians and from their pagan ideas. This doesn't mean we isolate ourselves on an island somewhere. What this does mean is that we are not to have friends who are not Christians. We will know people who are not Christians and we should be kind in all of our dealings with them, but we are NOT TO BE THEIR FRIENDS. If through our example and witness, these people become Christians; then we should befriend them and disciple them under the supervision of our parents. Otherwise, we are not to spend lots of time with them or closely associate with them. No matter how strong we think we are, we are always capable of sinning. So we must always be careful who we take into our lives because they will influence us—this includes both people we know and spend time with physically and people we "know" and spend time with in books, magazines, television, and movies.

The Bible says in I Corinthians 15:33, *Do not be deceived: 'Evil company corrupts good habits.'* And Proverbs 13:20 says, *He who walks with wise men will be wise, but the companion of fools will be destroyed.* These verses mean that we will become like the people we have as friends. NO MATTER HOW STRONG WE THINK WE ARE, the Bible says don't be fooled, unbelievers will influence us more than we will influence them if we spend time together. So choose your companions wisely.

Questions To Think About

1. Are all of your friends professing Christians—including those you listen to on CD's and watch in movies?
2. Do they live like Christians? How should this affect your relationship? Are they influencing you for GOOD?

Notes

September 20

Come and let us build . . . Nehemiah 2:17

Nehemiah was an Israelite who had worked his way into a position of authority under the Persian king, Artaxerxes. Remember the Persians were ruling Babylon at the time. The children of Israel had been given permission to return to the land of Canaan and many had gone home. When Nehemiah heard that his people needed permission and supplies to rebuild the walls of Jerusalem, he acted. Because of his position with the king, he was granted the authority and provisions to complete the walls around Jerusalem. His account of rebuilding the walls shows us what can be done when believers have a mission and a desire to accomplish that mission for the Lord.

First of all, read the whole chapter and check out how many times the words *built* and *rebuilt* and *repaired* are used. Also notice the words *next to him* and *after him*. These words and phrases show how the people worked together to accomplish their mission. God has put us here on earth with other believers to accomplish a mission. Each of our personal missions contributes to God's overall purpose for the earth. WOW! Isn't it exciting to know we are part of something so much bigger than ourselves and yet we are an important part of the whole?

Questions To Think About

1. What is God's mission for the earth? (Hint: Think about the commands He gave Adam and Eve in the garden and Jesus' last command to the Apostles.)
2. What is your mission right now?

September 21

"I am doing a great work." Nehemiah 6:3

In this verse Nehemiah's enemies were trying to trick him into coming and meeting with them so they could destroy him and stop the work on Jerusalem's walls. He answered them by saying, "I am doing a great work, so that I cannot come down. Why should the work cease while I leave it and go down to you?" Nehemiah didn't fall for their trick and he was also telling them that his work was God's will so it was more important than anything they might want to tell him. Nehemiah wasn't distracted from the path God had set before him.

So many times we are distracted. We are distracted by people who say, "Why do you have to go to church all the time? Why do you help the poor on Saturdays? You're always doing something like that. You think you're going to change the world or something?" Don't be distracted. When we help the poor and worship and fellowship with other believers we are obeying God's will and that is the GREATEST thing in the world that we can do. Sometimes "things" or the pursuit of things distract us. For example, we quit going to church so we can have a job that requires us to work on Sunday so that we can have nicer clothes or a motorcycle or whatever it might be that we want to buy. Don't be distracted. Remember, the greatest joy in life comes from obeying God. So stay focused on the goal.

Questions To Think About

1. Are you distracted? What are you going to do about it?

September 22

. . . for the joy of the Lord is your strength. Nehemiah 8:10

The Jewish people had just finished building the wall around Jerusalem and Ezra stood before them on a platform reading God's Law. When the people heard it they began to cry. Why did they cry? Perhaps it was because they recognized how sinful they rally were when they heard what God's Law required. Perhaps it was because they were moved by the fact that God had brought them home from exile and protected them from their enemies while they rebuilt the walls. Perhaps the power of God's Word which is *living and sharper than any two-edged sword,* had caused them to realize that they had been proud and stiff necked and had rebelled against the God of the universe. Perhaps it was all of these reasons.

Whatever the reason for their sorrow, the leaders comforted them and told them not to mourn. They reminded them once more that the Lord had wiped away their sin, He had given them freedom, and He was overcoming their enemies. Were all of these good gifts a cause for mourning? No! The leaders instructed the people to rejoice and give praise and glory and honor to God.

What does this have to do with us today? Everything. Jesus has done all these same things for us. We can rest in Him and have the strength and peace that only comes from being His child. So GIVE THANKS, PRAISE, REJOICE. *FOR THE JOY OF THE LORD IS YOUR STRENGTH.*

QUESTIONS TO THINK ABOUT

1. Why should Christians rejoice?
2. What is the result of rejoicing and praising God?

September 23

. . . *Remember me, O my God, for good!* Nehemiah 13:30

Today we read about Nehemiah again. He worked so hard to rebuild the wall and to teach the children of Israel to obey God's commands. But, when he left the people to return to Babylon, the people slipped back into their old ways and forgot God's Word and His commands once again. When Nehemiah returned to Israel and saw the people's wickedness, it grieved him deeply. He once more set out to establish things the way God had ordered. Nehemiah had been called by God to lead His people back to the Promised Land and to rebuild His temple. He had been called and he heeded that call.

All of us have good works that God has established for us to do. Sometimes the works are more public than others. For example, in the mid 1700's a man named William Wilberforce was born into a wealthy family in England. God's plan for his life was to free the slaves in his country. He was elected to the House of Commons and year after year he introduced a bill that would make slavery illegal in his country. Year after year that bill was defeated, but he never gave up and more than twenty years later his bill finally passed. That day 700,000 British slaves were freed.

Not everyone will be called on by God to do something so "big", but every good work that we do in answer to God's call is important. Being a godly father and mother and raising godly children is just as important as the work of William Wilberforce. The key is perseverance in doing whatever God calls us to do—our good works—our "job". If we persevere and do what God tells us to do—even the everyday things—"as unto the Lord" then we can say with Nehemiah, "Remember me, O my God, for good."

Questions To Think About

1. Are you listening for God's calling?
2. Are you doing everything "as unto the Lord"?

September 24

A son honors his father, and a servant his master. If then I am the Father, where is My honor? . . . Malachi 1:6

How are we to honor the Lord? We are told in Malachi that there are many ways to honor Him, but one way is with our tithes and offerings. God says that if we will give, He will open the windows of Heaven and pour out such blessing that there will not be room enough to receive it. Who wouldn't like to have that much blessing from the Lord? Of course God is talking about spiritual blessings in this passage, but He is also talking about material blessings as well. When God pours out His blessings sometimes they are spiritual and sometimes they are material—we don't get to pick which one—but remember that God always give us what is good for us and what we really need the most. So when God says, "Test me and see," He is promising blessings both material and spiritual.

So what does this have to do with honoring God? Well, we know that God doesn't need our money; after all He is master of everything. What He does want is for us to HONOR Him and tell others that He is the source of all our blessings. God has given us everything we have and we have no right to take credit for it. Even when we are obedient—and the Bible does tell us that if we obey God He will bless us—even then, God is still the source of all good things and every blessing we receive.

We need to tithe our income—that means allowances or payment for babysitting or mowing lawns or whatever. Then think about even adding to that a gift above the tithe. Whether the amount is small or large doesn't matter, it's the fact that we are willing and eager with a grateful heart to give something back to God. What a great way to HONOR Him.

QUESTIONS TO THINK ABOUT

1. How does tithing honor God?
2. What does tithing make us think about?

September 25

And Jabez called on the God of Israel saying, "Oh, that You would bless me indeed and enlarge my territory, that Your hand would be with me, and that You would keep me from evil, that I may not cause pain." I Chronicles 4:10

The prayer of Jabez is a prayer that each of us should pray every day. Jabez asked God for four things that would make his life a blessing to others. First, he asked that God would bless him. We know that God blesses us when we are obedient to His Word—Jabez had a desire to be obedient. Second, he asked that God would enlarge his territory, which means he wanted to be able to reach or interact with more people as a witness for God. Third, Jabez asked that God's hand would be with him. In this he was asking God to work through him in all that he did so that he might glorify God. Fourth, he asked God to keep him from evil so that he wouldn't hurt anyone—friends, family, and other believers.

This prayer covers so much in one sentence. And guess what, God granted Jabez's requests so we know that Jabez was asking with a pure heart for what was in God's will. For us today, we can be assured that whatever we ask for in God's will and for His glory we will be given!

Questions To Think About

1. What does it mean to ask for things that are in God's will?
2. What things can we ask for that we KNOW are in God's will?

September 26

. . . for they cried out to God in battle. He heeded their prayer, because they put their trust in Him. I Chronicles 5:20

Time and time again we read in Scripture that God graciously heard his children's cry for help and because they trusted in Him, He came to their rescue. This is still true for us today. We can know beyond a shadow of doubt that if we trust in the Lord, He will not only hear our prayers, but He will answer them. This would be a wonderful story if it ended here. But guess what—the children of Israel were influenced by the world and began acting like the unbelievers that surrounded them. They forgot their Heavenly Father and even began worshipping the pagan gods of the people in the nearby lands.

It would be easy for us to condemn the Israelites and say, "I would never turn from God's ways if He had done as much for me as He did for them." But let's think about this for a moment. There are many people today who call themselves Christians and they are really following the way of the world. They say they believe in God and His Word but they don't practice what it teaches. It's easy to turn to God and ask for His help when we are in a mess. When things are going well we tend to start thinking how great we are and how much we've accomplished and soon we forget that God has given us everything we have. But let us get into a mess and we are right there asking God to get us out of it even though it's our own fault. We owe everything to God and we should always keep this in mind and continually thank Him and praise Him for the many, many blessings He bestows on us. Remember, He promises if we put our trust in Him, He will answer our prayer.

Questions To Think About

1. What does "He heeded their prayer" in today's verse mean?
2. Why did God "heed their prayer"? What does this mean for us today?

September 27

Now these are the men whom David appointed over the service of song in the house of the Lord, after the ark came to rest. They were ministering with music . . . I Chronicles 6:31-32

Music has always been an important part in worshiping God. The Psalms are actually songs written by David and others to use in praising and worshiping God. As this verse says, David appointed musicians to "minister with music" in the temple. Remember how the Disciples and Jesus sang a song at the Last Supper before His death and resurrection? And Paul and Silas sang when they were thrown into prison for preaching the Gospel. Why is singing so important? Singing shows others how we feel in your spirit. Singing is a testimony of what is inside us. The world knows this and has tried to take over what God gave His children for their benefit and His glory. The world is trying to substitute its songs of immorality, death, and despair for the songs that glorify God and lift our spirits with a message of thanksgiving, hope, and love. We need to think about the songs we listen to and sing. Think about the words we are saying. Do they honor God, comfort us, and bring His hope and love to a lost world. If the words and songs we sing are not uplifting then we shouldn't listen to them. Sing unto the Lord a new song.

Questions To Think About

1. Are you listening to and singing songs that God would listen to?

September 28

There were mighty men of valor fit to go out for war and battle.
I Chronicles 7:11

What does the word valor mean? The dictionary says it means boldness and determination in facing danger. It comes from the Latin words that meant, "to be worthy". We might think that valor is a great characteristic to have if we are getting ready to go into battle, but why would we need valor in our day and time. Besides, why would we need valor when we are just kids—right? Well, as Christians we are in a battle. We are in a conflict that has been going on since the Garden of Eden. We are fighting against Satan and the fallen world and even our own sinful natures. We need to be bold and determined in this fight as much, if not more so, than in any other kind of fight.

There are so many battles! In fact, we encounter some sort of battle each and every day. The number one battle we have to fight is against our own natures. Jesus commanded us to show love for our brothers and sisters in Christ and sometimes that is hard enough. But more than that Jesus said we must love our enemies—talk about a battle! We must be bold and determined to love those who ignore us and are mean and hateful to us. This is hard to imagine, but if we obey and fight this battle—if we become "mighty kids of battle" just think how our actions could change our school, community, city, state, and nation. That's what it means to have VALOR—fighting on God's side in every circumstance. In other words, we must be obedient to all that God teaches us in his Word and fight against Satan and our own fleshly desires.

Questions To Think About

1. What does valor mean? Are you a "mighty kid of valor"?
2. What does it mean "to be worthy" in the sight of the Lord?

September 29

. . . carried away captive because of their unfaithfulness.
I Chronicles 9:1

This Scripture is specifically about the children of Judah who were physically carried away into Babylon because of their unfaithfulness to God. We might think, "So what does that have to do with me today?" The same thing is happening to God's children today. No, we aren't getting carted of to some foreign land when we are unfaithful, but let's examine what happens when we are unfaithful to Jesus. Sometimes we allow our friends or our own sinful desires to "carry us away" to places we don't really belong if we are Christians. One example might be when we go to a party we know is not pleasing to the Lord and we would be embarrassed and ashamed if our parents or the Lord happened to "catch" us there.

Sometimes we allow ourselves to get "carried away" in our thought life because of things we are watching on television, in movies, or reading in a book. We might think, "It can't be that bad, they are showing it on TV." Or we believe we can see any movie rated PG or PG-13. But we know in our hearts—or our conscience—when things aren't right. We feel "dirty" inside when we see, hear, and watch things that don't bring glory to the Lord.

We can get "carried away" by listening to gossip and repeating it. We can get "carried away" by coveting—wanting what wealthy people have that we don't have. The list could go on and on. We can see that we are still "getting carried away to Babylon". But PRAISE GOD, when we REPENT He forgives us. So let's THINK before we ACT and not get "carried away" by things that aren't pleasing to God. We want to be faithful to Jesus.

Questions To Think About

1. What does it mean to be "carried away into Babylon" in our day and time?
2. What can we do to stop being "carried away"?

September 30

For the law was given through Moses, but grace and truth came through Jesus Christ. John 1:17

Let's think about why God's law was given to us. God's law was given to man to show him how Holy God is and how unholy we are. The law points us to the fact that we are sinners and need a Savior because we can't live up to the law and save ourselves. But if we look at the rest of the verse we have so much hope because we see that God loved us so much that He sent His only Son Jesus to bring us grace and truth. That means that JESUS DID IT ALL! He lived a perfect life for us, He died to pay for our sins, He rose from the grave to give us eternal life. This is a hard concept for some people to accept. We want to be able to say, "look what I did" so we can have bragging rights and this goes back to PRIDE. Remember, "pride goes before a fall" and this fall will land people in hell for all eternity.

Even as Christians we have to be careful of letting pride creep into our lives. I remember having a Sunday school lesson on pride and I thought to myself, "well, that's one thing I don't have to worry about." I may have even said this out loud—I hope I didn't! What's wrong with that statement? My declaration that I didn't have pride and my attitude revealed the truth that I was actually FULL OF PRIDE. It's the same thing my Dad used to jokingly say, "I'm so proud of my humility!"

The Bible tells us that truth came through Jesus, and the Holy Spirit will lead us to the truth. Often we think we know so much about everything including what's true and what's not, but we find as we study God's Word that in many cases we have been influenced by the world and believed the world's lies. One BIG LIE that is going around today is that God is so loving that He would never send anybody to hell. God's Word doesn't teach this and we need to wake up and wake up others before it is too late.

We should all be so thankful that God is in control and that HE is the TRUTH and when we humble ourselves we can learn the real truth from Him. The REAL TRUTH is what will set us free!

Questions To Think About

1. Why did God give man the Law?
2. Can we live up to the Law? Can anyone?
3. What happens if we don't live up to the Law?
4. What provision did God make for us?

October 1

. . . for your prayer is heard. Luke 1:13

I've often wondered, "Why should I pray? I'm just talking to myself and no one, surely not God, hears or cares what I have to say." If we aren't careful this can end up being our attitude when we only go to the Lord in prayer when we need something or are in trouble. Under these conditions if we don't get an answer right away we get discouraged. BUT—do we have a right to be discouraged? There are many places in the Bible where we are told that our prayers ARE HEARD.

Our verse for today is one example of a man's prayers being heard. The man in the verse is Zechariahs. We don't know exactly what his prayer was but we do know that he had no children and when his prayer was HEARD and ANSWERED he and his wife were blessed with a son. In that day, having no children was considered a judgment from God because "they [children] are a gift from God and a blessing". Their son certainly was a blessing—he was John the Baptist. The amazing thing about Zechariahs is that he was an old man when this happened and considering the fact that he wanted children he had probably been praying for a son for a LONG TIME.

In our society we have become an impatient people and we think our needs and wants should be met NOW! We need to remember that GOD IS NEVER LATE. He has a timetable and He will always meet it; so let's not get discouraged when we pray and we don't get an "instant message" like we do on our computers. GOD DOES HEAR and is sending us what we need FOR OUR GOOD each and every minute of our lives. That is AWESOME! So keep praying every day. We should also keep in mind that we are to praise and thank God for His blessings too.

Questions To Think About

1. How do you feel if your prayers aren't answered immediately?
2. Do you only pray when you need something? Should you? Do you need to change this? If so, will you?

October 2

And when they had come into the house they saw the young Child with Mary His mother, and fell down and worshiped Him. And when they had opened their treasures, they presented gifts to Him . . . Matthew 1:11

This is the account of the Wise Men who traveled from a distant country to find Jesus. Their actions are very important for us to remember because it shows us how to act in the presence of God. Let's look at three ways we can come into God's presence and worship Him. We come into God's presence when we attend worship at church, when we read our Bible, and lastly when we pray. We are to praise Him in all of these situations.

When we worship, we should worship Jesus just like the Wise Men did. We should praise Him for who He is: our LORD and MASTER; our SAVIOR, who paid for our sins; and our HIGH PRIEST, who goes before the Father on our behalf and claims us as HIS CHILDREN. These are just a few reasons why we should WORSHIP HIM. So, let's think about how thankful we should be that Jesus loves us so much.

Questions To Think About

1. Can you think of other reasons we should worship Jesus?
2. How do we know Jesus loves us?

October 3

Therefore bear fruits worthy of repentance, and do not think to say to yourselves, "We have Abraham as our father."
Matthew 3:8-9a

In this verse John the Baptist was talking to the Pharisees and Sadducees who came to him to be baptized. He knew they thought that they were very holy and had all the answers, but He also knew that they were not true followers of God. They thought just being a descendant of Abraham made them special, but John set them straight. He said, "If you are really repentant then let me see some evidence (fruit) of the change in you."

It is the same today with us. Just because we are born into a Christian home doesn't mean that we are followers of Jesus. The Bible tells us that we are known for our love for one another and that all are known by their fruits. In other words, when we come to realize all Jesus has done for us, we should want to be obedient. Besides, if we are true believers we WILL PRODUCE FRUIT, or good works, because God promises that he will produce fruit in all of his children. This happens in true believers because God changes our hearts and then we WANT TO PLEASE GOD. Yes, we will mess up sometimes, but that's when we ask Jesus to forgive us and strengthen us to do better. Isn't that WONDERFUL!

QUESTIONS TO THINK ABOUT

1. Are you a true believer? If you aren't sure talk to your parents or pastor.
2. What "fruit" is evident in your life?

October 4

Nathanael said to Him, "How do You know me?" Jesus answered and said to him. "Before Philip called you, when you were under the fig tree, I saw you." John 1:48

This is the story of Philip who told his brother Nathanael that he had found the Messiah. Nathanael was skeptical, so Philip took him to meet Jesus. Jesus greeted him by saying, "Behold, an Israelite indeed, in whom is no deceit!" Then Nathanael said, "How do You know me?"

Nathanael couldn't believe that Jesus knew him, but just as Jesus knew Nathanael, He knows us. Isn't it great that even when we are young and aren't famous or rich, that Jesus knows us? Jesus told Nathanael that He saw him under the fig tree and Jesus sees us all of the time no matter where we are. We couldn't hide from Him if we wanted to. It isn't as if He is spying on us. Jesus always sees us because He is God. And He is constantly watching over us, protecting us, making sure that we are safe and taken care of and that we have what we need.

No one else can do this. Not even our parents. They can't see us at all times, only when they are with us. This is just another wonderful thing that Jesus does for us.

Questions To Think About

1. Do you thank God for watching out for you all the time?

October 5

And many of the Samaritans of that city believed in Him because of the word of the woman who testified, . . . John 4:39

There are three important words in this sentence which we need to examine today. The first word is TESTIFIED. Testify means to make a true and serious statement about something. In this case the woman in the verse had met Jesus at a well outside of her home village. After talking with Him, she went back to the people she knew in the village and told them about this man, JESUS. She told the people that He might be the Christ or Messiah that they had been looking for.

The second important word is WORD. Jesus talked to the woman and told her things that she needed to hear. He told her what the people of the village needed to know—that He was the Christ—the "living water". Since we live on this side of the cross, we know that Jesus is the Messiah, the "living water". We have the TESTIMONY of his disciples and followers written down in the WORD—the BIBLE. It is there to teach us all we need to know to be a follower of Jesus.

The third word we need to look at is BELIEVED. The woman at the well, believed what Jesus told her and she was brave enough to go back home and tell others about her experience with Jesus. Because of her courage, our verse says, "MANY believed". This is what all of us should do. Telling others about Jesus is both a privilege and a blessing.

Questions To Think About

1. Have you told someone about Jesus recently?

October 6

Then He said to them, "Follow Me, and I will make you fishers of men." They IMMEDIATELY left their nets and followed Him . . . and IMMEDIATELY they left the boat and their father, and followed Him. Matthew 4:19-20, 22

Today's Scripture tells us that when Jesus called the disciples to follow Him, they followed IMMEDIATELY. Let's ask ourselves, do we always obey IMMEDIATELY? Yes, the same thought went through my mind—but that was Jesus and if Jesus called me I would obey IMMEDIATELY. Well, every time our parents or teachers or anyone in authority over us calls it is like Jesus calling us to obey. Actually, if we don't obey IMMEDIATELY we haven't obeyed at all because we have said in our hearts, I will do the task when I want to do it. Even if it is only five minutes later because we want to finish watching a television show or finish a conversation with a friend or whatever the excuse might be, if we do not obey the call right away, we are being disobedient.

God wants us to obey IMMEDIATELY because not doing so is disobeying, but we also might miss out on a blessing. For example, when we know what is right, we must act IMMEDIATELY. For example, when we see someone standing alone at church or school and we know in our heart we should talk to them, we should do it IMMEDIATELY. If we don't school or church may start and it will be too late. If we obey IMMEDIATELY, we just might have made a great friend—what a blessing!

Questions To Think About

1. Do you obey your parents immediately?
2. Do you do what is right immediately?

October 7

And their scribes and the Pharisees complained against His disciples, saying, "Why do You eat and drink with tax collectors and sinners?" Luke 5:30

Our scripture today tells about Jesus calling Matthew, the tax collector, to become His disciple. Matthew was so thankful that he gave a big party to celebrate his salvation and of course he invited his friends. Who were Matthew's friends—tax collectors and the people he had been associating with for years. Jesus didn't reprimand him for the people he invited to the party, but the "religious" people of the day saw Jesus sitting and eating with those "sinners" and they complained about it. When they questioned the disciples, Jesus spoke up and said that He had come to seek and to save the lost, not people who didn't think they needed salvation.

Matthew gives us a great example to follow. He was so grateful that Jesus had chosen him to be a disciple that he wanted to share the news and introduce Jesus to all of his old friends. He wanted them to be as happy as he was and to know the true living God. This is exactly how we should feel and what we should do. Have you shared your faith with a friend?

Questions To Think About

1. When did you become a Christian? Have you told your friends?
2. How can you share the Gospel with your friends?

October 8

But Jesus answering them [the Pharisees] said,
"Have you not even read this, . . . Luke 6:3

God, through Moses, gave the Jewish people His law. The Pharisees, a group of religious leaders, insisted that the Law of Moses plus a bunch of laws they had added should be strictly interpreted and enforced. The Pharisees were jealous of Jesus and feared Him because they knew that He was TRUTH. They were supposed to know the Law of Moses frontwards and backwards and this is why Jesus said to them, "have you not even read this . . ." What Jesus was pointing out was the TRUTH and it contradicted one of their made-up laws.

There are people today who are a lot like the Pharisees who make up rules and regulations that they want us to follow. These rules will often have nothing to do with what the Bible teaches. This is another important reason why we need to KNOW THE WORD OF GOD so we will not be fooled by untruths. The Bible covers every possible circumstance that we might encounter and is a Christian's guide for living a godly life. The Bible warns us not to be fooled by people who will try to mislead us. They might say something like, "Well, I Believe . . ." Unfortunately people can believe lies and misinformation, so check what people say with your parents and your Bible. Remember, TRUTH is what counts not what someone "believes".

Questions To Think About

1. Are you studying your Bible to be prepared to combat lies?

October 9

You are the light of the world . . . Let your light so shine before men, that they may see your good works and glorify your Father in heaven. Matthew 5:14a & 16

When a person becomes a follower of Jesus, the true light, then that person becomes the light of Christ that others see. We reflect this light of THE SON as the moon reflects the light of the sun. What is this light that others see in us? Do we glow? No. The light reflected from us is manifested in our works, what we do and what we say. We know that Jesus was perfect and while we won't be perfect until we are in Heaven, we can reflect Jesus by doing and saying good things like Jesus did while he was here on earth.

How do we know what Jesus would do? We study His Word. We read about and then practice the things He did. Jesus was Kind to people regardless who they were. He ALWAYS told the truth even when it wasn't what the people wanted to hear. He ALWAYS gave all the praise and honor and glory to God the Father. These are the characteristics of Jesus we should be reflecting, not because we have to, but because we want to be like Jesus. SO GO SHINE FOR JESUS and brighten someone's day.

QUESTIONS TO THINK ABOUT

1. Are you reflecting Jesus?
2. What do you need to do to know what Jesus would do? Will you study?

October 10

"Therefore whoever hears these sayings of Mine, and does them, I will liken him to a wise man who built his house on the rock: and the rain descended, the floods came, and the winds blew and beat on that house; and it did not fall, for it was founded on the rock. But everyone who hears these sayings of Mine, and does not do them, will be like a foolish man who built his house on the sand; and the rain descended, the floods came, and the winds blew and beat on that house; and if fell. And great was its fall."
Matthew 7:24-27

Remember this story about the wise man who built his house on the rock and the foolish man who built his on the sand? We have a song about it that we have sung since we were very small. However, sometimes we miss the message of the song—and these verses. Jesus was teaching His disciples two very important things in this passage. Jesus gave the disciples two verbs—HEARS and DOES. In this story, Jesus explains that the foundation of a person's life is not just HEARING God's Word, but also DOING what God commands.

Jesus is saying that when we HEAR and DO what he commands, we are like a wise man. If we study and listen to our parents, pastor and Sunday school teachers and then act on what we learn, we have a rock solid foundation that makes us wise. Like the man in the story, we will have problems or *storms* while we are here on earth, but how we handle it goes back to our foundation. If we build our foundation on God and His word and are HEARERS and DOERS of the Word, we have built our lives on the ROCK. When the storms come we will be strong. We will be wise.

Questions To Think About

1. Are you a wise hearer and doer of God's Word? If you are, give examples. If you are not, what can you do to become a wise hearer and doer of God's Word?
2. Are any of us ALWAYS wise? How can we work on this?

October 11

Come to Me, all you who labor and are heavy laden, and I will give you rest. Matthew 11:28

In this verse, Jesus is referring to the Jewish people of his day. The people had so many demands placed on them by their religious leaders, that it was impossible for them to follow them all. These were not commands given to the people by God, these were "man-made" rules and regulations added to the law. This caused the people to think of God's Law as a great burden.

Sometimes adults think that kids don't have any troubles or even know what "heavy laden" means. The dictionary says laden means "weighed down with a heavy load, oppressed, or burdened with grief." Have you ever felt like this? People of all ages feel this way at times—even kids. BUT—the GOOD NEWS is that we have a way out from under this HEAVY BURDEN. As Christians we have someone to go to that will help us carry the load. Who? Jesus! Jesus listens to our prayers and helps us work through anything that is giving us a hard time. He helps us work through any heavy BURDERN. He will give us strength to deal with whatever comes our way. He will give us rest.

QUESTIONS TO THINK ABOUT

1. Do you have any burdens? Have you talked to God about them?
2. Have you talked to your parents, pastor, Sunday school teacher about your burdens?

October 12

A sower went out to sow his seed. And as he sowed, some fell by the wayside; and it was trampled down, and the birds of the air devoured it. Some fell on rock; and as soon as it sprang up, it withered away because it lacked moisture. And some fell among thorns, and the thorns sprang up with it and choked it. But others fell on good ground, sprang up, and yielded a crop a hundredfold.
Luke 8:5-8a

This is one of the parables that Jesus told to the crowds as they gathered to hear Him speak and it has a very good lesson for us today as well. The parable teaches that there are four different kinds of people who hear God's Word—represented by the seeds. First, there are the people who listen; but "then the devil comes and takes away the word out of their hearts, lest they should believe and be saved." Secondly, there are those who hear the stories from the Bible and enjoy church for a while but these people have no root. They "believe for a while and in time of temptation fall away." Thirdly, there are those who hear, but "go out and are choked with cares, riches, and pleasures of life, and bring no fruit to maturity." Finally, there are those who hear the Word of God and truly believe the Gospel and love God and they take the seed, "and keep it and bear fruit with patience."

We have to ask ourselves, where do we fit into this parable? We must not be misled by the Devil or the world or be concerned with pursuing riches and pleasures or be afraid and worried about things. Are we the fourth kind of person—A TRUE BELIEVER?

Questions To Think About

1. As explained in this parable, what kind of person are you?

October 13

Another parable He put forth to them saying: "The kingdom of heaven is like a mustard seed, which a man took and sowed in his field, which indeed is the least of all the seeds; but when it is grown it is greater than the herbs and becomes a tree, so that the birds of the air come and nest in its branches."
Matthew 13:31-32

When Jesus talks about the Kingdom of Heaven in these verses, He is referring to the Gospel, the Church and Us. The Gospel began like a weak little seed but soon spread to the whole Roman world. So even though the Gospel message started out small, with a little band of disciples, it eventually "conquered" all of Rome and is still being spread throughout the world

Today, the Church is the kingdom of God among us and grace working in our hearts is the kingdom of God within us. As a KINGDOM KID, we are called to help spread the Gospel to the ends of the earth. That doesn't mean we have to go off far away to tell someone about Jesus. We all know people in our neighborhood, or school, or maybe even our church who don't know Jesus as their Savior. And just like that mustard seed representing the Gospel, Jesus "planted" us right where we are so that we could spread the Gospel and help it grow to envelope all of our neighborhood, then our town, then our state, then our nation, then our world. Let's get GROWING!

QUESTIONS TO THINK ABOUT

1. Are you studying the Word, learning in church and Sunday school and following what your parents are teaching you so you can help spread the Gospel?
2. Why is it important for people preach the Gospel?

October 14

"As soon as Jesus heard the word that was spoken, He said to the ruler of the synagogue, "Do not be afraid; only believe."
Mark 5:36

The dictionary definition of believe is, "to have confidence in the truth." To have confidence in something means that we are so sure that something is true and real that we ACT accordingly. So believing is more than just SAYING we believe or have confidence in something; it means we ACT on what we believe.

My Dad once told me the story of a man who walked across Niagara Falls on a tight rope. He had quite an audience and the people who were there cheered him on and thought he was wonderful. The crowd heard the next day that he was going cross the Falls again but this time he was going blindfolded pushing a wheelbarrow. As he arrived that morning all the people were cheering and yelling, "You can do it. We know you can do it. We BELIEVE you can do it." The tightrope walker said to the crowd, "so you think I can really do it?" The crowd yelled, "Yes! We believe you can." So the man turned to them and questioned, "Ok, which one of you wants to get into the wheelbarrow?" There was complete SILENCE.

Believing is not only SAYING you trust, but DOING the things that PROVE you believe. It is easy to say we believe in Jesus, but Jesus said, "If you love Me keep my commandments." OBEYING Jesus is how we know that we truly BELIEVE. And remember Jesus words in our verse, "Do not be afraid; only believe." Jesus is always with us to help us so we don't have to be afraid like all the people who wouldn't ride in the wheelbarrow. We can fully BELIEVE Jesus without fear.

Questions To Think About

1. What does it mean to believe?
2. Do you believe you can trust Jesus for anything?

October 15

Then He said to His disciples, "The harvest truly is plentiful, but the laborers are few. Therefore pray the Lord of the harvest to send out laborers into His harvest" Matthew 9:37-38

True followers of Jesus are in the minority and in this passage Jesus is telling His disciples that many people need to hear the Gospel and be taught how to follow Jesus, but there are not enough preachers to teach everyone who wants to hear. So what did Jesus tell his disciples to do? He said, "Pray the Lord of the harvest to send out laborers into His harvest." The same thing is true today. Compared to the number of people who NEED to hear the Gospel and who NEED to be taught how to follow Jesus, the preachers, teachers and workers are few. So what can we do about this?

First and foremost we need to follow what Jesus said and PRAY that the Lord will send laborers. Some of these laborers are already on hand, like our pastors and Sunday school teachers and our parents so we need to pray for them. We need to ask God to bless their work and give them wisdom to teach us what we need to know. Then we need to pray for missionaries and church planters who leave their homes to take the Gospel to different cities and countries here in America and all over the world.

We also need to pray that God will direct our lives and help us to learn everything we can from our pastors and Sunday school teachers and parents so we will be equipped to do whatever he calls us to do with our lives in the future. Who knows God may call YOU to be a pastor, Sunday school teacher, parent, or missionary someday.

Questions To Think About

1. Are you praying for you pastor, Sunday school teacher and parents?
2. Are you learning everything you can to equip yourself for God's calling?

October 16

So He commanded the multitude to sit down on the ground. And He took the seven loaves and gave thanks, broke them and gave them to His disciples to set before them; and they set them before the multitude. Mark 8:6

This is easy to recognize as one of the times that Jesus fed the multitude with just a few fish and loaves of bread, but what can we learn from this incident? Before this verse, Mark tells us that the multitude had been following Jesus for three days and He didn't want to send them away hungry. So the first thing we learn here is that Jesus loves His children and has a plan to take care of them. This means that we never have to worry about ANYTHING. God has EVERYTHING under control. He loves us and has a plan to care for our every NEED.

Secondly, we learn from this story that Jesus asked the Disciples to bring him what they had. They said they only had seven loaves. Instead of Jesus saying, "Well, that won't be nearly enough," He commanded the multitude to sit down and prepare to be fed. This teaches us that Jesus BELIEVED His Father would provide—so much so that he had the people prepare for the meal. What about us? Do we TRUST God and BELIEVE that He is sovereign and will provide for us whatever our circumstances?

Lastly, Jesus thanked His Father and broke the bread apart and we all know what happened. They all ate, were filled, and had seven baskets of food left over. Do we THANK God for providing everything for us? Remember, this verse shows us that God is SOVEREIGN over all and because He LOVES us, he PROVIDES for our needs; so we should TRUST Him, BELIEVE His promises, and THANK Him for all that He does for us.

QUESTIONS TO THINK ABOUT

1. Do you believe God is sovereign over everything? Do you live your life like you believe it? (If you have trouble with this question, talk to your parents or Sunday school teacher about it.)
2. Do you trust in God's promises and believe He will do what He promises?
3. Do you thank Him for all He does for you?

NOTES

October 17

. . . You are an offense to Me, for you are not mindful of the things of God, but the things of men." Matthew 16:23b

Jesus was telling his disciples that He was going to Jerusalem, where he would have to suffer and die. This offended Peter and he told Jesus that HE (Peter) would never let that happen. Jesus then turned to Peter and said what we read in our verse above. Before we condemn Peter, let's think about what Jesus said, "Peter, you are only looking at the circumstances around you, but God sees the whole picture." Do we ever do this? Of course we all do. Sometimes we "can't see the forest for the trees" and this is true of all people, even Peter. Peter was comfortable with the way things were going right then. He thought he had Jesus' plan all figured out. He thought Jesus was going to defeat the Romans, kick them all out of Israel, and rule as king. But that was never Jesus' plan. Jesus was being obedient to His heavenly Father and would not be swayed from the course that God had set for Him. He was being "mindful of the things of God."

How can we be mindful of the things of God? We have to know His WORD—that means the Bible. We learn about God through worship, study, and listening to sound teaching. Then, we need to apply what we learn and be obedient. We need to look at ourselves often and ask, "Who is influencing us most, God or the World? Are we being mindful of the things of God, or the things of men?

QUESTIONS TO THINK ABOUT

1. Who has the greatest influence in your life—God or the World? In other words, do you look more like Jesus or the World?

October 18

"But when he saw that the wind was boisterous, he was afraid; and beginning to sink he cried out, saying, "Lord, save me!" And immediately Jesus stretched out His hand and caught him, and said to him, "O you of little faith, why did you doubt?"
Matthew 14:30-31

Being afraid is something that we all have to deal with and there are lots of different situations that cause us to be afraid. Anything from being alone in the dark to speaking in front of an audience can scare us or make us afraid.

In the above verses, Peter and the other disciples were surprised by a sudden storm when they were crossing the sea. They had gone ahead of Jesus and planned to meet him later. When Peter saw Jesus walking toward them he wanted to walk with Jesus on the water. He was fine as long as he had his eyes on Jesus; but, when he took his eyes off of Jesus and saw the waves crashing and the wind howling around him he was afraid and started to sink. When this happened he certainly cried out to the right person. I like the next part. Jesus didn't hesitate to help. He IMMEDIATELY caught Peter and saved him, even though Peter didn't have very much faith.

Jesus promises to do the same for us. When we are afraid, we can call on Jesus to calm our fears. We can count on Jesus. This is what it means to have faith. We don't just have faith in some abstract "thing" out there somewhere in the universe. When we know Jesus, we believe His promises because he is always faithful to keep His promises. We believe IN HIM. That is faith. So let's not forget to call on Jesus the next time we are afraid. He will always answer our call.

QUESTIONS TO THINK ABOUT

1. Are you keeping your eyes on Jesus and trusting in HIM?

October 19

"These people draw near to Me with their mouth, and honor Me with their lips, but their heart is far from Me, and in vain they worship Me, teaching as doctrines the commandments of men." Matthew 15:8-9

This scripture reminds us that just because we can "talk the talk" doesn't me we "walk the walk". We must have a changed HEART to truly belong to God. We know when the Holy Spirit changes our heart because He gives us a desire to study God's Word and do what is right. And, when we mess up, the Holy Spirit convicts us of our sin so we can repent. However, as the verse says there are those who go through the motions of being a Christian, "but their heart is far from God."

These verses are definitely referring to people who don't have a changed heart and are not really Christians, but we also want to be careful that these verses aren't talking about us. Sometimes when we get comfortable with our lives and put our minds on "auto pilot" we just go through the motions in the worship service without really thinking or really listening and we don't apply the lessons to our heart. Or perhaps when we read the Bible or pray, our minds are wandering all over the place thinking about what's for dinner or if we made an "A" on a test. The Bible calls people who just "go through the motions", HYPOCRITES. We don't want to be HYPOCRITES, so we need to stop and make sure that we are truly participating with our hearts and minds in worship and Bible study.

Questions To Think About

1. Has the Holy Spirit changed your heart? If not talk to your parents or pastor or Sunday school teacher about it.
2. Have you asked yourself if you are "just going through the motions"? If you have been repent. If not, keep up the good work!

October 20

"For everyone will be seasoned with fire, and every sacrifice will be seasoned with salt. Salt is good, but if the salt loses its flavor, how will you season it? Have salt in yourselves, and have peace with one another." Mark 9:49-50

In these verses, Jesus is talking to His disciples and He is making three points clear to them and to us Christians today. First, we will have to go through some "fire for Jesus" if we are true witnesses for Him. When we meet at school to pray or have a Bible with us or present the Gospel to an unsaved friend, someone may make fun of us. Jesus said that the world hates Him so if we are living for Him, the world is going to hate us as well.

Secondly, Jesus says salt that loses its flavor isn't much good. When I was a kid, if something were really good, we said it was "SALTY". It meant the same thing as "cool" means today. As Christians, we are called to be salt in this world. What does that mean? Well, salt helps preserve things and brings out the good flavor in what we eat. That means we are to "salt" the world by proclaiming the Gospel, through our lives and words, wherever we go. He also uses our lives to encourage others and bring out the good flavor of their talents.

Thirdly, Jesus says to His disciples and us, that we are to "have peace with one another." This doesn't mean that we are to have peace at any cost or do whatever it takes to keep the peace. He did mean that we are to love each other and live together without fighting, but we are always to love God more. If "keeping the peace" would cause us to compromise on what the Bible teaches, we must always do what God says. And even in the midst of the fire, we will have true peace that only God can give. So let's be "SALTY" and God will give us a PEACE that passes all understanding.

QUESTIONS TO THINK ABOUT

1. Are you being salty?
2. If you aren't what do you plan to do about it?

October 21

Then Jesus said to those Jews who believed Him, "If you abide in My word, you are My disciples indeed. And you shall know the truth, and the truth shall make you free."
John 8:31-32

We hear this scripture or at least part of it quoted a lot. Usually what it means today is that some group or other wants to be free to do whatever they want in this life. But that is not what Jesus was talking about at all. Notice what the whole verse says. "IF YOU ABIDE IN MY WORD", then "YOU ARE MY DISCIPLES". What did Jesus mean by abiding? First of all we have to be a Christian to be "abiding" in Christ. But once we become a Christian we have to live like we are Christians. How do we do that? We become His disciples. A disciple is someone who learns from a master, so we must study His Word and then LIVE out what we have studied or been taught. If we do this, what happens? We will "KNOW THE TRUTH". We will understand that Jesus is God's Son and through His grace we have been made FREE.

What does it mean to be made free by the truth? It means that we will be free from the guilt of sin. In other words, IF we truly are Jesus disciples (Christians) and abide in His Word, we know the truth (SALVATION and SANCTIFICATION) and we are free from the penalty of sin, which is eternal death. So Jesus is telling the people who heard the Gospel and believed it that they have "passed from death unto life".

Questions To Think About

1. Have you passed from death unto life? If you don't know or are unsure talk to your parents or pastor.
2. Are you living like a disciple of Jesus? If not, repent. If you are, keep up the good work.

October 22

So he answered and said, "You shall love the LORD your God with all your heart, with all your soul, with all your strength, and with all your mind, and your neighbor as yourself."
Luke 10:27

When a lawyer tested Jesus by asking what he should do to inherit eternal life, Jesus made him answer his own question. The lawyer answered correctly and Jesus said; now you must DO IT. So let's take a look at what Jesus is talking about.

First, we see LOVE. Since TRUE love comes from God, we need to have Jesus in our hearts as the lawyer rightly stated. Then we see that the heart is involved. We know from Scripture that our heart is where we make decisions and whatever is in our heart we will act out. So we need to have a pure heart which will only result from a relationship with Jesus. The verse goes on to say that we must love with our soul. Our soul is the "self" that lives in our bodies and makes us who we are. We will only be joyful when our hearts and souls are filled with GOD. Then we see that we are to love with ALL our strength. This is really important because it takes lots of strength to discipline ourselves to do all of the above and this discipline is impossible without the Holy Spirit living in us and helping us. Another part of us that comes into play in this verse is our mind. This is what Satan is trying to control. Whoever controls our mind has won the battle. This is why it is so important to be careful what we see and hear, because these are the things that feed our mind. Lastly we are to love our neighbor as ourselves. This is a tall order, but, we have Jesus to thank for making this all possible. We should thank Him every day for being so free with His wonderful gifts.

QUESTIONS TO THINK ABOUT

1. Do you love the Lord your God with all your heart, soul, strength, mind and your neighbor?

October 23

"And do not seek what you should eat or what you should drink, nor have an anxious mind. For all these things the nations of the world seek after, and your Father knows that you need these things. But seek the kingdom of God, and all these things shall be added to you." Luke 12:29-31

If we could obey this scripture, that Jesus himself gave us, we would be so much happier. Jesus tells us not to be anxious, but this is really hard sometimes. Let's say Dad loses his job or perhaps Mother is ill or maybe we are worried we won't pass a class at school. Any one of these situations can make us VERY ANXIOUS.

But Jesus says that our Father knows our needs. So, instead of becoming fearful, we need to trust in the LORD. We need to focus on Jesus' instructions for furthering His Kingdom. In other words, we are going to have to take our minds off of ourselves and ask for guidance to do and be what our Heavenly Father wants us to do or be. If we live by this promise we will get what we need. Isn't that the greatest PROMISE? And all we have to do is to seek God first. WOW!

Questions To Think About

1. Are you ever anxious? If so, what makes you anxious?
2. How do you "get over" feeling anxious? (You might need your parents' help on this one.)
3. What is the difference between what you WANT and what you NEED? Does Jesus promise to fulfill all of our WANTS?

October 24

Now we know that God does not hear sinners; but if anyone is a worshiper of God and does His will, He hears him. John 9:31

Right before this verse, Jesus healed a man who had been blind since birth. The church leaders were upset because they were afraid of losing their grip on the people of that day. Instead of rejoicing over this miracle, they accused Jesus of having a demon and said that He was a sinner. The blind man didn't know who Jesus was when He healed him, but he refused to let the Pharisees get away with this lie. Scripture says, the blind man BOLDLY said, "If he is not of God, how could he open my eyes?" The church leaders were so angry; they kicked the formerly blind man out of the church. Jesus heard about this and found the man he had healed and told him that He was Jesus the son of God. The man believed, rejoiced, and worshiped Jesus.

Even though someone has a position in the church, it does not guarantee that he knows Jesus. What the once blind man told the Pharisees is still true today; God does not hear the prayers of those who are not His children. The man continued *but if anyone is a worshiper of God and DOES HIS WILL, He hears him.* The Bible tells us of many wonderful things God promises to do for us when we are OBEDIENT. How do we know what to do to OBEY God? We read His Word, listen in Sunday school and church and obey our parents. So READ, STUDY, AND OBEY.

QUESTIONS TO THINK ABOUT

1. Are you obeying God BOLDLY?

October 25

"When you are invited by anyone to a wedding feast, do not sit down in the best place, lest one more honorable than you be invited by him; and he who invited you and him come and say to you, 'Give place to this man,' and then you begin with shame to take the lowest place. For whoever exalts himself will be humbled, and he who humbles himself will be exalted."
Luke 14: 8-9, 11

Even though we may never be invited to a wedding feast, this verse is still important because it is about so much more than seating. Jesus is not worried about where we sit when we eat, he is pointing out that we should have a right attitude. What right attitude—HUMILITY. If everything is "easy" and we "always win", we have a tendency to think we are "really something special" and PRIDE sets in. BUT, we should never forget that everything comes from God. If we are good at something, it is a gift and we should give Him the glory.

OR, perhaps we just like to be "seen with the important people". We push ourselves past others to get to hang out with them. Jesus warns in this verse that we need to watch out, because things can happen that will bring us down a notch or two. We should be HUMBLE. Humble doesn't mean that we let people run over us. It does mean that we listen and are interested in others more than ourselves. It has much more meaning when someone comes to us and thanks us or honors us than if we BRAG about what we do. Besides, we don't have to worry about getting CREDIT for every "good deed", because Jesus knows everything and HE WILL HONOR US. Remember things done in secret will be rewarded openly for everyone to see.

Questions To Think About

1. Do you have a humble attitude? Do you put others first?

October 26

"Does he thank that servant because he did the things that were commanded him? I think not. So likewise you, when you have done all those things which you are commanded, say, 'We are unprofitable servants. We have done what was our duty to do.'"
Luke 17:9-10

We all like complements don't we? Sometimes we may not deserve compliments but we still want them. I can remember when my older sister was complimented and I would say something like, "Well, I did that too. What about me?" We feel important even when we have to ask for a compliment. In these verses, Jesus is telling His disciples that when we do what we are supposed to do, we don't really deserve a compliment and there is really no reason to expect praise. It is so much more rewarding when we sincerely complement others and take our minds off of ourselves.

We need to understand that God EXPECTS us to OBEY. We shouldn't get rewarded just because we obey our Mom and Dad and our teachers. That is expected of a Christian. There will be plenty of rewards for our truly great accomplishments when we get to Heaven. God is a REWARDER of those who diligently seek Him. And we may even be complemented because we are always ready and willing to complement those who really deserve it.

Questions To Think About

1. Do you recognize others when they do something good or nice?

October 27

Then they brought little children to Him, that He might touch them; but the disciples rebuked those who brought them. But when Jesus saw it, He was greatly displeased and said to them, "Let the little children come to Me, and do not forbid them; for of such is the kingdom of God. Assuredly, I say to you, whoever does not receive the kingdom of God as a little child will by no means enter it." And He took them up in His arms, laid His hands on them, and blessed them. Mark 10:13-16

Isn't it interesting how man looks at children and how Jesus looks at them? So much of the time kids get little or no respect from anyone. They seem to be a necessary evil to some and people "put up" with them because they have to. But Jesus looks at children in an entirely different light. He scolded his disciples for telling them to "get lost" and taught the disciples an important lesson about faith that day.

It is as if Jesus were saying, "Don't you guys get it? When kids know who I am, they want to be near me. When they are told that I will always take care of them, they believe me. When they hear that I love them, they love Me back. This is what the kingdom of God is like. They have the faith that everyone needs."

Isn't it great that Jesus loves children? Jesus didn't treat them like second class citizens. God created each of us to be our unique selves and He wants us to be a part of His kingdom. That's why it's so wonderful when kids ask Jesus into their hearts. They have so much longer to love Jesus and do His will.

Questions To Think About

1. Have you praised God today for loving you?
2. Have you asked Jesus into your heart? If you haven't, ask your parents of pastor about it.

October 28

"And whoever desires to be first among you, let him be your slave—just as the Son of Man did not come to be served, but to serve, and to give His life a ransom for many."
Matthew 20:27-28

We all want to be number one. It's just the way we are. We want to be first in whatever we do, but that's not the way to be happy. Jesus spelled it out for us when He told us that we are here in this life to serve or help other people. Look at Jesus. He is the creator of the universe, but when He came to earth what did He do? Jesus served people. Jesus helped people wherever He went and as Christians, He wants us to do the same.

Why does Jesus want us to serve others? Well, one reason is because serving others will make us truly happy. We might picture ourselves in front of crowds of people who say they love us. Maybe they are shouting, "Long live _____! Long live _____! We may dream about being a big name—someone famous; but, Jesus said that isn't what makes us happy or great. What makes us both is helping someone, serving someone in need.

Jesus didn't just TELL us to serve; He did it first. He came to earth *not to be served, but to serve* . . . So think about it. If Jesus, God who created the universe, came as a servant to heal the blind, sick, lame, demon possessed, and helpless, shouldn't we become a servant too. We can humble ourselves and serve others. Everyone is someone's servant. We either serve Satan or Jesus. WHOSE SERVANT DO YOU WANT TO BE?

QUESTIONS TO THINK ABOUT

1. Are you serving God by serving others?

October 29

So Jesus answered and said to him, "What do you want Me to do for you?" The blind man said to Him, "Rabboni, that I may receive my sight." Mark 10:51

This is the story from Scripture about the blind man, Bartimaeus. We might think, "What can I learn from a blind beggar who lived so long ago?" Well, Bartimaeus is definitely a good example of how to follow Jesus. First of all, Bartimaeus was going about his usual business, when he heard that Jesus was coming: Jesus, the one everyone said could perform miracles; Jesus, who had healed many blind people. Bartimaeus wanted to see; he wanted to be healed. So Bartimaeus called out for mercy. Even though the people around him tried to shut him up he kept yelling. Because he was persistent, Jesus asked him to come to Him and then He asked him what he wanted. Bartimaeus said, "I want to see." Jesus answered him, "Your faith has made you whole." From that second on Bartimaeus was healed. The Bible doesn't stop there. It goes on to say that Bartimaeus followed Jesus.

So what can we learn from "a blind beggar who lived so long ago"? We can learn how to "follow Jesus". First, he called out to Jesus for mercy (not what he deserved). Second, he kept calling until Jesus heard him. Third, he went to Jesus when Jesus called him. Fourth, he told Jesus what he needed. Fifth, he received his sight (we are all blind until Jesus comes into our hearts). Sixth, he followed Jesus. Seventh, he was joyous and praised God. There it is, just what we need to do to follow Jesus.

Questions To Think About

1. Are you a Bartimaeus?

October 30

Nevertheless even among the rulers many believed in Him, but because of the Pharisees they did not confess Him, lest they should be put out of the synagogue; for they loved the praise of men more than the praise of God. John 12:42-43

We look back at these people who lived during Jesus' lifetime and wonder, "Why wouldn't they believe Him? Why wouldn't they follow Him?" The answer applies not only to those who lived during Jesus' day, but to us as well. The answer is FEAR. Let's think about it. What if, we were in a group of kids and they were making fun of Christians. Would we have the courage to stand up to them and say, "I'm a Christian and I think you have it all wrong?" OR, what if we were asked to do something that we didn't feel reflected Jesus. Would we have the courage to say no or would we go along because we didn't want the other kids to make fun of us or think we were different? OR, what if we wanted to "fit-in" and in order to do that the kids said we had to steal something from the mall, just something small, would we walk away? OR, what if everyone else said mean things to someone or called him names, would we join in? The examples and questions could go on and on, and this is what the verses are talking about.

As Christians, we have to have the courage to stand tall and not let the approval of others be more important to us that the approval of God. Remember, Jesus said, "If you deny me before men, I will deny you before my Father." We need to stop and think about the direction others are pulling us. Are they leading us into temptation? We need to flee from those situations. And remember, Jesus is right there with us, giving us the strength to withstand temptation and bringing us the joy of OBEDIENCE.

Questions To Think About

1. Are you living as a courageous Christian should? If not, what do you need to change?

October 31

"But what do you think? A man had two sons, and he came to the first and said, 'Son, go, work today in my vineyard. He answered and said, 'I will not,' but afterward he regretted it and went. Then he came to the second and said likewise. And he answered and said, 'I go, sir,' but he did not go. Which of the two did the will of his father?" Matthew 21:28-31a

"Which of the two did the will of his father?" We probably would answer that the first son did and this is what we need to talk about today. Sometimes we are like the first son in this story. We have a "mean streak" in us and we don't want to do what we know we should. We really don't have any good reason; we just don't FEEL like it. It is sort of like when we are supposed to clean our rooms, take out the trash, or watch our baby sister. It doesn't have to be anything big for us to be rebellious, but the way we act in little things shows how we will probably act when the BIG things do come along. In these verses, the son who said he didn't want to go work, started thinking about what he had said and decided that he was wrong and that he was being DISOBEDIENT. So he REPENTED and did go work in the vineyard. This was the right thing to do, but he should have obeyed right away. However, it is a good thing that he repented.

Then we have the son who LIED. He said he would go right away to work in the vineyard but he never went. He might have fully intended to go when he told his father that he would go, and maybe he just got caught up in doing things he wanted to do and forgot all about what he told his father. Or maybe he never really intended to go. Whatever the case, the fact is that HE WAS DISOBEDIENT and didn't seem to care that he didn't do his part or that he lied to his father.

We all know that we aren't perfect and there will be times when we disobey; but, if we REPENT (ask for forgiveness) and then OBEY, our HEAVENLY FATHER will FORGIVE us. But if we don't repent we are rebelling against God. Isn't it great that our Heavenly Father, who is King of ALL, will forgive us as if we hadn't been rebellious at all?

QUESTIONS TO THINK ABOUT

1. Have you been disobedient and rebellious lately?
2. Have you repented and asked for forgiveness?

NOTES

November 1

And no one was able to answer Him a word, nor from that day on did anyone dare question Him anymore. Matthew 22:46

This verse is really kind of funny because the Pharisees, Sadducees and Scribes thought they were so smart that they could trick Jesus into making a mistake by asking Him some hard questions. The Pharisees asked Him if they should pay taxes. Jesus told them to give to the government what they owed and to God what He was owed. So the Pharisees didn't cross Him up.

Now it was the Sadducees turn and they asked Him about the resurrection. Of course, they didn't even believe that there was life after death. Once again Jesus answered them with the truth, but evil people are not ready to hear the truth. So when He told them that people would not marry when they were resurrected but would be like the angles, they didn't know what to say. Jesus was not tricked into giving an untrue answer.

Then came the Scribes and they just knew they could get the job done and find some reason to put Him to death. They asked Him what was the greatest commandment. They just knew they had Him this time, but Jesus told them the first and greatest commandment was to "LOVE God" with everything in us and the next was to "LOVE YOUR NEIGHBOR as yourself." They couldn't argue with that and as the Scripture says they didn't DARE ask Him another question so they just kept SILENT. God is truth and He can not lie. Isn't that exciting? GOD IS TRULY AWESOME !

Questions To Think About

1. How do we know what the truth is?
2. Can you think of a time when it was hard for you to tell the truth?

November 2

Now Jesus sat opposite the treasury and saw how the people put money into the treasury. And many who were rich put in much. Then one poor widow came and threw in two mites, which make a quadrans. So He called His disciples to Himself and said to them, "Assuredly, I say to you that this poor widow has put in more than all those who have given to the treasury; for they all put in out of their abundance, but she out of her poverty put in all that she had, her whole livelihood." Mark 12:41

This verse points out a very important fact. I know sometimes we think because we don't have much money that we don't need to give at Sunday School or Church; but, this story of this poor woman is told to us for a reason. Why do you think this story is in the Bible? I'll tell you why I think it is.

First of all, the money that she had is less than pennies to us. The mite was the lowest denomination of coins in circulation. A quadrans was a Roman coin worth ONE SIXTY-FOURTH of a denarius, which was one day's wage. However, the important point wasn't that it was such a small amount but that it was ALL that she had. It was her willing attitude to give.

When we get an allowance or are given some money is our attitude like the widow's? Do we even think about giving some of it to help others? We may think it is such a small amount it wouldn't even count; but, think of this verse. If we give from our heart, God can use it for His glory. God established long ago that when His believers came to worship Him they were to bring a gift. It is still a part of worship today.

QUESTIONS TO THINK ABOUT

1. Why do you think we should bring a gift to a worship service?
2. Why doesn't the amount of the gift matter?

November 3

Who then is a faithful and wise servant, whom his master made ruler over his household, to give them food in due season? Blessed is that servant whom his master, when he comes, will find so doing. Matthew 24:45-46

Do you ever wonder "How can I faithfully serve the Lord?" When we are young we think when we get older we will be able to do something great. Then, when we're older, we think that it's time for the young people to serve. God's Word says regardless of our age we can serve Him. How? We serve Him by serving each other.

Jesus said what we do for other people, we do for Him. All through the Bible He encourages us to visit the sick, feed the hungry and clothe the naked. We don't have to go to some far off place to help people. When God puts others in our lives we are to minister to their needs, whatever they are.

The key word in our Scripture today is faithful and the next one is servant. We are all here on earth to do something for others. Every single one of us—NO excuses!

All that is really necessary is to be very SENSITIVE to others, see their needs and HELP them however we can. The more we serve, the more Jesus will send others in need our way. If every Christian will just do this, "God's will, will be done on earth as it is in Heaven." So TODAY when we see someone with a need—MEET it. HAVE A GREAT TIME SERVING THOSE AROUND YOU! Jesus did!

Questions To Think About

1. How has another Christian ministered to you?
2. Name one thing you can do for someone today.

November 4

. . . And those who were ready went in with him to the wedding: and the door was shut. Afterward the other virgins came also, saying, "Lord, Lord, open to us!" But he answered and said," Assuredly, I say to you, I do not know you.
Matthew 25:10-11

This is the parable of the ten virgins; five were ready and waiting for the bridegroom to come. Another five were there also; but, they did not have their lamps ready. They were not prepared to meet the Bridegroom.

It is the same with us. Just because we go to the church every time the doors are open does not mean that we are prepared to meet Jesus. Some people think if they just show up and go through all the motions that they are Christians. Jesus told this parable so people would know that they must be prepared for His coming. Jesus is preparing a great feast for all of His followers and some day He will come for His followers.

There are two things that we need to remember about being prepared. First, we have to have Jesus living in our hearts. When we are drawn to Him by His Holy Spirit, we see our sin and repent. Then Jesus comes to live in our hearts; and, He changes us completely. We are now a new person. Love is more important in our lives and we act differently to others. We are READY to put others first which shows that Jesus really did change us. Now we watch for things we can do to help others showing our love for them. This is how we glorify God.

The five unwise virgins showed up but they were not prepared. They had lamps to light the way but not enough oil to last. They had not taken the time to prepare. They wanted to borrow oil from the prepared virgins; but, Jesus tells us that each person is responsible for himself.

Questions To Think About

1. Are you like the wise or unwise virgin in the parable?
2. How do others know that we are Christians?

November 5

A new commandment I give to you, that you love one another; as I have loved you, that you also love one another. By this all will know that you are My disciples, if you have love for one another.
John 13:34-35

Let's stop and think how this is a new commandment. When Jesus told his disciples this, loving others certainly wasn't a new command. Remember the commandment "love your neighbor as yourself"? Let's look how Jesus changed this idea to make a new commandment. He changed neighbor to one another. Then He said, love as I have loved you. He also added that this is how we know that people are Christians, His followers.

This thread of LOVE runs throughout the Bible because God wrote it and HE IS LOVE. This is a command not just a suggestion that we MIGHT do if we want to or if we feel like it. We are commanded by Jesus to love fellow Christians. He said to His disciples, and to us, that if we are one of His, we will love each other, not as we love ourselves, but with a much higher kind of love, a SUPERNATURAL love. We can love in this way because Jesus first loved us in this way.

Questions To Think About

1. Do you love your fellow Christians?
2. How do you show it?

November 6

. . . Let not your heart be troubled, neither let it be afraid.
John 14:27

I guess all of us have been afraid of something or someone at one time or another; but, Jesus is telling us here that there is no need to be afraid. He has done all that is necessary for us not to fear anything. When we fear something we are to go to Him. The next time we are tempted to be afraid, no matter what the situation is, we just need to whisper a short prayer. It doesn't have to be a long one; He will hear us and help us stay calm.

One time I was driving down the highway on a rainy day and a car passed me going very fast. Suddenly, the other driver lost control and his car was spinning around right in front of me. All I had time to do was say; "Jesus, Jesus." The Holy Spirit knew that one of His children was in need and immediately He was in control of the situation. The other car went off the road and I was safe. We can always call on Jesus because He promised that He would never leave us.

Jesus also says that our hearts are not to be troubled. This means we should not worry. Jesus understands our fears and concerns and because He loves us, He will work everything out for us. He will never let us down. Isn't it wonderful to know that He is never too busy to hear from us? Remember, He likes to hear from us, so don't forget to pray and thank Him for taking away our fears, doubts and worries.

Questions To Think About

1. Why do you think you should thank Jesus for watching over you?
2. Why shouldn't we worry about anything?

November 7

Watch and pray, lest you enter into temptation. The spirit indeed is willing, but the flesh is weak. Mark 14:38

Jesus said this to His disciples when He went into the garden to pray just before He was betrayed by Judas. The disciples didn't do what He asked; instead, they fell asleep. Rather than standing by Jesus like they said they would, they ran away. Remember when the girl recognized Peter as one of Jesus' disciples, Peter said he didn't even know who Jesus was. Then Peter heard the rooster crow. Peter was very sorry, but if he had only WATCHED AND PRAYED, he would not have fallen into this sin.

It is the same with us today. If we don't pray, (I don't mean just once in a while on Sunday or when we get into trouble), regularly in our everyday life, we will fall into sin. Jesus understands that we live in a world where evil is everywhere. That is why He tells us to watch and pray. He is there to help us but we have to ask for His help and let Him guide us through the temptations we come up against.

God gave us the Bible so that we can know right from wrong, but we have to read it. The more we read the Bible and know how Jesus wants His followers to act the easier it is to OBEY Him. When we obey it makes us HAPPY.

Questions To Think About

1. What does it mean to be betrayed?
2. Why should we read the Bible regularly?

November 8

Then he began to curse and swear, saying "I do not know the Man!" Immediately a rooster crowed and Peter remembered the word of Jesus who had said to him "Before the rooster crows, you will deny Me three times." So he went out and wept bitterly.
Matthew 26:74-75

Peter was a lot like us, wasn't he? He had told Jesus that he would go to his death for Him, but just a few hours later he had forgotten about his pledge and was shouting curses saying that he had never even known Jesus. We all remember this part of the story but to me the most important part is the very last sentence, "So he went out and wept bitterly."

When Peter realized what he had done he was very sorry. First of all, he recognized that he had sinned. So much of the time we think: "Oh well, it wasn't that bad, everyone is doing it and so it must be okay." We need to realize that sin is anything that separates us from God and call it what it is, SIN.

Peter and Judas realized that what they had done was sin, but they responded so differently. Peter repented with bitter tears, but Judas didn't go to Jesus and ask Him to forgive him.

Repentance does not mean we are sorry because we got caught doing something wrong. Repentance means that we are truly sorry that we did what was wrong. When we ask for forgiveness, it makes us stronger. Then, the next time we are tempted we can say: "No, I'm not going to do that. I got in trouble last time and Jesus forgave me and I don't want to go through that again."

The Bible says that Peter wept bitterly. There is something about tears that shows that we are really, really sorry. We know Peter was truly sorry because he became one of the greatest disciples. Peter's repentance made him grow as a Christian. If we do as Peter did when we sin we will GROW in CHRIST as well. Thank You, Father for forgiveness.

QUESTIONS TO THINK ABOUT

1. What does it mean to repent?
2. What was the difference between Peter and Judas?

November 9

For he (Pilate) knew that the chief priests had handed Him over because of ENVY. Mark 15:10

Isn't this terrible? Here the church leaders were so jealous of Jesus because some of the people followed Him that they wanted to kill Him. It just blows my mind to think that the very ones who were supposed to lead the people in their spiritual lives could do this. Envy is one of the worst sins that we can commit.

Just stop and think about it. Most of the crimes today are because someone wants something that someone else has. Envy has caused thefts, murders and wars. Remember the reports when kids were killing other kids to get their Nike shoes? Then there was the high school girl's mother who tried to kill another girl because she made cheerleader and her daughter didn't. It goes on and on. That's how envy works. It may start small but if we don't repent, it can lead to every sin imaginable and ruin our lives.

The very worst thing that ever happened because of envy was when the High Priest wanted Jesus, our Lord and Savior, put to death because he wanted to be more popular and have more POWER than Jesus. The religious leaders were willing to lie or do whatever they had to do to get Jesus out of the way. We too could end up doing terrible things if we let envy get a foothold in our lives. If we know we are envious of someone we need to repent immediately.

Questions To Think About

1. How does envy start and what part does jealously have in envying someone?

November 10

"Father, forgive them, for they do not know what they do."
Luke 23:34

Jesus, who came to earth to save us by dying for our sins, was condemned to die by crucifixion. And, as Jesus hung on the cross, dying, He asked God to forgive the ones who were crucifying Him. Crucifixion is a horrible, extremely painful, slow death. And yet Jesus asked God to forgive the men who were in essence torturing Him to death. And, even before He was hung on the cross, these men made fun of Him, spat on Him, beat Him and pushed a crown of thorns down on His forehead. This Jesus is the one who created everything. This Jesus created the very men who were doing all these horrible things to Him. While He was on the cross these men gambled for His clothes, tried to give Him sour wine and still mocked Him. Yet Jesus asked His Father to forgive them.

If I had been as innocent as Jesus and the authorities were putting me to death, it would have been very hard to forgive them. Yet, because Jesus was sent to go through all this so that we could be spared, He felt compassion toward the people who were doing and saying all these terrible things to Him. He was being OBEDIENT to His Father's will. Therefore, He had a peace that only comes when we are obedient to God. This doesn't mean that He didn't suffer both mentally and physically but it means that He knew whatever His Father wanted Him to do He would do it.

We all want forgiveness for the bad things that we do, but we need to remember that He forgives us as WE FORGIVE OTHERS. Jesus gave us this perfect example of forgiveness. "Oh Father, help me to have a forgiving spirit like Jesus."

QUESTIONS TO THINK ABOUT

1. Is there someone you need to forgive?
2. Why is it important to forgive others?

November 11

But the angel answered and said to the women, "Do not be afraid, for I know that you seek Jesus who was crucified. He is not here; for He is risen, as He said. Come; see the place where the Lord lay. Matthew 28:5

Mary Magdalene had not always been a follower of Jesus. She had been a sinner just like all of us until she met Him. She then faithfully followed and loved Jesus. She knew how much Jesus had done for her and we can only imagine how she felt after she saw Him Crucified. Even though she did not fully understand what had happened, her mind was still on the Lord. She had to wait to prepare his body for burial until the Sabbath was over but BEFORE DAYLIGHT she was at the tomb eager to serve her Lord.

It wasn't until later when the Holy Spirit of God came to Jesus' disciples that they finally understood all that had happened. Now they realized why Jesus came down from Heaven and died on the cross. Now they knew they had to tell others about their Lord.

Mary Magdalene was a great SERVANT of Jesus. She gave us an excellent example to follow. We should be obedient, available, and THANKFUL for what Jesus has done for each one of us.

Questions To Think About

1. How can we show our love for Jesus?
2. Why did Jesus come to earth?

November 12

Go therefore and make disciples of all the nations . . . I am with you always . . . Matthew 28:19-20

Jesus was just about to go back to Heaven because His work on earth was finished, for now. He gave His disciples instructions before He left. He told them to GO. Now we, as His followers, know what we are to be about.

I noticed that Jesus didn't mention age when He gave this command. Sometimes we use our age as an excuse for not doing anything for the Lord. When we're just KIDS, we say we are too young; but, when we get older, we say we are too old. Jesus says to ALL His disciples GO. Often we think this means we have to go around the world; but, we are to go to those right around us. Many times that is the hardest thing to do. Answering Jesus' call may mean that we eventually travel far away, but in the meantime we are to begin where we are. When we do a good job right where we are, it may be in His plan to send us somewhere else. We have to listen to our hearts and then we will know just what Jesus wants us to do and where He wants us to do it. He will make the way for us whether it is at home or in a foreign nation.

One of the greatest things Jesus promises in His Word is that HE WILL ALWAYS BE WITH US. Stop and think about that. WOW! Isn't that awesome? Just think, Jesus is so concerned about US that He never leaves us by ourselves. Where He is there is peace, love and understanding. But we can shut Him out of our lives and not receive all He has for us by ignoring Him and His Word.

QUESTIONS TO THINK ABOUT

1. Why is it important to listen to what Jesus tells us?
2. How does it make you feel to know that Jesus is always with you?

November 13

Then Peter said to them, "Repent, and let every one of you be baptized in the name of Jesus Christ for the remission of sins: and you shall receive the gifts of the Holy Spirit. For the Promise is to you and to your children, and to all who are afar off as many as the Lord our God will call." Acts 2:38-39

We have heard a lot about the Holy Spirit, but we may still be kind of in the dark as to who He is and how we are filled with the Holy Spirit. Here, Peter is telling the people how to be saved and receive the Holy Spirit. Peter says, "First, we must repent. We tell Jesus that we are sorry and really mean it for all the bad things we have ever done. After repentance, so that we are identified with Jesus, we are baptized. Then by grace, the gift of the Holy Spirit comes to live in us." He comes to teach us as we read the Bible, to comfort us when we are sad, and to discipline us when we sin.

Peter wasn't just talking to the people who were in the crowd that day. He knew that from that day forward, everyone who believes in Jesus would be given the gift of the Holy Spirit. The Holy Spirit is for all who are called by the Lord our God. This is a PROMISE by God and God always keeps His promises.

Questions To Think About

1. Does the Holy Spirit live in everyone?
2. What does the Holy Spirit do for us?

November 14

. . . for if this plan or this work is of men, it will come to nothing; but, if it is of God, you cannot overthrow it—lest you even be found to fight against God. Acts 5:38

I think all of us have really wanted to do something great for God? Perhaps being in the Christmas play at church is something we think is "great" and we are doing it for Jesus. However, when we stop and think about it we know we really just wanted to "show off" our acting ability? Or, it could be any number of things.

This is what Gamaliel, a teacher of the law, was telling the church leaders. "If Peter and his crowd are just showing off, it won't amount to anything, but if it really is of God, then no one can stop them."

This is a great rule to go by. We should always check out why we are doing what we say we are doing for God, the church, or other people. Are we helping feed the homeless at Thanksgiving because we want to get "credit" for doing something good, or do we sincerely feel sorry for the people because they don't have food like we do? Do we truly want them to see how Christians really love others and give unselfishly?

We need to listen to the Holy Spirit and let Him lead us so that we can be sure that it isn't just us wanting to be noticed. We should always be available for whatever comes our way, and if we act out of love for others, we will all be blessed.

QUESTIONS TO THINK ABOUT

1. Have you ever done something for someone that no one knew about?
2. What is a blessing?

November 15

When they heard these things they were cut to the heart and they gnashed at him (Stephen) with their teeth. Then they cried out with a loud voice, stopped their ears and ran at him with one accord and they cast him out of the city and stoned him.
Acts 7:54 & 7:57

Stephen was a young man who, as Scripture says, was "full of faith and the Holy Spirit." He was not afraid to tell the truth about God and Jesus. He knew that there were many who would not believe and that they might run him out of town or even kill him, but he had to tell the truth about his Lord.

There are people today, both young and old, who are just like those in Stephen's day. They do not want to hear the truth. Jesus tells us that evil men hated Him and that they would hate us as well. Today, there are those who won't let the word of God be heard in our schools, public places, or government buildings. These people are saying to us, just as the people said to Stephen, "We're not listening to your talk about Jesus or your God. We are a free people who will determine our own path in this life, so we aren't interested in your Christian ideas."

We have heard about missionaries who have lost their lives trying to tell a lost world about Jesus. In this day and time, more people are killed for their faith in Jesus than ever before in the history of the world.

Questions To Think About

1. Could you die for your Christian faith?
2. Can you name someone who did?

November 16

As for Saul, he made havoc of the church, entering every house, and dragging off men and women, committing them to prison. Therefore those who were scattered went everywhere preaching the word . . . Acts 8:3-4

Saul, whose name became Paul after he was saved, was being very cruel to the Christians in Jerusalem, but Jesus' followers didn't hide or stop telling others about His Kingdom, instead they left Jerusalem and preached in a number of different places. What was meant to be a way to destroy the new Christians, God turned around and the good news was spread throughout the land. Many more people heard the word and believed.

Isn't it great how God works everything out for His glory? I get excited when I stop and think about how He will work out our lives so that others can be blessed by us. God has put us in this very place so that we can be His witnesses in our family, our church, our school, and our community. The neat thing about living the Christian life is that it is so exciting. I recently asked one of my sons if he had ever dreamed that he would be living in Hong Kong when he as a little boy. He answered, "Not in a million years." We never know what God has in stores for us, but we can be sure it will be exciting. There is a whole big world out there just waiting for us to spread God's word just as those early Christians did. All we have to do is be faithful and listen.

QUESTIONS TO THINK ABOUT

1. When and where do we start serving Jesus?

November 17

Then Peter opened his mouth and said: "In truth I perceive that God shows no partiality. But in every nation whoever fears Him and works righteousness is accepted by Him. The word which God sent to the children of Israel, preaching peace through Jesus Christ—He is Lord of all." Acts 11:34-36

Peter had a vision that made him realize that God wanted the Apostles to go to "all the nations" because God wanted all people, as well as the Jews, to be part of His Kingdom.

This is a clear picture that points to us and says, "It doesn't matter who we are—white, yellow, brown or black, American, Chinese, Mexican or Russian, beautiful or ugly, rich or poor—Jesus is LORD of ALL."

Sometimes we Americans think of ourselves a little higher than we ought to. I never will forget, when we lived in the Marshall Islands, hearing a missionary preach an outstanding message and thinking, "He shouldn't be wasting his time here in the islands. He is such a good preacher, he should be preaching to large crowds of people in the United States." I've asked for forgiveness for that thought but often this is the way we feel even if we don't say it.

Jesus is not a respecter of people. He calls who His Father has given Him, and He uses us to help Him spread the GOSPEL. We must never let pride get in the way of reaching others who are different from us. Isn't it wonderful that when we get to Heaven we'll all be beautiful to Jesus? Pray that Jesus will use us to reach anyone He sends our way.

Questions To Think About

1. What makes us think that we are better than others?
2. Why should we treat everyone with love?

November 18

Then he (Herod) killed James the brother of John with the sword. And because he saw that it pleased the Jews, he proceeded further to seize Peter also. Peter was therefore kept in prison, but constant prayer was offered to God for him by the church.
Acts 12: 2, 3 & 5

This scripture is telling us about the worst of times and the best of times as well. The Christians were being persecuted but their numbers were also growing in size and faith. This gives us a great example to follow. When someone in our church is hurting or in need whatever it might be, we should also have them in our prayers and thoughts. For example, if a friend is sick even if it is just a cold we should pray. When someone hasn't been coming to church for a while we should pray. When someone is acting hateful toward us or others we should pray. When someone doesn't seem to have a friend we should pray.

After we pray, it's time to listen to what the Holy Spirit is saying to us. Are we the one who needs to go and help that person? It may be that God is calling us to be a friend who will listen and share our time, money, clothes, food or whatever to meet the person's need at that time.

We pray for others so that God can use us any way He wants. Isn't it neat that even though God doesn't need us to meet other's needs that He lets us get in on it and get a blessing?

QUESTIONS TO THINK ABOUT

1. Do you know someone you need to pray for right now?
2. Can you think of a time when you needed help and someone helped you?

November 19

So God who knows the heart acknowledged them by giving them the Holy Spirit, just as He did to us and made no distinction between us and them, purifying their hearts by faith.
Acts 15: 8

You know it is an awesome thought that God knows our hearts. It doesn't really matter what people think about us from our looks on the outside but what counts is what is in our hearts. Many times we may be misunderstood by other people, and it may seem no matter what we say or do, we can't change their minds about us. It doesn't matter because God knows exactly what we meant by our actions and our words.

I knew a boy that was very shy and everyone thought because he wasn't outgoing and talkative that he was stuck up. He was really hurting on the inside but he just didn't know how to make the other kids realize he wanted to be their friend. He was afraid they wouldn't like him, and he just couldn't make himself say anything to them.

Jesus always included the people that on one else seemed to care about. He always had a good word for them. We just need to think about how we would feel if we were in their place and always be kind to everyone. There are always those around us that need a kind word so let's make it our mission to be the one who finds and accepts them. A new friendship will begin and we will be blessed.

Questions To Think About

1. How does God look at people?
2. How should we see others even if they are not like us?

November 20

Therefore the law was our tutor to bring us to Christ, that we might be justified by faith. But after faith has come, we are no longer under a tutor. Galatians 3:24-25

When Paul wrote this letter to the Galatians, a tutor was a slave responsible for a child's training, especially for pointing out and punishing misbehavior. The tutor was to separate and protect the child from the influence of outsiders. This is what God's law was to do. It was to point the Jews to their Messiah, Jesus the Christ. The law couldn't save them. Faith in the Messiah was what they needed to be saved just as it is with us today.

I have heard people say that we don't have to obey the Ten Commandments any more, but that isn't true. We are not saved by obeying them, but if we love Jesus we will want to obey them. Jesus said, "If you love me obey my commandments." They show us what to do and what not to do so that we can have a rewarding and happy life. This is one reason that "the world" wants the Ten Commandments banned from our schools and many public places. They want to live the way they want and not have anything put a guilt trip on them. They want to believe only in themselves and not rely on God's plan for their lives.

When we follow Jesus, the Holy Spirit will lead us through the Ten Commandments and other lessons we learn from His Word. We show our love to Him by our obedience to Him and our love for others.

Questions To Think About

1. Why did God give us the Ten Commandments?
2. How do we show our love to Jesus and other people?

November 21

Have I therefore become your enemy because I tell you the truth?
Galatians 4:16

Sometimes it is hard to hear the truth, isn't it? Paul was having this trouble with the churches he had started. Practices had gotten into the churches which were not supposed to be there and when he told them about it the church members were angry with him.

Often, we don't like to hear the truth either, especially when it's about something that we want to do but it won't be the best thing for us. We fight or argue with the people who bring us this news even though down deep, we know that they are right. If our parents say we can't go to a party on a school night, chances are we will try to "talk" them into it. We know that they are our parents and that as a Christian we are to obey them. As we grow in our Christian life we are able to listen and understand the truth better.

However, listening to the truth is something that we will always have to think about and work on.

When someone tells us the truth, there is no reason to dislike them. We should thank them. Lies are from the devil, even though they may be what we want to hear. The Bible tells us that the devil is the author of lies. We certainly don't want to listen to what he has to say.

Questions To Think About

1. Why should Christians obey rules?
2. Why do we not want to hear the truth sometimes?

November 22

So then, my beloved brethren, let every man be swift to hear, slow to speak, slow to wrath; for the wrath of man does not produce the righteousness of God. James 1:19-20

James, Jesus' brother, gave us some good advice in these two verses. There are three things he mentions that we should always remember. The very first thing and probably the hardest of all, is to be swift to hear, which means listen. It has often been said that is why God gave us two ears and only one mouth, that we should listen twice as much as we speak. Just listen when a group gets together and you'll hear them interrupting each other almost every sentence. And when we do this what we are really saying is "what I have to say is more important that what you have to say." We never LEARN anything when we are talking. It is only when we listen that we learn.

The second thing we can learn from this Scripture is to be slow to speak. This means we should think before we say anything. We have all said things that we wish we hadn't said? The problem is, once something is said, we can never take those words back.

The third thing James tells us is to be slow to wrath. That means we shouldn't "fly off the handle" and get angry at every little thing. It is very difficult to be around someone who is this way. We are afraid to say anything or do anything in his presence because we don't know how he will react. No one likes to be around someone like that. We need to realize that we shouldn't be like that either. James tells us that people who act like this aren't setting a very good example as followers of Jesus.

QUESTIONS TO THINK ABOUT

1. Have you ever said anything that you wished you hadn't?
2. How did you feel afterwards?

November 23

So he (Apollos) began to speak boldly in the synagogue. Acts 18:26

Apollos was a Jewish man who had become a Christian and he was so "on fire" for Jesus that he spoke boldly in the synagogue. He is a great example for us in our Christian walk. Even though he didn't know all there was to know about his new found faith he went ahead and told what he did know. So often we don't think we could be a very good witness for Christ because we don't know a lot. But if we just tell people what Jesus has done for us others can believe in Him. When Apollos heard from other Christians, he listened and learned even more. The Bible tells us that he greatly helped others.

So when we first meet Jesus we start on a wonderful journey that will last forever, and every day we will learn new things if we study our Bible, listen to other Christians, and ask the Holy Spirit to help us. He will help us understand more and give us wisdom.

One of the best things I've heard on answered prayer came from an eight year old girl. She said that she had a cow that she had to milk and that the cow had gotten into a barbed wire fence and hurt its udder and she didn't want to milk her that evening. She was afraid the cow would kick over the bucket and she would loose all the milk. Then she remembered to pray and she asked God to please make the cow stand still and she would be very gentle with her if she would just not kick over the bucket. She told me, "You know that my cow didn't move at all and I just was so happy that I had prayed and that God had heard me and answered me." What a great testimony. We can go to God in prayer just as she did and he will hear us also.

Questions To Think About

1. What are some things you might talk to God about today?
2. Have you ever told anyone about one of your answered prayers?

November 24

But concerning brotherly love . . . you are taught by God to love one another . . . But we urge you, brethren that you increase more and more, that you also aspire to lead a quiet life, to mind your own business, and to work with your own hands . . . that you may walk properly toward those who are outside, and that you may lack nothing. I Thessalonians 4:9-12

This is a long passage, but it is so important for us to know. Those who are outside are people who are not Christians. Paul says that we are not only to love other Christians but everyone who we come in contact with. Sometimes it is hard to be nice and kind to people who mistreat us or say untrue things about us, but we are to treat them as we would want to be treated. If we are Christians, we can do it because Jesus will help us with all things.

Paul tells us to lead a quiet life which means not to stir up trouble. We all know someone who enjoys causing trouble, and no one really likes to be around people like that. It certainly isn't the way we should act as followers of Jesus.

We are also to mind our own business. We can accomplish this by not gossiping or telling others what they should do. If they ask for our help, then we gladly give it to them, but we should wait for them to ask.

We are also to work with our own hands. This includes a list of dos and don'ts. We are not to cheat, we are to do our part, and we are to be dependable whatever our tasks are.

When we act as Paul says in this scripture, we are promised that we will lack nothing that God has for us. That sounds like a good deal to me.

QUESTIONS TO THINK ABOUT

1. What should you do when someone starts talking bad about someone?
2. Why is cheating bad?

November 25

But as for you, brethren, do not grow weary in doing good.
II Thessalonians 3:13

I've had days when I didn't want to get out of bed. I didn't want anyone messing with me, and doing anything nice was not in my plans for the day. I guess we've all been there, thinking only of OURSELVES. But this isn't what Jesus has in mind for us in our Scripture today.

One reason Paul wrote this to the people of Thessalonica was because some of the believers were not doing their part. Instead they were busy causing trouble.

It's the same today. Maybe our Sunday school class has planned a trip to the rest home to sing. A number of the members don't show up because they had something more fun to do.

Doing things for others isn't easy. It takes sacrifice. That means sometimes we will have to give up something that we want in order to serve others. It takes dedication. This means no matter how we feel, we go ahead and help out anyway. It takes love for others and putting them before our own needs and desires. We are always rewarded when we do good for others. It not only makes us feel good inside, we're glad we did get out of bed and we did change our attitude and we put our selfish plans aside to help someone else. Now, that's not growing weary in doing good.

Questions To Think About

1. Can you think of a time when you didn't do what you wanted to but helped someone instead?
2. How are we rewarded for doing good?

November 26

I do not write these things to shame you, but as my beloved children I warn you. I Corinthians 4:14

None of us likes to be scolded. Many times when we think we are being treated badly, we are just being told the truth. It's like a baby who heads for the cup of hot coffee and her Mom says, "No, no, hot." She is warning the baby that if she grabs the cup that she is going to get burned. What would we think of a mother who just sat there and let her baby grab the coffee and get burned? We would think that she wasn't a very good mother, wouldn't we?

God gave us His Word to warn us against the many dangers we will be exposed to in our daily living. The Bible is full of stories of people who didn't pay attention to what God had warned them about and then they had to pay the consequences. The Bible tells us what we need to know to keep us safe and happy. All through the Bible, God is telling us that we must listen and be obedient to His teachings so that we can live a rewarding life.

Questions To Think About

1. Why is it important to be disciplined?
2. How do people act who have never been disciplined?

November 27

But if anyone loves God, this one is known by Him.
I Corinthians 8:3

We like to be able to say, "I know him, and he is famous." Or, "I met her and she is really somebody." Or, "I saw them at the air terminal and they said, 'Hi." There is just something in us that makes us want to be associated with the rich, famous, and the "in" group. Perhaps we feel that if other people know we "know" someone famous, they will think we are someone special. We've all felt like this—I like to let everyone know that a Governor calls me by my first name; that I knew a Broadway actress, was in a play with her and even took acting lessons from her; that I went to church with Billy Graham's cousin; and I could go on and on. But, when I say those things, does it make me a better person or someone very special? No.

The Bible tells us something that does make us very special. It's the verse above. That is if we love God, then HE knows US. Now that is really something. The God of the Universe who is in control of all governors, all Broadway actresses and Billy Graham's cousin KNOWS ME. My only response is to love God and in turn He will know me in a very special way. It's hard to really understand how awesome this is. God knows us personally and He even knows our name. WOW!

We love those whom we know, so it's our great privilege to get to know God better. We do this by reading about Him and praying to Him and listening to others talk about Him.

Questions To Think About

1. What are you doing to know God better?
2. How do we know that we truly love God?

November 28

Do you not know that those who run in a race all run, but one receives the prize? Run in such a way that you may obtain it.
I Corinthians 9:24

I hope everyone reading this can run faster than I can. Even when I was a kid, I always came in last or at best near the last. Everyone called me "Slow Poke" and I wouldn't even run in a race because I knew that I would never win. But guess what. When I got older, my kids talked me into running with them for exercise. I ran with them as they trained for a marathon, and then they talked me into running a 5K race. And I WON a trophy in my age group. WOW, old "Slow Poke" made it. I have it on my desk to remind me no matter how impossible something seems we should never give up.

This is what Paul is talking about in our Scripture today. Our life is an endurance race and sometimes living like Jesus is very HARD. If we don't stay in there and run with our eyes on Jesus (our goal) we won't win the crown of life.

So, no matter how difficult the circumstances get, keep your eye on winning the greatest prize of all eternal life with Jesus. The Bible tells us that things are going to be so WONDERFUL that we can't even imagine how great life with Jesus will be. That sure beats a little wood and metal trophy sitting on my desk.

Questions To Think About

1. What are some things that make us want to quit being faithful to Jesus?
2. What do we have to look forward to as Christians?

November 29

For if the trumpet makes an uncertain sound, who will prepare for battle? I Corinthians 14:8

In Bible times when soldiers were preparing for battle, their leader would tell the trumpeter to play certain notes. These trumpet blasts would tell the troops exactly what they were supposed to do and where they were to go. Some notes were for going forward, some for retreating, and some for other orders. The trumpet was the only way the officers could make their orders heard above the noise of battle. If the trumpeter slurred the notes or stopped and started in the wrong place, the soldiers would not know what to do.

Today, we are Christians in God's army and we are in a battle every day. So it is very import ant that we hear a sure sound and listen only to those who send a clear message. A message that is consistent with what God tells us in the Bible. When my grandson was small his pastor preached a sermon on abortion. When the sermon was over , my grandson leaned of to his dad and asked, "Dad, was he for abortion or against it ?" The preacher had given an uncertain sound.

It is not just preachers who might send wrong messages. It could be teachers, friends, and world leaders. Even we can be guilty of sending unclear messages when it comes to what we believe. This is why it is so import ant to study and KNOW what the Bible says. Then we will be able to tell others what we believe and why we believe it.

QUESTIONS TO THINK ABOUT

1. Do you know why you are a Christian?
2. Can you tell others what you believe?

November 30

Do not be deceived: "Evil company corrupts good habits."
I Corinthians 15:33

I once knew a boy who seemed to really love the Lord. He came to Sunday school and church and belonged to the youth group. He even talked about becoming a minister or a missionary someday. Out of all the students I ever taught, I *KNEW* he would be a strong Christian all of his life. We moved away and one day I heard that he was not the same kid I had known. It seemed that he had started running around with some boys who weren't interested in the things of God and he had gotten into some trouble at school. His Mom was really worried about him.

What happened to this boy? I couldn't help but wonder. Was it something that the pastor or his Sunday school teachers neglected to do for him? Was it something going on in his home? OR was it the guys he ran around with who were influencing him? Had he bought THE LIE that "all that church stuff isn't important?"

Evil is sometimes dressed up in very beautiful, glamorous, and exciting wrappings. We have to be very careful not to fall into Satan's trap. We should never think, "Oh, that couldn't happen to me." Remember, the world will tell us anything to deceive us and get us off track. However, as children of God, we have the Holy Spirit living us who will guide us if we will listen. Paul said, "Do not be deceived." We are all capable of doing evil so we need to surround ourselves with people who love the Lord and stay in the Word and in church. Then we will be able to discern what is true, and right, and good.

Questions To Think About

1. What are some ways we can fall into temptation?
2. What can we do so we are NOT deceived by the world?

December 1

" . . . while we do not look at the things which are seen, but at the things which are not seen. For the things which are seen are temporary, but the things which are not seen are eternal."
II Corinthians 4:18

Just take a look around. See that favorite game, the paper with an "A", the bedroom set, the picture of friends at the back to school party, and the stuff that no one knows about saved in that special box hidden under the bed. All of that stuff is only temporary.

So, why do we spend so much time looking at it and thinking about it? It just might be because that's where our hearts are. I don't mean we have to become a monk and live on bread and water and sleep on the floor, but we do need to get our priorities right.

All those things are great but we need to know just as Paul was telling the Corinthians that only the things that are not seen are going to last FOREVER. What in the world are things not seen? How can we know and think about something we can't even see?

Well, the things we don't see are things like the love that flows between our parents and us, the kind word we say to someone who really needs a friend, the good deeds we do for our teachers, the smile we share with a passer by, the "thank you" we speak to someone who does us a favor, the volunteering to help out at church, the prayer we say for the missionaries, the holding the door for our grandmother, and a million other thing that we can't put in our room and look at, but things that are hidden in our hearts where God looks. Those are the things not seen that last forever and ever.

Questions To Think About

1. What are some things that you cherish?
2. Name some unseen things you have or can do for others.

December 2

For we know that if our earthly house, this tent, is destroyed, we have a building from God, a house not made with hands, eternal in the heavens. Now He who has prepared us for this very thing is God, who also has given us the Spirit as a guarantee. II Corinthians 5:1 & 5

It's always a good idea to get a guarantee when we buy something. A car may have so many miles or years which ever comes first, a new house has a one year builder's guarantee and some clothes we buy are guaranteed not to fade or shrink. So when we get a guarantee it means that we can be sure that whatever and however long the guarantee is for, the product is going to do what it promises or the seller will fix it or get us a new one.

As a Christian we have the best guarantee that is out there and that is the Holy Spirit. God gave the Holy Spirit to us when we were born again. All Christian have the Holy Spirit living in them to guide, strengthen, teach, and correct them. And since He is there we can KNOW that we have eternal life. It is a guarantee.

Our guarantee, which God has promised us in His Word, is that when we have finished doing what God wants us to do on earth, we are going to get a new body and live forever with Jesus.

So we have nothing to fear EVER if we belong to Jesus. He is right here with us taking care of every detail. That should make us feel really good. Just to know that Jesus, who created the entire world, not only knows us by name but has the time to be with us PERSONALY all the time is a wonderful guarantee.

QUESTIONS TO THINK ABOUT

1. What does guarantee mean?
2. What is eternal life?

December 3

". . . bringing every thought into captivity to the obedience of Christ."
II Corinthians 10:5

Paul is telling the Corinthians that every one of their ideas, motives, desires, and decisions belongs to Christ. The Corinthians were having problems with leaders in their church who were teaching them false doctrine. They were not Christians at all but were trying to lead the people astray. This happens today and we must realize that there is a war for our minds going on in our world. So we must bring everything to Jesus and ask Him to help us with our very thoughts.

First let's look at our ideas. Where do we get them? From all around us, don't we? Of course we know that every influence that we come in contact with is not from Jesus. So we have to ask Jesus to protect us and help us know when the ideas are not from Him.

Then there are motives; the reason we do what we do. Sometimes we don't have the purest of motives and selfishness or pride is behind how we act. The third thing is our desires. Desires come from our heart and the Bible tells us that if we are obedient that God will give us the desires of our heart. The key word here is OBEDIENCE. In other words we have to make sure that our desires are good and not evil or hurt others. The last thing is our decisions. We should always go to Jesus and ask for guidance in making good decisions.

Wow, Paul sure said a lot in that little short sentence, didn't he? This is what it means to live our lives unto the Lord. We must make sure He is involved in everything we do so we can make sure we live according to His will.

Questions To Think About

1. Why is it important to ask Jesus about things in our lives?
2. How do our actions show that we are obedient?

December 4

"For I am not ashamed of the gospel of Christ, for it is the power of God to salvation for everyone who believes . . ."
Romans 1:16

Have you ever been ashamed of something? I know I have. I can think of a lot of thoughts and actions that I have been ashamed of. Along with being ashamed goes embarrassment. Sometimes we feel like we would like to crawl under a rug and disappear.

We like to act as if it never happened and some of the time we try to lie our way out of it, don't we?

I had a friend once and his mother was a minority and I was ashamed of that. Why? I don't know. When some of my friends found out I told them not to tell anyone because he didn't want anyone to know. This was a LIE. He didn't have a problem with his mother. I DID.

I guess I thought that if people knew I had a friend whose mother came from another country that they would think less of me. Sounds pretty stupid, doesn't it? Well, it was and if the friend had known I felt this way, I'm sure it would have hurt his feelings.

This is what Paul is talking about. Maybe at one time or another all of us have been ashamed to let people know that we are Christians? We show we are ashamed by doing things like hiding our Bible so no one will see us carrying it; or, we won't join a Christian Club at school because someone might think we are freaks. Maybe when we are asked to pray in public, we won't do it for fear of what someone might think. This is being ashamed of the gospel of Christ.

Some people might think less of us, but usually others admire those who will stand up for what they believe. Besides, so what if they do make fun of us? The Bible tells us that it is a great honor to be persecuted for Christ's sake. Jesus will always give us the POWER to be saved and the POWER to tell anyone that we are Christians. He will also help us invite others to become a Christian too.

Questions To Think About

1. Why do you think we are afraid to talk to others about Jesus?
2. Can you think of a time when you didn't let someone know you were a Christian because you were afraid?

Notes

December 5

"For the wages of sin is death, but the gift of God is eternal life in Christ Jesus our Lord." Romans 6:23

There are two jobs that I had when I was a kid where I got wages that I will never forget. The first one was picking cotton. Picking cotton looks like a lot of fun going down the rows and pulling the white fluffy cotton out of the bowls. BUT, it is VERY hard work. I picked all morning and made sixteen cents. So I decided I would try my hand at some other job and I found an orchard where the pecans needed to be harvested. A machine would go up and down the rows and shake the trees and we would sit under them and pick the pecans out of the pile of leaves and hull them. This was more rewarding because I made six dollars a day and I thought I was in the big money even thought I stained my hands and knees until I was ashamed to be seen in public.

What Paul is telling us here is that we always get paid for what we do whether it is a job or the way we live our lives. We can act the way we want and it may seem like we're really doing great, but, just like I was paid at the end of the week for harvesting pecans, we will also receive wages for the way we live. That's why it is so important to be a Christian.

The Bible tells us that we are known by our actions and that we reap what we sow. What is so great about being a Christian is we get paid for what Jesus did, not what we do. Jesus is the only one who doesn't give wages. He gives gifts. We can't earn a gift. That sounds like a pretty good deal to me. I would rather get gifts than wages any day.

Questions To Think About

1. Do you ask Jesus to help you live a life that pleases Him?
2. What is the difference in wages and gifts?

December 6

"And we know that all things work together for good to those who love God, to those who are the called according to His purpose."
Romans 8:28

There are not a lot of things in this world that we can KNOW beyond a shadow of a doubt. But just look what WE as Christians can KNOW. Paul is reminding us that ALL, that is every little thing that happens to us, is going to end up being for our good. But there is a condition to this promise. It says to THOSE WHO LOVE GOD AND ARE CALLED. Who are these people? No one can love God unless he is a Christian, so the "called who love God" are Christians.

So if we are Christians, we will love God. How can we love God so that we will know we are Christians? One way is by being like God, by being Holy. He tells us to do this. He says to us "Be ye Holy as I am Holy." This doesn't mean we won't mess up. We will. It means that in our hearts we want to be Holy, we want to do His will, and we want to show His love to others. We also do things like pray, read our Bibles, and worship at church to equip us to be holy.

When we are one of God's children, we don't have to worry, even if things seem bad at the time. God's plan for us is at work and nothing can stop it from happening and we wouldn't want to stop it if we could, because for us—"all things work together for our good."

Questions To Think About

1. Do you know what God's purpose for you is?
2. What does it mean to be Holy?

December 7

How then shall they call on Him in whom they have not believed? And how shall they believe in Him of whom they have not heard? And how shall they hear without a preacher? And how shall they preach unless they are sent? Romans 10:14-15a

These are four questions that are very important to all of us both before and after we became Christians. Before we became Christians, we would be the "they" in the first question. In the beginning we did not believe, we didn't even know who or what to believe because we hadn't heard of Jesus. Then, someone told us about Jesus. It may have been our mother, father, friend, Sunday school teacher, pastor, or a Christian friend, but, someone told us about Jesus.

We may not remember the first time we heard about Jesus? God had it all planned out. He planned for us to hear about Jesus and His death and resurrection so we could have eternal life. The way God has chosen to work on earth is through His people so he sent someone to talk to us about Jesus.

This brings us to question two. In order for those who haven't heard, to hear, someone must go. Who will it be? We must always be open to the Holy Spirit's call on our lives to be a preacher, missionary, or a lay person who has the good of others at heart. God always provides a way for us to prepare and then to serve.

Let's move on to question three. This is where we come in if we haven't been called to be a preacher or missionary. There are those who SEND the preachers and missionaries. The Bible tells us the Christian's reason to work and make money is so that we can help those in need. Therefore, we are to give so we can send some out so others can hear like we did.

It's a never ending cycle if everyone does his part and helps either as one being sent or one who sends. We need to listen for God's call on our lives. It is a great opportunity to give ourselves and our gifts.

Questions To Think About

1. Why do you think God lets us help Him?
2. Why is it important to let others know about Jesus?

Notes

December 8

Rejoice with those who rejoice, and weep with those who weep.
Romans 12:15

Paul is telling the Romans how to act as Christians. It sounds pretty simple doesn't it? If someone is happy, be happy with them. But let's stop and think. Are we always happy when someone else has a reason to be joyful. When a friend wins a position on the team that we want, can we truly REJOICE with them or does jealously take over. Do we want to yell out, "I should have gotten that spot on the team. I deserve it more than he does. No, I'm not happy he got it. Why should I be?" It takes a very BIG person to truly rejoice with someone who receives what we want. It is hard in this situation to be happy, but if Jesus is in our hearts, we CAN DO IT. Talking to Jesus about it in prayer will help us work through it.

It seems so much easier to cry with someone who has had something bad or sad happen to them. It is easier because we wouldn't want it to happen to us. Still sometimes it is very hard to show another person who has been hurt deeply that we are sorry and want to help him. Again, Jesus will help us know what to say and how to comfort this person. All we have to do is ask Him. He is with us and knows our needs. We just need to call on Him and listen carefully to His Word. All the answers are there for us to show us the way we should act.

Questions To Think About

1. Can you remember a time when you were jealous and how you acted?
2. How can we know how to treat others when they are happy or sad?

December 9

. . . And remember the words of the Lord Jesus, that He said, 'It is more blessed to give than to receive.' Acts 20:35b

At this time of the year when we are nearing Christmas, we are usually making a list of things that we want. We haven't given too much thought to what we might give. The Bible tells us that Jesus said that it was more blessed to give than to receive. This means that we will receive greater joy in giving than in getting.

This may be hard for us to believe, at first. After all, our entire lives have been centered on ME and what I want and what I need and what I desire. So now we hear we're going to get more joy out of giving something to someone else than getting something for OURSELVES? This might take some work.

When we really think about it we may get what Jesus is talking about. Let's do a little reasoning here. Here are the facts: 1) We are Christians. 2) As Christians, we are to be like Jesus. 3) To be like Jesus, we look at what He did. 4) Jesus' first concern was not about Himself. 5) He GAVE all He could for others. 6) Therefore, if we are to be like Him, we are to give all we can to others. 7) What does Jesus want us to give? 8) Our money to feed the poor, our time to visit the widows and orphans, our lives to go make disciples. How can we do this? 10) Jesus will be with us always helping us to give. 11) THEREFORE, if we are doing what Jesus wants us to do, which is GIVING, we WILL BE BLESSED. Now I see how it works.

Questions To Think About

1. What is one thing we can do for someone else today?
2. What does it mean to be blessed?

December 10

So I said, "What shall I do, Lord?" Acts 22:10a

Paul was on his way to Damascus to persecute more Christians because he thought he was doing the will of God. He had been brought up as a Jew and what these *Christians* were doing was against his religion. He was so devoted that he was putting men, women and children in prison where some were probably executed. But God had a plan for Paul. When he was on the road God blinded Paul with a great light and asked him why he was doing this to the Christians. As the Scripture tells us Paul asked Him what he should do. There is a great lesson here for us. Now we are not like Paul who was putting Christians in prison, but what are we doing? We need to ask God, just as Paul did; "What shall I do, Lord?"

God has a wonderful plan for each of us and if we just ask He will lead us in His plan for our lives. We may think that we are too young or too old to be asking God what He wants us to do, but He wants us NOW and He has things for us to do NOW, regardless of our age. Jesus will put us in places where He needs us to be His light. Maybe it will be at home being obedient to our parents. Maybe it will be at school or work where non-Christians need our love. Maybe it will be somewhere with complete strangers who need a smile or a kind word. One thing is for sure, God can use each of us wherever we are IF we will say as Paul did, "What shall I do Lord?"

Question To Thing About

1. What are some of the ways we can be obedient?
2. Where are some places that we can be used by God?

December 11

Then Agrippa said to Paul, "You almost persuade me to become a Christian." Acts 26:28

These are some of the saddest words in the Bible. Agrippa was a king who knew all about the Jewish religion and it was his duty as the political leader of Palestine to appoint the high priest of the Jewish temple. He listened to what Paul had to say but would not humble himself to accept that Jesus was the Messiah.

"Almost" is not good enough. You either are or you are not a Christian. There is no middle ground. How wonderful it would have been for a person in Agrippa's position to have accepted Paul's teachings concerning Jesus. Unfortunately at this point, Agrippa rejected the good news of the gospel and remained in his fallen condition.

As children of God, we are blessed by the fact that on judgment day when we stand before God, He will see us through Jesus. He will see us washed white by the blood of the Lamb. Now that's the greatest thing that could ever be done for us.

Another thing we should realize from this scripture is that Paul could never PERSUADE Agrippa to come to Christ. The Holy Spirit must first put a new heart in us and make us alive before we, who were "dead in trespasses and sin", can see that we are sinners without hope of saving ourselves. Then we turn to Jesus.

We, like Paul, can't persuade anyone to become a Christian, the Holy Spirit is in complete control of that; but, we can tell people about Jesus and what a wonderful life we can have. It's our job to TELL but it's Jesus who saves. So don't worry about someone not accepting Jesus when you tell them about Him, you have planted the seed. The Holy Spirit has to do the rest.

Questions To Think About

1. Have you ever told anyone about what Jesus did for you?
2. Why is it important to share your faith with others?

December 12

For the hearts of this people have grown dull. Their ears are hard of hearing, and their eyes they have closed, . . . Acts 28:27

Paul was speaking to the Jews and they had problems just as Isaiah the great prophet had said they would. There were three areas that he talked about which we should also be concerned with today. First, he says their hearts had grown dull. How does a heart grow dull? This happens when we don't fill our hearts with the right "stuff" but let evil and worldly desires take over. Worldly desires and evil can be disguised in many ways. They can come into our hearts through music, movies, books or other things we come into contact with on a daily basis. That is why we are warned to be IN the world but not OF the world. We can only live righteously through the work of the Holy Spirit in our hearts and lives.

Secondly, Paul says our ears are hard of hearing. He means we won't listen to God's Word but prefer to listen to the ways of the world. Our ears become hard of hearing when we don't listen to our parents, other Christians and when we won't study God's Word. It means more than just saying, "I'm a Christian." It means living like a Christian, which we learn to do by listening to God's Word.

Thirdly, the Scripture says we close our eyes. That means we refuse to see the evil around us and pretend it isn't there. It means we refuse to see the evil in ourselves and repent. We need to keep our eyes wide open by studying the Word and turning away from evil TV, movies or books.

So let's keep our hearts, ears and eyes in good shape by staying close to Jesus.

QUESTIONS TO THINK ABOUT

1. What is meant by worldly?
2. Name three ways to stay close to God.

December 13

For we are His workmanship, created in Christ Jesus for good works, which God prepared beforehand that we should walk in them.
Ephesians 2:10

In this verse Paul is telling the Ephesians that because they have been born again they should live to glorify God through good works that He calls them to do. The specific acts may vary from person to person but the underlying basis for our actions should be love. The Bible tells us that if we are born of God we will love each other.

Another important aspect of this Scripture is the fact that "we are His workmanship". That means that we don't have to walk in the good works God has prepared for us in our own strength. In fact, we can't do good works without God's grace. Through God's grace we are able to be obedient to His call. Because of God's grace we are able to walk in good works that God prepared for us "beforehand".

How often do we think about how GREAT this truth really is? There are good things that need to be done. It's awesome that God chose to use us to accomplish his work in this world.

Questions To Think About

1. What are we to do while we are here on earth?

December 14

Therefore take up the whole armor of God, that you may be able to withstand in the evil day, and having done all, to stand. Stand therefore, having girded your waist with truth, having put on the breastplate of righteousness, and having shod your feet with the preparation of the gospel of peace; above all, taking the shield of faith with which you will be able to quench all the fiery darts of the wicked one. And take the helmet of salvation, and the sword of the Spirit, which is the word of God; praying always . . .
Ephesians 6:13-18a

We need to realize that we are in a battle. It's the greatest battle we will ever fight and God Himself has provided us with the equipment we will need for the war. We need to be alert, battle ready and have all the weapons that God has provided. So let's take a look at the weapons. First, there is TRUTH. We get our truth from the Bible and this is the first place the enemy will try to stop us. The world will say the Bible isn't TRUE, but we know it is and must study God's Word and hide His TRUTH in our hearts by memorizing Scripture.

Our second weapon is RIGHTEOUSNESS. There is no law against being HOLY and again the enemy will work to get us to do unholy things, but God's Words says if we resist the Devil he will flee from us.

Thirdly, we have the GOSPEL of PEACE. We have peace in our hearts because we know the gospel, the good news. The good news is that as a Christian we are no longer an enemy of God. We are fighting on God's side, so we have stability and confidence to march onward without fear. If God is for us who can stand against us?

Next we have FAITH. Faith is a gift God gives us to believe and know the TRUTH. We will be victorious because God has promised victory.

We also have the helmet of SALVATION which is our last piece of defensive armor. Our salvation makes us alive through Christ and we will someday actually see Him face to face. Christ has given us victory over death.

The SWORD of the SPIRIT is the Word of God. The Word is our ammunition against the enemy. So the more we study and learn and memorize Scripture, the more ammunition we have in our arsenal. There is no weapon that the enemy has that can overcome the Bible.

Lastly we have PRAYER. As we go into battle every day we need to keep our lines of communication with our Commander open. We need to talk with the Lord "continually" and draw wisdom and strength from our fellowship with Him.

My prayer is that we all FIGHT THE GOOD FIGHT. Put on your gear and charge!

Questions To Think About

1. As a Christian what kind of battle are we in?
2. What is our job in this battle?

December 15

Therefore, as the elect of God, holy and beloved, put on tender mercies, kindness, humility, meekness, longsuffering; bearing with one another, and forgiving one another, if anyone has a complaint against another; even as Christ forgave you, so you also must do. Colossians 3:12-13

In these verses Paul was talking to the Christians in Colossi. He was telling them how to get along with other Christians. Now I know we think we don't need to learn how to get along with other Christians, but actually this is often one of our biggest problems. As we all live out our lives here on earth as Christians we will still sin and that means other Christians will sometimes sin against us or hurt us. For example, if we are called on to read in Sunday school often because we can read well, or sing well, or whatever it may be, others may become jealous. Perhaps another Christian has said something mean about us and isn't at all sorry. Or, maybe we don't like the way our teacher is conducting our class and we don't think he is a very good teacher so we just happen to mention that to several people. This list is endless. So we can see that we need some guidance here.

Paul gives a list of what we should be like, and it isn't easy, that's for sure. First, we are to be KIND regardless of anything (that's a hard one for sure). We are also supposed to FORGIVE. This is really hard for most of us and I have often said, "I'll forgive them, but I don't know if I will ever forget . . ." Forgiveness means that we forget. This is tough but with God's help we can do this.

I know I have my work cut out for me and this is only with our Christian friends. I pray God will help us to be CHRISTIANS like Paul tells us to be.

QUESTIONS TO THINK ABOUT

1. Do you have anything a Christian friend has done to you? Did you forgive him?
2. Do you need to ask a Christian friend for forgiveness?

December 16

Do all things without complaining and disputing, . . .
Philippians 2:14

Whoa, wait a minute. We have to do ALL things without complaining or arguing? It isn't very practical to think we can actually do this. Is it?

Well, it does come straight out of the Word of God and we say we believe every word it said? What really jumped out at me in this verse was the ALL. That includes everything! We must even do things we don't like to do without complaining and arguing. This means doing chores, following rules our parents give us, getting along with sisters and brothers, doing homework, not getting to do everything that our friends do, not getting our way about things, not getting to pick our teachers, having to stay after school because no one would confess who wrote on the board, sitting on the bench instead of playing in the game, not getting a big part in the school play, not winning the election for president of the class, practicing our music for an hour, wearing a dorky shirt that our grandma gave us for our birthday, sitting and listening in church, getting our Sunday school lesson, memorizing our Bible verses, having to work at the work day at church, and the list goes on and on.

It's so hard not to complain or argue about anything. However, we know that Jesus will give us the strength to do it. He will never ask us to do anything that we can't do with His help. Remember our verse for today and go for it. We can do it.

Questions To Talk About

1. How can we guard against complaining and arguing?

December 17

For we have great joy and consolation in your love, because the hearts of the saints have been refreshed by you, brother.
Philemon 1:7

Paul wrote this short (one chapter) letter to Philemon because he had a slave, Onesimus, who had run away and found Paul in Rome. Paul had led him to Christ and he is asking Philemon to take Onesiums back as a brother in Christ. We don't know if Philemon took Onesimus back or not. Did Philemon forget the past and forgive Onesimus or did he say "no" and punished him for what he had done, which may have included stealing money from him.

What would we do if a person we had known for a long time and thought we were good friends with decided not to be our friend any more? They might even have taken something that was ours and wouldn't give it back. What if someone led them to the Lord and they came to us and told us how sorry they were and asked for forgiveness. What would we do? What SHOULD we do? We know the right answer and I hope we would act as all Christians should.

Because of the way Philemon had shown love to others in the past, I'm sure he took Onesimus back with open arms. Not because Paul had asked him to but because he had the LOVE of Jesus in his heart.

QUESTIONS TO THINK ABOUT

1. What does it mean to have the love of Jesus in your heart?
2. What do you think about holding a grudge against someone?

December 18

Let no one despise your youth, but be an example to the believers in word, in conduct, in love, in spirit, in faith, in purity.
I Timothy 4:12

Paul was giving Timothy some good advice as a young man in the ministry, but it is something that is really good for all of us today. This is a picture of what a Christian should be. First, we are to be an example to other believers in what we say. This means everything that comes out of our mouths. Second, we are to act like Christians from the time we get up in the morning until we go to sleep at night. We are to act like Christians at home with our families and wherever we go the rest of the day whether we are with other Christians or are among unbelievers. It even includes when we are alone, because God always sees us and Jesus is always with us.

Next Paul tells Timothy the qualities that a Christian should have. The first on the list is LOVE. It is always first because if we act in love and have a loving spirit everything else will fall into place. Then he lists faith, which is what keeps us going in our Christian walk. We don't always SEE the outcome of our Christian beliefs, but we KNOW that what God says in His Word is true.

Lastly he speaks of purity. It is hard to be pure in every though, word, and deed but remember we have the Holy Spirit living in us to help us in every circumstance. These are just a few good words to guide us day by day. Let's make it happen!

Questions To Think About

1. What does it mean to be an example?
2. Should we act differently around those who are not Christians?

December 19

But know this, that in the last days perilous times will come., For men will be lovers of themselves, lovers of money, boasters, proud, blasphemers, disobedient to parents, unthankful, unholy, unloving, unforgiving, slanderers, without self-control, brutal, despisers of good, traitors, headstrong, haughty, lovers of pleasure rather than lovers of God having a form of godliness but denying its power and from such people turn away.
II Timothy 3:1-5

This is the last letter Paul ever wrote. In it he tells Timothy to carefully follow his instructions. He tells Timothy not to be like men who love themselves more than others. This is what the world is still teaching today (to look out for number one) and if we don't read God's Word daily we tend to believe this lie. No one likes to be around someone who is always bragging and because we all like to be noticed and loved this is a big thing that we have to be careful not to do.

Slanderers are people who talk about other people. We must be careful not to participate in gossip. If we find ourselves in this situation we should walk away and tell the one talking we don't want to hear it. Even when gossip is true it can hurt people almost more than any other thing.

We have heard many times how important it is to OBEY our parents but sometimes we get tired of hearing about it. However, if God thought it was important enough to make it one of the Ten Commandments He must have thought it was VERY important.

Paul also talks about lovers of pleasure and this sometimes slips into our lives and we haven't even realized it. Just think what might happen if we spent more time reading the Bible, giving others a helping hand, and praying than watching TV? The Bible tells us that true happiness comes from the Lord. We are happiest when we are obedient. This doesn't mean we aren't to have fun, relax, and do things that let us have a good time, but we shouldn't make seeking pleasure the main activity of our lives. This is what Paul is explaining to Timothy. Following God's plan is always the best way and makes us truly happy.

Questions To Think About

1. What should we do when someone starts to gossip?
2. How should pleasure fit into our lives?

Notes

December 20

"And if you call on the Father, who without partiality judges according to each one's work, conduct yourselves throughout the time of your stay here in fear. I Peter 1:17

Our Scripture today is only one sentence but there is so much to learn from it. Let's look at "call on the Father". The first time we called on the Father was when we repented and asked for forgiveness and He gave us the gift of life forever. From that time on we have continued to pray to Him. Our prayers have included praising Him, seeking His advice, asking forgiveness for our mess ups, and seeking help for others. So as a Christian we have called on Him often.

This Scripture also talks about Him being a judge and judging what we do. The word JUDGE makes us kind of nervous because we always feel we're guilty of something and we're going to get into trouble. God is not judging whether or not we're going to Heaven because that was already decided when Jesus came to live in our hearts; He is judging what we do here on earth with what He has given us. What Peter is saying is that we need to "make hay while the sun shines". While we are here on earth it is never too early to start using our gifts to honor Jesus and further His kingdom. We are to give of our time and our talents, not because we are trying to get the biggest reward in Heaven, but because we love Jesus and want to serve Him.

Questions To Talk About

1. What is God judging Christians about?
2. How can we show Christ's love?

December 21

These are grumblers, complainers, walking according to their own lusts; and they mouth great swelling words, flattering people to gain advantage. Jude 1:16

I'm sure this doesn't describe us, but I'm sure we know people like this and the Bible warns us not to be like them or hang around them. Jude says these are people who cause Christians trouble and divide them. He says we should have nothing to do with them. They could be leaders or they may be followers who never think anything that is from Jesus is right. They act this way because they don't want to act like Christians so they decide to belittle anyone who is a Christian and make fun of what they believe and cause them all kinds of trouble. Sometimes these guys are even in our churches. They may sit next to us in Sunday school and even act NICE in class, but when they are not at church they seem to be someone entirely different. They are walking "according to their own lusts".

All people are a slave to someone, whether it is God, the world, our flesh, or Satan. The Bible says we need to be wary of grumblers, complainers, and people who want to "do their own thing". They believe they are in control, but they are actually slaves to their own lusts and the old saying "misery loves company" is true. The only ones who are truly free and happy are God's children. We should want everyone to be free and happy as we are so we should pray for the rebellious ones and witness to them but not fall into their ways.

Questions To Think About

1. How should we treat people who are always negative?

December 22

For the word of God is living and powerful, and sharper than any two-edged sword, piercing even to the division of soul and spirit, and of joints and marrow, and is a discerner of the thoughts and intents of the heart. And there is no creature hidden from His sight, but all things are naked and open to the eyes of Him to whom we must give account.
Hebrews 4:12-13

Isn't it awesome that God gave us His Word? It is our most faithful guide as we live our lives in this world. No matter what happens we can go to God's Word and find help. This Scripture says that the Bible can tell us what our thoughts and intentions are. All we have to do is READ the Bible and it will let us know when we are on the wrong track or if we are living according to God's will.

Isn't it wonderful that we have a God who cares what we do every day? Isn't it amazing that God, the Creator of the universe, is interested in each of us? He is interested in EVERY little thing. He is interested in what we THINK because that is where our actions start. He knows us better than we know ourselves. There is nothing about us that He doesn't know because, as this Scripture says, all things are open to Him.

This should keep us on our toes since we know that God is going to ask us if we have obeyed and glorified Him in all things.

Remember we need to have fellowship with God through Jesus every day so we can learn how to obey and glorify and enjoy Him forever. This is very IMPORTANT. So talk to Him and study His Word daily.

Questions To Think About

1. Why are our thoughts important?

December 23

. . . and behind the second veil, the part of the tabernacle which is called the Holiest of All, which had the golden censer and the ark of the covenant overlaid on all sides with gold, in which were the golden pot that had the manna, Aaron's rod that budded, and the tablets of the covenant; . . . Hebrews 9: 3-4

The tabernacle which God had instructed the Israelites to build in the Old Testament was a type of things to come later on. A "type" in the Bible is like a model of the real thing. We have miniature planes and cars that are not the real thing but they have the same characteristic, that's what the Old Testament tabernacle and its furnishings were. God dwelt in the tabernacle at that time but after Jesus came He dwells in us because we are the tabernacle of the Holy Spirit. In the Tabernacle there was a veil that separated the people from God and only the High Priest could go behind it once a year. When Jesus died on the cross the veil in the Tabernacle was torn in two, so we no longer need a high priest to go between us and God. Jesus is our High Priest.

The Ark of the Covenant was to remind the people of the promise of God to always protect His covenant children and how He would always provide for them.

Aaron's rod represented God's authority and calling. Just as Aaron was called by God we are called to a position in God's Kingdom. The tablets that had the Ten Commandments written on them were there again as a reminder of God's law which He had established for His children so that they might have a good productive life. God was not only concerned about His people who lived before Christ but all the Christians who have lived after Jesus as well. He gave the early believers symbols but we have experienced the real thing. What a loving Father.

Questions To Think About

1. Where is the Ark of the Covenant today?
2. What was in the Ark of the Covenant?

December 24

But without faith it is impossible to please Him, for he who comes to God must believe that He is and that He is a rewarder of those who diligently seek him. Hebrews 11:6

Faith is a hard thing to understand because we can't see it, taste it, or feel it. It is something that is inside us and makes us believe certain things, but it is very important as we can see that this Scripture says without it, it is IMPOSSIBLE to please God. Thankfully faith is a gift from God so we must first ask God for faith to believe His Word.

Some things are easier to explain by showing how they work or what they do. Take wind for example. We can't see the actual wind but we can see what it does. We all have faith. For instance when we sit down on a chair, we have faith that it will hold us up. We don't have proof of that right on the spot. There is not a tag that says how much weight it will hold or what condition it is in. We just sit down on it because that is what a chair does. It holds people when they sit down.

Faith in God and all of His promises works the same way. We know that what God says is true and we have seen God's faithfulness to others. Just like we have seen chairs hold up people who sit in them, we have witnessed God's faithfulness in keeping his promises in others' lives. Hebrews reminds us of some of those people. What all these people had in common was that they were diligently seeking to glorify God because they believed (we can't separate faith and believing) that He would do what He said in His word, because He always has and always will. We are to take God at His word. Faith is a gift from God and He grows our faith as we use it, as we TRUST God to keep His promises.

Questions To Think About

1. Name someone in the Bible who had faith in God.
2. How can you tell if someone has faith in God?

December 25

If you endure chastening, God deals with you as sons; for what son is there whom a father does not chasten? . . . Furthermore, we have had human fathers who corrected us, and we paid them respect. Shall we not much more readily be in subjection to the Father of spirits and live? . . . Now no chastening seems to be joyful for the present, but painful; nevertheless, afterward it yields the peaceable fruit of righteousness to those who have been trained by it. Hebrews 12: 7, 9, 11

Now none of us like the idea of being punished. We can all remember the dread of punishment we knew was coming. We didn't enjoy it because it was painful. Even if it didn't involve physical punishment, it was emotionally painful. God's Word says that if our parents do not correct us we will grow up to be "out of control". Even if we don't understand right now, we will be glad our parents loved us enough to correct us when we are adults. I am certainly thankful for my parent's correction.

Our heavenly Father knows what is best for us. He knows when we need to be corrected even as adults. Many times we can't see why things are going the way they are but, as we look back on events, we see that we needed to be corrected and are so grateful that God loved us enough to get us back on the right track. I am so thankful that God corrects us just as our earthly fathers do.

Questions To Think About

1. Why does God correct us?
2. How should we react when He does?

December 26

Now by this we know that we know Him, if we keep His commandments. He who says, "I know Him," and does not keep His commandments, is a liar, and the truth is not in him. But whoever keeps His word, truly the love of God is perfected in him. By this we know that we are in Him. He who says he abides in Him ought himself also to walk just as He walked.
I John 2:3-6

There have been times in my life when I've wondered, "Am I really a Christian?" I'm sure at some time we have all wondered if we were really a Christian or if we were just kidding ourselves. We can know the answer to our question. I John pretty well spells it out for us. Remember we believe the entire Bible to be the truth and here in the Bible is says we can KNOW that we are followers of Jesus if we keep His commandments. That doesn't mean that we never sin because the Bible also says that if we say there's no sin in us we are liars. It does mean that our life style, our mind set, and the way we live our lives every day should be different from the world and that we will desire to be obedient to God's commandments.

In addition, as Christians, when we sin we can ask God to forgive us. We feel comforted in this promise. If we weren't Christians, we wouldn't feel the need to ask for forgiveness. I feel so privileged to be a Christian who can ask God's forgiveness and KNOW that He promises He will forgive us.

Questions To Think About

1. How can you know that you are a Christian?
2. Why do Christians ask for forgiveness?

December 27

Blessed is he who reads and those who hear the words of this prophecy, and keep those things which are written in it; for the time is near. Revelation 1:3

When I was a little girl I looked forward to going to my grandmother's and spending the night. I looked forward to this for two reasons. First of all, I got to sleep on the living room floor. My grandmother would pile up homemade quilts and to me that was the best bed in the whole world.

Second, we would talk about something from the Bible. My favorite topic was hearing about things that were going to happen in the future. I thought that my grandmother knew all there was to know about the Bible and I would just lie there on my quilt bed and soak in all her wisdom and knowledge. She always made it so exciting.

This is still important to me, to know what is going to happen in the future because what we do now affects what will happen to us later. In the prophecy of Revelation it tells us about God's sovereignty (His all powerfulness), our redemption (being born again), and the second coming of Jesus.

In today's Scripture we are told we will be blessed if we do three things: read this word, hear what we read and keep what we hear. First, we have to READ. When we pray "give us this day our daily bread" we are talking not only about the food that we eat but the Heavenly food that we receive from reading our Bibles. We are to read God's Word daily to get the strength for TODAY. Next, we are to HEAR. This means we need to understand what we read. We may not understand everything we read at first, but if we don't we are to study and work at finding out what it means. Look up the references in the margin of your Bible, or read other books that your parents' trust, and ask your Sunday school teacher or pastor to explain things.

The most important thing that this scripture brings out is that we must KEEP what we read. This is the hard part. But we can do it with

God's help and He is always there for us. We need to remember these three words when we are thinking about God's Word: READ, HEAR, and KEEP. God will help us with all three.

QUESTIONS TO THINK ABOUT

1. What are we to read daily?
2. What does hear mean in this scripture?

NOTES

December 28

And they sang a new song, saying: You are worthy to take the scroll, and to open its seals: for You were slain, and have redeemed us to God by Your blood out of every tribe and tongue and people and nation. Revelation 5:9

Sometimes as Americans we think we are the greatest nation on earth and that every other nation is just a little below us. It's great to have pride in our nation and our heritage but this Scripture says that as Christians, "every tribe and tongue and people and nation" are brothers and sisters in Christ. Jesus redeems (saves) people regardless of where they are born, where they live or what language they speak.

So we should learn a great lesson from this Scripture. We shouldn't base how we feel about someone on their nationality or ethnic background because Jesus doesn't. In fact, Jesus doesn't care what we look like on the outside at all. So we should never think of ourselves as better than others. Isn't it wonderful that as Christians we can just be ourselves and love others and not have to worry about how we look or speak or where we live?

Questions To Think About

1. How should we treat those who are not like us?
2. Why do you think we sometimes feel that we are better than other people?

December 29

Then I saw another angel flying in the midst of heaven, having the everlasting gospel to preach to those who dwell on the earth—to every nation, tribe, tongue, and people—saying with a loud voice, "Fear God and give glory to Him, for the hour of His judgment has come; and worship Him who made heaven and earth, the sea and springs of water." Revelation 14:6-7

There are some wonderful things in this Scripture to remember and practice every day. First, after the Gospel or good news is preached to us then we are to do three things. Number one is FEAR GOD. That means we are to hold God in awe. We are to realize who God is and give him the glory and honor and respect that He deserves. It's sort of like when we have done things that we know we shouldn't and our father finds out and we are afraid of what he will do and say to us. We are ashamed that we have disappointed him. That's the kind of fear we should have for our Heavenly Father as well. God has given us His Word to tell us how to act and it also tells us that He corrects those He loves just as our earthly father does.

The next thing we see is that we are to give him GLORY. We've talked about this before. Being obedient to His Word is how we glorify God. It's not just singing songs in church on Sunday morning, it's being OBEDIENT every day of our lives.

The last thing in this Scripture is WORSHIP. As we read this, and take to heart what we read, we are worshiping Him. Sunday morning as we sing, pray and listen to His word, we are worshiping Him.

Questions To Think About

1. Name some ways we worship God. Why is it important to worship God?

December 30

"These will make war with the Lamb, and the Lamb will overcome them, for He is Lord of lords and King of kings; and those who are with Him are called, chosen, and faithful.
Revelation 17: 14

This Scripture should give us goose-bumps. Here is the GREATEST person who ever lived, and not only that, He is God. There we are, the Christians, with Him in the midst of the battle. We know Christ wins because it says right here that He will OVERCOME the evil ones who have tried to take His place since the beginning of time. It is the evil one who wants to be as great as He is and who has been behind all the trouble, heartache, and sadness here on earth.

Wow! We are not only going to be with Him and known as His, but He is going to call us CHOSEN and FAITHFUL. We know how important it is to us to be chosen, whether it's on a team that's playing ball, a group that we want to be a part of, or for some award that we've always wanted. Being chosen is a wonderful thing but when we are chosen by the Lord of Lords and the King of kings. WOW!

It is the best compliment anyone can receive to be called faithful. That means so many things. It means that when we have a chance to stand up for Jesus we do. It means when we have to go through some tough times we do. It means when others try to get us to compromise, we hang in there. Now we see why this verse should give us goose-bumps. What a great way for our story to end.

Questions To Think About

1. What does Lord of lords and King of kings mean?
2. Who chose us to be on the Lord's side?

December 31

"And God will wipe away every tear from their eyes; there shall be no more death, nor sorrow, nor crying. There shall be no more pain, for the former things have passed away." Then He who sat on the throne said, "Behold, I make all things new."
Revelation 21:4-5a

It's a great time of the year to think about NEW things. We have new stuff we got for Christmas and new things we're going to do this year. There is just something about anything new that always gives us hope. Just imagine what it will be like for ALL things to be made NEW. Our Scripture tells us this will happen.

Something else we have to look forward to is no more CRYING. Remember all the things that have made us cry? Remember the hurts, both physical and mental, all the sad things that have happened, all the people we were close to who have died. NONE of that will happen ever again. It is such a big thing that it's hard for us to imagine. We know, however, beyond a shadow of a doubt that it is going to happen and we as Christians have this NEW LIFE to look forward to.

God has done His part. Our part is to repent of our sins, believe with our hearts that Jesus died on the cross, that He rose the third day to live forever, that He paid for all our sins and set us free to live for Him and with Him FOREVER. YES!!! Have a great NEW Year.

Questions To Think About

1. What are we to believe as Christians?
2. What are your plans for the New Year?

CPSIA information can be obtained
at www.ICGtesting.com
Printed in the USA
LVHW032232061021
699771LV00002B/2